THE HEALING BODY

Northwestern University
Studies in Phenomenology
and
Existential Philosophy

General Editor Anthony J. Steinbock

THE HEALING BODY

Creative Responses to Illness, Aging, and Affliction

Drew Leder

Northwestern University Press
Evanston, Illinois

Northwestern University Press
www.nupress.northwestern.edu

Printed in the United States of America

10 9 8 7 6 5 4 3 2 1

Library of Congress Cataloging-in-Publication Data

Names: Leder, Drew, author.
Title: The healing body : creative responses to illness, aging, and affliction / Drew Leder.
Other titles: Northwestern University studies in phenomenology & existential philosophy.
Description: Evanston : Northwestern University Press, 2024. | Series: Northwestern University studies in phenomenology and existential philosophy | Includes bibliographical references.
Identifiers: LCCN 2023017280 | ISBN 9780810146372 (paperback) | ISBN 9780810146389 (cloth) | ISBN 9780810146396 (ebook)
Subjects: LCSH: Human body (Philosophy) | Medicine—Philosophy. | Aging—Philosophy. | Aging—Psychological aspects.
Classification: LCC B105.B64 L4334 2024 | DDC 128.6—dc23/eng/20230411
LC record available at https://lccn.loc.gov/202301728

To my father,
Dr. Harold Leder,
who was himself such a dedicated healer

Contents

Acknowledgments

There are so many to thank for their contributions to this book. I will start by appreciating friends and colleagues who have dealt honestly and skillfully with their own forms of illness and incapacity. These include those whose stories are represented in the book, such as Kevin Aho, Havi Carel, S. Kay Toombs, Arthur Frank, Missy Gugerty, and Joan Boor, the last of whom, as a close friend, has spoken to me for years about her journey with Parkinson's.

Then too, there are the dedicated medical healers who have educated me, such as my good friends Mitchell and Carol Krucoff, and Michelle Burack, who liberally shared her work with Parkinson's patients. Crucial to my own understanding of healing are those who have treated my own ailing body and spirit: the acupuncturist Heather Dorst; massage and energy worker Leyan Darlington; teachers of meditative breath and qigong, Adhikari Sacha and Durga Handley; and Eric Williams, great guy, great surgeon. My own father, Harold Leder, a sensitive internist who actually made house calls, is throughout a guiding light.

There are others who have educated me on specific subjects; for example, Joseph Straus, Eva Kittay, and Gail Weiss, on topics of disability and caregiving. Ram Dass and Rupert Spira have provided spiritual teachings that resonate throughout my life and this book. I wish to thank colleagues like Lenart Škof, Manos Tsakira, Helena De Preester, Espen Dahl, Cassandra Falke, and Thor Eirik Eriksen for their invitations to write on topics that then transmuted into book chapters. The chapter on imprisonment is inspired by the many incarcerated citizens I have had the privilege to work with—and I am delighted that John Woodland, Arlando Jones III, and Vincent Greco are now friends on the outside. I also thank all those at Marymount Manhattan College for an inspirational semester, albeit Covid-interrupted, as the Ferraro Fellow in Prison Education and Public Philosophy.

More generally, I received useful suggestions and support from my friends and colleagues Rick Boothby, Bret Davis, Kirsten Jacobson, Susan Bredlau, Mary Watkins, and Edward S. Casey. My debt to the latter is incalculable—I would not even be in philosophy if it weren't for his unfailing care and friendship.

There are others who were partners in bringing the book to fruition. Rachel Cicoria and Jeremy Ahearn were great research assistants. Kevin Aho helped with the publication of the book, and Elizabeth Davidson in lessons on how to reach readers. Andrea Cacase provided the excellent figures that give graphic visualizations of the book's healing strategies.

I want to thank Anthony Steinbock and Faith Wilson Stein, my expert editors at Northwestern University Press, for helping with the final publication. Feedback from the press's anonymous reviewers proved very useful. My colleagues in the philosophy department, our program assistant, Lisa Flaherty, and Loyola University Maryland in general have also been unfailingly supportive. More specifically, much financial support was provided by Loyola's Summer Research Grant program and the Center for the Humanities.

On a more personal note, I want to thank my wife and fellow philosopher, Janice McLane, and our two daughters, Sarah and Anna-Rose Leder. What can I say but that you are very cool people who have filled my life with joy and meaning. Then too, thanks to my canine partners, Maggie and Remy, who accompanied me on the forest walks where I did my best thinking.

But pivoting back in a professional direction, I am grateful to the publishers who have permitted me to present work of mine that has been revised, sometimes extensively, from the following sources in which they originally appeared:

Chapter 2: "The Phenomenology of Healing: Eight Ways of Dealing with the Ill and Impaired Body," *Journal of Medicine and Philosophy* 47, no. 1 (February 2022): 137–54.

Chapter 3: "Healing Time: The Experience of Body and Temporality When Coping with Illness and Incapacity," *Medicine, Health Care and Philosophy* 24, no. 1 (2021): 99–111.

Chapter 6: "Coping with Chronic Pain, Illness and Incarceration: What Patients and Prisoners Have to Teach Each Other (and All of Us)," *Medical Humanities* 44 (June 2018): 1–7.

Chapter 7: "What Is It to 'Age Well'? Re-visioning Later Life," in *Existential Medicine: Essays on Health and Illness*, ed. Kevin Aho (New York: Rowman and Littlefield, 2018), 223–34.

Chapter 8: “Inside Insights: A Phenomenology of Interoception,” in *Interoception*, ed. Manos Tsakiris and Helena De Preester (Oxford: Oxford University Press, 2018), 307–22.

Chapter 9: “Breath as the Hinge of Dis-ease and Healing,” in *Atmospheres of Breathing: The Respiratory Questions of Philosophy*, ed. Lenart Škof and Petri Berndtson (Albany: SUNY Press, 2018), 219–31.

Chapter 10: “The Body in Advaita and Phenomenology (Two Non-Dualisms and Three Null-points),” *Prabuddha Bharata* 125, no. 1 (January 2020): 124–32.

THE HEALING BODY

Figure 1

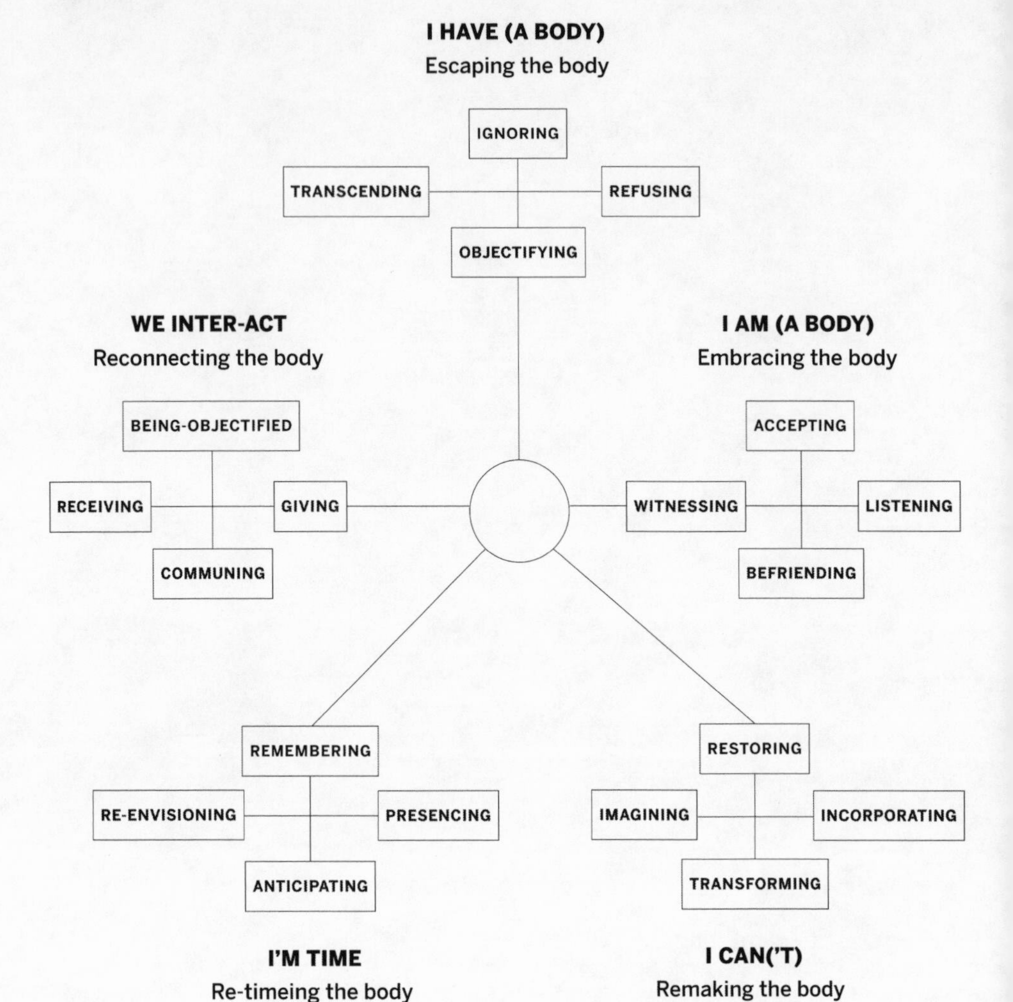
I HAVE (A BODY)
Escaping the body
IGNORING
TRANSCENDING
REFUSING
OBJECTIFYING
WE INTER-ACT
Reconnecting the body
BEING-OBJECTIFIED
RECEIVING
GIVING
COMMUNING
I AM (A BODY)
Embracing the body
ACCEPTING
WITNESSING
LISTENING
BEFRIENDING
REMEMBERING
RE-ENVISIONING
PRESENCING
ANTICIPATING
I'M TIME
Re-timeing the body
RESTORING
IMAGINING
INCORPORATING
TRANSFORMING
I CAN('T)
Remaking the body

Figure 2

FEATURES OF EMBODIMENT:	I HAVE (A BODY)	I AM (A BODY)	I CAN('T)	I'M TIME	WE INTER-ACT
HEALING ORIENTATION:	Escaping the body	Embracing the body	Remaking the body	Re-timeing the body	Reconnecting the body
	Ignoring	Accepting	Restoring	Remembering	Being-objectified
	Refusing	Listening	Transforming	Anticipating	Communing
	Objectifying	Befriending	Incorporating	Presencing	Receiving
	Transcending	Witnessing	Imagining	Re-envisioning	Giving

Six Questions to Keep in Mind While Reading This Book

1. Of these twenty healing strategies, which ones do you make the most use of in coping with your problem(s)? (You might circle or highlight these on one of the charts above—for example, on Figure 2, what spaces do you occupy on the "chessboard" of healing?)

2. Are there particular times—for example, moments of flare-up or fatigue, or special challenges and tasks of everyday life—when you turn to a particular strategy for help?

3. In what ways do your favorite strategies serve you well?

4. In what ways might your favorite strategies fail or limit you?

5. What other strategies might be most helpful to you? Have you perhaps been overlooking them? (Again, you could mark these on one of the charts above—using Figure 2, this is comparable to asking what new places you might move to on the "chessboard" of healing.)

6. Are there times in your life when these new and different strategies might be helpful? How so? Be specific.

In conclusion, you might consider keeping a diary of the challenges you face, the coping strategies you now use, are experimenting with, or would like to try—and what seems to work, or not, at different times. Don't be judgmental of yourself. Simply use this as a tool for exploring, and perhaps expanding, the universe of healing strategies you have at the ready.

Introduction

Before Siddhartha Gautama became the Buddha, his father had gone to the utmost lengths to shield him from the sight of human suffering. One day, in the midst of his privileged life, charioting through his princely domain, Siddhartha happened to see a sick person, an old person, and then a corpse. He realized that these were not simply their personal tragedies, but universal to the human condition. Despite his current youth, beauty, and riches, this fate awaited him as well. Siddhartha also saw a renunciate representing the possibility of existential healing, and so he embarked on the arduous journey to become the Buddha, the "awakened one."

Sooner or later in our lives all of us replicate this archetypal pattern. Some enter this world laden with challenges from birth. Many, for a time, enjoy the vigor and seeming invulnerability of youth. But then come periods of illness, which can settle into chronic and disruptive patterns as we age. Sudden injuries may also derail our lives and leave lingering aftereffects, both physical and psychological. We may struggle with sensorimotor impairments, energy deficits, modes of incapacity, or sites of pain that isolate us from others. These issues are all but universal. For example, a recent estimate from the Institute of Medicine suggests that more than one hundred million Americans suffer some form of chronic pain (Dusenbery 2018, 176). In many ways this is an impersonal process. Few of us fully escape physical suffering, and none of us gets out of this world alive.

Yet, these afflictions are also very personal. They are unique, contextualized by one's own life-narrative. Many people find ways to thrive despite their struggles. This involves coming to terms with the intimate, yet alien nature of our embodiment. Especially when encountering affliction, our very own body—the foundation of our perception, movement, habits, abilities, and relationships—can seem an enemy, or a mysterious stranger. Why do I feel so unwell today? Where has my energy gone when there is so much to be done? Why is my stomach chronically in turmoil; or my back always aching; or this cancerous growth senselessly threatening my life?

And yet, again people find ways to flourish despite, and sometimes even because of, these challenges. They develop strategies for coping, resilience, adaptation, and growth. This book begins by examining the healing strategies individuals employ, often quite independently of the medical system. Modern medicine may excel at forms of diagnosis and treatment but is often sadly deficient at the business of "healing"—that is, finding wholeness in the face of the breakdowns which threaten to disintegrate our lifeworld.

In the first half of this book I examine no less than twenty different healing strategies that people utilize in the face of bodily challenges, either largely on their own or in concert with others. From whence is this table of strategies derived? To some degree I draw on personal experience. I have hardly escaped illness, aging, and intimations of mortality; for example, chronic back pain which ultimately demanded emergency surgery, as well as a searing peripheral neuropathy (nerve pain in my leg) which has led to two surgeries. Along the way I have investigated and used probably every strategy I write about, discovering both their benefits and limits.

Philosophically, I am engaged in "phenomenology," the search for essential and repeated structures of human experience. First-person introspection is one point of entry, but this can also be misleading if we seek to universalize our own idiosyncratic experiences. As such, this book also relies on a number of "pathographies," that is, memoirs of illness, impairment, and healing by acute self-observers. My own medical training is also a useful background, along with my acquaintance with some clinical, anthropological, and psychological research. I also draw on many years of volunteer teaching in maximum-security prisons which revealed the resonances between chronic illness and long-term incarceration. Much studying, teaching, and engaging in practices drawn from Hinduism, Buddhism, and Daoism has helped provide me with non-Western contexts.

But most directly this book depends on work in the phenomenology of the lived body conducted in the twentieth and twenty-first century by so-called continental philosophers. Figures such as Edmund Husserl, Maurice Merleau-Ponty, and many others who followed in their footsteps have explored essential structures of embodiment: for example, that I both "am" my body and "have" a body which I don't entirely understand or control; that the body is the root of an "I can" structure of habitual abilities, but also the "I can't" of weakness and disability; and so forth.

These structures help determine the kind of "chessboard" of moves that are possible in response to bodily breakdown. For example, when assaulted by illness, I can either move toward my body, listening to and embracing it (I *am* my body), or I can distance myself (I *have* a body), and choose to ignore, objectify, or transcend its limits. In total, I examine *five essential structures of human embodiment*—and *four variant possibilities of healing response* that pertain to each area, hence twenty in all.

Figure 1 gives an overview of these healing strategies in the order they are taken up by successive chapters. **Figure 2** presents them through a chessboard analogy as a five-by-four matrix of possible healing strategies. I have purposely not arranged the strategies in any hierarchy, which might classify certain ones as superior to others. There are many books that tout, often quite well, a particular approach (mindful witnessing, listening to your body, revising your life-narrative, etc.), but my goal is to survey the broad set of possibilities, all of which may be of use to different individuals at different times.

To employ this book as a tool for healing, whether for yourself or when working with a patient or client, these diagrams can help track which strategies an individual is using, and others which that person might beneficially try. For this purpose, following the figures is a list titled "Six Questions." These questions will help one survey the strategies one has tried, the ways that they have worked or failed, and other available healing approaches. *This turns a somewhat academic book into more of a workbook for active healing.* Similarly, a clinician can use these diagrams and questions as a tool to help patients negotiate the challenging process of adapting to an illness or incapacity.

I do not claim this list of twenty healing strategies to be definitive in a transhistorical and transcultural sense. Phenomenology has progressed away from claiming to present one essentialist, universalized account of human experience. "Critical phenomenology" analyzes, and often critiques, the particular sociohistorical conditions that shape human lives. Our embodied experience can be influenced by racism, sexism, ageism, homophobia, and other modes of discrimination. (I focus more on this in part 2 of the book.) Nonetheless, I believe that the body—and consequently bodily experience—is not infinitely plastic. The body, considered both biologically and experientially, does have built into it a variety of features that serve to constrain and vector possible interpretations. We have bones that can break; acutely sensitive skin; inner organs less accessible to immediate experience; and needs for breath, nutrition, and thermoregulation. These are elements in embodied life that are meaningfully invariant, though they also serve as the launching pad for much societal and personal variation.

My analysis of twenty healing strategies thus grows out of fundamental features of the lived body, but with the recognition that these are enacted in a wide variety of ways in our own time and place. There is a tendency in postmodernist philosophy to thematize "the body" a great deal, but also to overlook it. As Prosser (1998, 13) notes, in key figures like Foucault and Lacan, "materiality figures only in reference to discourse and signification . . . The body is rather our route to analyzing power, technology, discourse, language." While I certainly take on such topics, my primary focus remains on our direct experience of the body and how we can cope with its challenges and breakdowns.

Of course, many in the clinical and psychological sciences have tried to codify our adaptive responses to illness. Yet the overall result can be a bit inchoate: different authors are often working with different disease entities, patient populations, and ways of organizing data from various survey protocols. In this book I use a distinctive approach. I suggest how the edifice of healing strategies is built directly upon the basic structures of lived embodiment.

I hope this book will be accessible not only to scholars in the philosophy of the body/medicine, but also to the educated layperson. At the time of publication well over one hundred million Americans suffer from some sort of chronic illness. The "chessboard" of healing strategies I survey may help name and affirm strategies they are already using or suggest new possibilities that could bring relief. Nor are the "healthy" immune to facing these issues, especially at a time when we are recovering from a global pandemic. In the words of a *New York Times* article: "The pandemic has brought many able-bodied people for the first time into territory intimately familiar to the chronically ill, the former speaking with wonder and pain of what, to the latter, is commonplace" (El-Mohtar 2020, 7). Unfortunately, not only Covid-19, but its aftermath, "long Covid," casts a dark shadow on many lives—so we are even more in need of methods for healing.

This typology of strategies may also be of interest to those in the healing professions, whether physicians, nurses, physician assistants, psychologists, or those in complementary and alternative medicine. It is imperative for them to understand the array of strategies their patients are using, or which they could use with the proper coaching and support. It is equally important to be aware of the potential shadow-sides of healing strategies: for example, the person who refuses to be limited by illness, but overdoes it to the point of risking self-injury.

For me, this book also constitutes the last in a trilogy, albeit one that has taken more than thirty years to unfold. In *The Absent Body* (1990), I used phenomenological methods to examine the many ways in which the body seems to disappear from experience, and the ways it surfaces when things become problematic. I suggest this to be an experiential basis for Cartesian dualism, which separates the essential self from its body. Then, in *The Distressed Body* (2016), I looked deeper into the experience of chronic pain, illness, and incarceration, as well as how these are dealt with by the medical and carceral systems (hint: not always well). This last book, *The Healing Body*, is more a celebration of human resilience in the face of affliction.

The book begins with "A Musical Overture" (chapter 1) stating a number of themes that will later be further modulated and developed. Using an example from the violinist Itzhak Perlman, I give an overview of the dis-integrating impact of illness and impairment, and our capacity for healing—that is, the recovery of an integrated life, perhaps one even enriched by its challenges. This first chapter is deliberately nontechnical: feel free to skip it if you wish to proceed to the more systematic analysis.

Over the course of the next three chapters composing part 1, I lay out the *twenty healing strategies* previously mentioned. Chapter 2 focuses on how the body-self disruption caused by illness can be coped with either by distancing from the body "*I have*," or by choosing to embrace the body "*I am*" and "*am-with*." I explore four subvariants of these fundamental moves away from or toward the problematic body.

Chapter 3 turns to the body as the source of what Husserl and Merleau-Ponty called the "*I can*"—our reservoir of abilities and habits—and also of the "*I can't*," our limitations. Yet these change over time, bringing into focus lived time itself. The ill person can seek to reclaim previous capacities, or transform their way of being-in-the-world to compensate for illness or injury. They can gain strength from remembering the past, anticipating a better future, or putting down roots firmly in the present. Serious illness can make us reexamine, and perhaps even reconstitute, our whole life-narrative. In the face of chronic illness or aging, these strategies can support what I call "chronic healing," that ongoing process of adaptation which also helps to heal time (*khronos*) itself.

Chapters 4 and 5 turn to the intersubjective nature of embodiment. This topic is so rich and significant that greater space is given to its unfolding: whereas previous chapters had taken on eight strategies at a time, each of these chapters focuses on only two. From before the time of birth, one's body has been intertwined with and nourished by other bodies. Healing the self-body relationship is no private matter but is often mediated by (or sometimes interfered with) by others. The physical body is an *object* in the world and can often benefit from diagnostic and therapeutic objectification. Yet the lived body is also an experiencing *subject*, and the empathic communion offered by loved ones and fellow sufferers is crucial for relieving isolation and building a community of mutual empowerment. For the ill or aged person, learning to *receive* help is often one of the hardest lessons, especially in a culture that values independence above all. Also crucial is the discovery that one can still *give* despite having an impaired body, and that this giving may be deepened by experiences of struggle and loss.

Thus concludes the survey of twenty healing strategies that constitutes the first part, and roughly the first half, of this book. As mentioned, I have diagrammed them using a two-dimensional chessboard surface representing different "possibility spaces" through which one can respond to the recalcitrant body. But it must be understood that one has multiple chess pieces at one's disposal such that one can, and in most cases will, be using multiple strategies in conjunction. Or instead of imaging a two-dimensional chessboard surface, one might think of healing as a *five-dimensional chess game*. For example, in the face of serious illness, communing with others with a similar condition may help one seek out appropriate clinicians, better care for one's own body, and re-envision one's life narrative in a positive way, knowing one still has much to enjoy and give. One is "playing the game" on different dimensions simultaneously and they synergistically work to enable one another.

Yet there is still more to explore. In part 2 I turn away from this generalized focus on bodily affliction to the predicament of those groups who are particularly challenged and marginalized. This unfortunately is a huge topic insofar as ableism, racism, sexism, ageism, heterosexism, xenophobia, and so on, devalue certain bodies. There are many excellent books that examine such topics in detail. I briefly present an overview of "embodied injustice," and then turn to two examples most familiar to me from my teaching and research: the position of *prisoners* and of *elders*.

Chapter 6 suggests that those suffering from chronic incarceration deal with many of the same life-disruptions as those experiencing chronic illness, and often employ similar healing strategies. There is much the two communities could teach one another, and all of us, about how to survive, and even thrive, in the face of embodied assaults.

In chapter 7 I turn to *elders*, who are often struggling with health challenges as well as ageist discrimination. Drawing on wisdom traditions the world over, I critique our usual models of "successful aging" and suggest different ways the challenges of later life can become a catalyst for personal/spiritual growth and social contribution. Again, I articulate a variety of healing archetypes rather than a one-size-fits-all model of holistic elderhood.

The last part of the book, part 3, seeks to deepen our analysis of what I term the "inside-out" nature of the lived body, along with the implications of this for healing. In chapter 8 I examine "interoception" (our sensory experiences of our own body), which is a hot topic in medicine and the neurosciences. I analyze how our visceral functions and awareness profoundly intertwine with outer-world relations such that the very division between "inner" and "outer" is called into question. Western culture, while celebrating the interiority of mind, thought, and reason (what I call the "superior interior"), tends to devalue and override what has been judged the "inferior interior"—our visceral self-awareness. Yet the ability to hear messages from our inner body is, I suggest, often a key to self-healing independent of the medical system.

Chapter 9 then works with the paradoxical nature of *breathing*—a bodily function that forms a hinge between the bodily interior and the outside world; is ordinarily automatic, but available to voluntary control; and forms a bridge between what we customarily divide up as "mind," "body," and "spirit." The breath can thus serve as a key to mental/physical healing and, as used in meditative techniques, can further our liberation from the confinements of the isolated self.

This latter becomes the focus of the book's final chapter. I closed *The Absent Body* by turning to the neo-Confucian notion that "we form one body" with the universe. Similarly, in chapter 10 of this book I draw on non-Western inspirations (this time primarily the Hindu tradition of Advaita Vedanta, though supplemented by Buddhist and Daoist references) to examine the personal body as a channel for transpersonal awareness. Diverse wisdom traditions suggest that to fully "heal," become whole, is not only to cope with bodily misfortune but to dissolve the very sense of a rigid and limited body, that which imprisons us as a separate self. I explore what I call the "transparent body," as well as practices that may help us experience its expansive and healing effects. The chapter is purposefully provocative and speculative, but with due attention paid to ordinary lived experience.

Thus concludes our survey of healing responses to those sights encountered by the Buddha, and by us all: the sick person, the old person, and the corpse. To be healed—to find wholeness even in the face of bodily and existential afflictions—is one of the greatest challenges and accomplishments of human life.

1

A Musical Overture

Re-possibilizing Life after Illness and Incapacity

Prelude

Sometimes, rather than beginning with technical analyses, it helps to start with a story. As recounted by Jack Riemer in the *Houston Chronicle*, the famed violinist Itzhak Perlman was launching into his New York concert when something went wrong. One of his violin strings snapped. Perlman walks slowly on crutches, a legacy of his childhood polio—would he now leave the stage in search of a new violin or string?

> But he didn't. Instead, he waited a moment, closed his eyes and then signaled the conductor to begin again. The orchestra began, and he played from where he had left off. And he played with such passion and such power and such purity as they had never heard before.
>
> Of course, anyone knows that it is impossible to play a symphonic work with just three strings. I know that, and you know that, but that night, Itzhak Perlman refused to know that. You could see him modulating, changing, recomposing the piece in his head. At one point, it sounded like he was de-tuning the strings to get new sounds from them that they had never made before . . . and then he said—not boastfully, but in a quiet, pensive, reverent tone—"You know, sometimes it is the artist's task to find out how much music you can still make with what you have left." (Riemer 2001)

It should be noted that there are questions about the accuracy of Riemer's account. It was written down several years after the concert, and contemporary records show no reviewers referring to this onstage incident (Mikkelson 2007). The story may be embellished or apocryphal. Nonetheless, we can use it as a parable to help us explore healing from illness, injury, and impairment. When a string snaps—when we lose bodily capabilities that were present before, thereby threatening our physical and existential integrity—how can we still make music with what we have left?

In this first chapter I will take as my paradigm case of "string-snapping" the onset of a serious physical illness or an injury with long-term implications. Ram Dass, the spiritual teacher who did much to bring Eastern wisdom to the West, suffered a late-life stroke, placing him in a wheelchair and severely damaging his language abilities. He writes, "Whether their bodies have been incapacitated by physical trauma, disease, or old age makes little difference, since the results are the same" (Ram Dass 2001, 71).

There is truth to this, but there are also important differences to explore. Some incapacities may be present from birth. As those in the field of disability studies point out, having a body differently-abled from what is judged normative does not make it diseased. Being deaf, for example, can enable its own rich ways of engaging the world. Much of the dysfunctionality associated with such conditions may arise from the stigmatization of "non-ideal bodies," and from obstacles to their full social engagement (Wendell 1996; Kafer 2013; Davis 2016; Clare 2017; Reynolds 2022). Similarly, aging should not be equated with affliction. Despite our ageist prejudices, many elders are leading healthy and vigorous lives, not to mention enjoying the fruits of wisdom and liberty that can grace the later years (Leder 1997; Chernikoff 2021). This will be a focus of chapter 7.

Yet it is true that old age almost inevitably brings its pains and impairments, and that many with disabilities are so as the result of chronic diseases such as arthritis, diabetes, or heart or respiratory disease (Wendell 1996, 20). While there is truth to the focus in disability studies on the prejudicial treatment of non-normative bodies, it is also true that there are biologically based modes of incapacity and suffering (Reynolds 2022, 78–80). At some point, most of us will face the issue of "how much music you can still make with what you have left."

In harmony with the Perlman example, I give a somewhat musical organization to this first chapter. The prelude now done, we turn to "three movements," followed by a coda in place of the usual scholarly conclusion. I will speak of illness and healing as incorporating (1) "*impossibility*" (the loss of previous capacities), (2) "*I'm possibility*" (the reclaiming of creative response), and (3) the "'*I am*' *possibility*" (the experience of a level of Being, which I term the "*I am*," that transcends the limitations that illness/injury make so apparent). The themes introduced in this chapter will later be modulated and developed throughout the book.

First Movement: *Impossibility*

"Of course, anyone knows that it is impossible to play a symphonic work with just three strings." Serious illness and injury can make us unable to do or be things that previously characterized our identity. There are many excellent pathographies, ethnographies, and phenomenologies of illness experience (for example, Toombs 1992; Couser 1997; Kleinman 1988). I will start by drawing on a few unusually reflective memoirs by those who are medically, sociologically, or philosophically trained.

Paul Kalanithi, in the midst of a highly successful life as a top Stanford neurosurgeon, describes how he suddenly found himself incapacitated by metastatic lung cancer.

> My body was frail and weak—the person who could run half marathons was a distant memory. . . . Because I wasn't working, I didn't feel like myself, a neurosurgeon, a scientist—a young man, relatively speaking, with a bright future spread before him. Debilitated, at home, I feared I wasn't much of a husband for Lucy. In fourteenth-century philosophy, the word patient simply meant "the object of an action," and I felt like one. (Kalanithi 2016, 140–41)

While I wrote earlier about the impersonal nature of illness, aging, and death, the impossibilities faced by an ill person are also particular and personal. Kalanithi is unable to run a half-marathon. This is not something illness would take from *me* because I have never even contemplated running such a race, but Kalanithi did and loved it. Then too, he was an accomplished neurosurgeon at work and an engaged husband at home, yet all these personal investments are suddenly threatened. Thus, the impossibilities brought about by serious illness/injury are not *logical* in form—such as "A" cannot equal "not A"; nor are they merely *imaginative*—Kalanithi cannot sprout wings and fly; nor are they *universal* in nature; but rather real, specific, and individual.

As the above suggests, serious illness can threaten not only a repertoire of actions but one's very identity and life-narrative. Kalanithi no longer feels he is the "subject" of his life, but rather the "object," a body under treatment by others. This subject-object split can seem to divide the self in two, with one's own body now rendered an antagonist. Moreover, the ill person may simultaneously feel split off from others. At the very moment we most wish for compassionate aid, we may feel most alone, as if exiled to some island of the ill (Leder 2016a, 13–23). This can also upend any sense of cosmic connection—why would God or the universe do this to me?

There is a special price to be paid for having *invisible impossibilities*. In the midst of a vigorous midlife, Susan Wendell developed a form of chronic fatigue immune dysfunction syndrome (myalgic encephalomyelitis). Because this disease is largely invisible to others, she found herself trapped in a double bind: she could either seek to power her way through the disability "like a normal person," without receiving understanding and accommodations from others—or she could draw attention to her condition and feel like a complainer (Wendell 1996, 27).

But so too is there a price for those with highly *visible impossibilities*. Nancy Sherman, writing of soldiers who have lost limbs in combat, notes that "amputees often feel stigmatized by their injuries, self-conscious that others view them as freakish or disfigured or just different" (Sherman 2011, 197). She recounts the story of Dawn Halfaker, who had her right arm blown off in an explosion in Iraq:

> She told herself, "I'm never going to be normal. It's never going to be easy. . . . When I lost an arm, that went out the window." There is a tension in her images of herself, then and now, of who she would like to be and who she is, filtered through the eyes of others and her perception of their gaze, and through her own grief. (Sherman 2011, 203)

Though Halfager makes dramatic progress and eventually becomes the CEO of a large company and an avid left-handed tennis player, she cannot be the person she once was, as the gaze of others ceaselessly reminds her. And working with "only three strings," to use the Perlman metaphor, is made harder by modes of social discrimination. As Wendell (1996, 86) writes, "Body ideals include not only ideals of appearance, which are particularly influential for women . . . but also ideals of strength, energy, movement, function, and proper control." Incapacities can feel like shameful inadequacies in the face of the pressure to fulfill rigid norms, often vectored by one's gender identity.

This may be reinforced by a phobic response to those who remind us of illness and mortality. Havi Carel one day found herself short of breath: a workup revealed the devastating news that she had lymphangioleiomyomatosis (LAM), a severe, progressive, and at the time, uniformly fatal disease. She experienced this burden as increased by others' discomfort and denial. "With many the fact of my illness is never mentioned and I have come to experience it as something highly secretive, grossly inappropriate for conversation. My dirty little secret" (Carel 2014, 65).

One would hope that at least medical professionals would surmount this evasiveness and aversion, but encountering bodily *impossibilities* can be hard for them as well. They may be disappointed in the ineffectiveness of their treatments, fearful of failure, or of death itself, and even sometimes ready to blame the patient. Arthur Frank, the well-known sociologist, recovering from both a heart attack and testicular cancer, writes: "In society's view of disease, when the body goes out of control, the patient is treated as if he has lost control. Being sick thus carries more than a hint of moral failure; I felt that in being ill I was being vaguely irresponsible" (Frank 1991, 58). Having myself both received and studied medical training, I remember the expression "the patient failed the treatment"—when of course the reality was that the treatment itself had failed.

Second Movement: *I'm Possibility*

Though starting with the theme of *impossibility*, that is hardly where the music ends. In the face of illness and incapacity, the healing process involves a reclaiming of the sense of possibility. Classic existentialist philosophy, for example, that of Jean-Paul Sartre (1956), emphasizes the freedom that distinguishes the human being as "for-itself" from an "in-itself" material object governed by deterministic laws. Though humans have a factical life-situation they also transcend it—they retain the capacity to define the meanings and purposes of their life and to choose their actions. In this sense, bodily *impossibilities* are embraced within the framework that *I'm possibility*. Again, Riemer describes Perlman as "modulating, changing, recomposing the piece."

Sartre's stark dualism of for-itself and in-itself, transcendent consciousness and brute materiality, fails to acknowledge the truth that illness reminds us of—that we, in our subjectivity, also *are* our bodies; our freedom is intertwined with our embodied capacities. As Sartre's colleague, Maurice Merleau-Ponty, explored in depth, there is a bodily "*I can*" (2012, 139), a complex ability-structure based on our physiological capacities and cultivated habits. This structure may be massively disrupted by illness and injury (what I will later term the *I can't*), but at the same time, like Perlman, one can still respond in creative ways.

The experience that *I'm possibility* may seem the reverse of that of *impossibility*, but the linguistic echo (they are the same sequence of letters) is meant to suggest their interconnection. After all, a healing process does not simply get rid of illness's existential dissonance, but finds a way of incorporating it into a new music. Perlman has broken a string but despite this, or perhaps even as a result of it, he summons up the flexibility, persistence, skill, and humor to carry on with his playing.

In such ways might an ill or injured person learn to accomplish customary tasks, but now through a different deployment of bodily resources. Carel, adjusting to her severe respiratory disease, writes: "I adapted to my breathlessness by finding circuitous routes to the shop to avoid walking uphill; I pause several times while climbing up a flight of stairs. . . . Finding a new way of performing an old task, given an altered set of capacities, is challenging; successful performance leads to a sense of achievement" (Carel 2014, 97).

In other situations one's physical body needs supplementation. In a famous passage, Merleau-Ponty (2012, 144) writes of how a blind man learns to use and experience his stick not as an external object but as part of his subjective intentionality, that *from* which he senses and negotiates the world. The stick has been *incorporated* into the structure of his bodily *I can.* Of course, something similar can be said of Perlman's violin: through long years of practice, the instrument has become his own expressive voice. In chapter 3, I will explore such healing through *incorporation*: for example, a wheelchair used by someone rendered paraplegic, or a hearing aid or cochlear implant for a person grown deaf.

We also need to consider where this wheelchair, this cochlear implant, came from. They required an investment of social resources to make them available to the impaired individual, as well as professionals to help train someone in their use, and/or build appropriately accessible environments. This reminds us that re-possibilizing the ill and disabled body is an *intersubjective* endeavor. After all, Perlman needs a symphony orchestra to accompany him, an audience to listen, and an acoustically built concert hall that allows his music to sing. Similarly, someone with a serious illness, injury, or impairment benefits from medical and financial support; competent and caring professionals; understanding friends and family; workplace policies that incorporate medical leave and flexible work hours; architecture, elevators, and ramps that ensure accessibility; and so on. Earlier I discussed how social rejection can intensify the experience of illness *impossibility*; conversely, social support can enhance the "*I'm possibility*" experience by showing that there is, implicitly, a "we" involved. This healing power of intersubjective relations will be the focus of chapters 4 and 5.

For Kevin Aho, an athletic philosopher (and friend) who had a shockingly unexpected heart attack, a consequent deepening sense of "we" reconfigured his world:

> The people in my life that I ordinarily took for granted became luminous and fragile. And this extended beyond my family, partner, and intimate friends, but to colleagues, neighbors, and even complete strangers at the supermarket or gas station. The masks came off, and I sensed

> how helpless and dependent we all are, and this made me love even more. (Aho 2019)

Whether accomplished with others or on our own, paradoxically, it is often accepting impossibilities that opens up the process of re-possibilizing. After all, Perlman "waited a moment, closed his eyes," and took a little time to assimilate the new reality before signaling the conductor to recommence the piece. In Ram Dass's words, if you have developed arthritis, it would often be best to "give up the model of being somebody without arthritis" (Ram Dass 2001, 71). "Instead of will, I've found in myself a peaceful surrender to the karmic unfolding of my life—an unfolding that's like a tree growing or a flower blooming" (Ram Dass 2001, 194). Long a famously adept and sought-after public speaker, Ram Dass learned to enjoy the silence and essential truths that emerged when verbiage was stripped away by his stroke. Long an itinerant wanderer, he found that the stroke grounded him, making it easier for him to meditate in stillness.

Carel similarly writes of new modes of appreciative presence that the impossibilities posed by her grave illness now made possible:

> I no longer save money. . . . I care much less what people think of me. . . . I found to my surprise that I experienced amplified enthusiasm and joy, echoing against the narrow confines of the present. All my energy and happiness are funneled into the *now,* into today: how nice it feels to be *here,* in the sun, having a massage, listening to beautiful music, laughing until I am dizzy, sitting by a warm fire, experiencing friendship, love, sunshine, the lazy sensation of waking up after a deep sleep, the sharp authority of beauty. (Carel 2014, 146)

These examples grow from an *acceptance* of illness, a healing strategy I explore in the next chapter. But I also write there of the potential value of *refusing* the limitations of illness—in fact, these attitudes can stand in dialectical and complementary relation to each other. While Perlman accepted the fact of the busted string, he simply "refused to know" that he couldn't complete his symphonic piece. In the history of music, the most famous example of such a principle is found in the life of Beethoven who, after much inner struggle, determined not to be destroyed by his growing deafness but rather to put it to liberatory uses. Without his "disability" we would likely have missed out on the wild and brilliant experimentation of the late string quartets.

Third Movement: The *"I Am" Possibility*

That which Buddha saw, and we all encounter—illness, aging, dying—may ultimately lead to a search for that which overleaps bodily limits. As Carel (2014, 83) writes in a stoical vein, "Even in cases of extreme physical disability there is always a freedom of thought, imagination, emotion and intellect." This need not imply a metaphysics of mind–matter dualism or a wholesale rejection of embodiment. Wendell, drawing on her experience with chronic myalgic encephalomyelitis, writes:

> To choose to exercise some habits of mind that distance oneself from chronic, often meaningless physical suffering increases freedom, because it expands the possibilities of experience beyond the miseries and limitations of the body. . . . Nor do I think we need to devalue the body or bodily experience to value the ability to gain some emotional and cognitive distance from them . . . since it is bodily changes and conditions that lead us to discover these strategies. (Wendell 1996, 177–78)

Still, *physical* illness often leads to *metaphysical* yearnings—for many people, deep healing has an implicitly or explicitly spiritual dimension. Ram Dass writes: "What was changed through the stroke was my attachment to the Ego. The stroke was unbearable to the Ego, and so it pushed me into the Soul level also, because when you 'bear the unbearable,' something within you dies" (Ram Dass 2001, 201). This facilitated a realization he had long sought: "My Awareness doesn't have a locus, and so my consciousness isn't trapped in my body. I had *experienced* that—not as an abstract understanding, but as a real event" (Ram Dass 2001, 194). I worked with Ram Dass when we were both writing books on aging around the same time, but his publisher told him his treatise wasn't quite finished: he needed a last chapter that would convey the experience of the truly "old old." Shortly afterwards he had his devastating stroke, but one which also provided him with that missing finale. He titled the last chapter "Stroke Yoga" (Ram Dass 2001, 183–204): his catastrophic illness proved a *sadhana* (spiritual method) that was just as powerful or even more so than the many others he had built his life around.

Taking many forms—near-death experiences, existential realizations, a deepening of religious faith, a sense of transcendent interpersonal love—I refer to this as opening up the *"I am" possibility*. In Exodus 3:14, God, when asked his name, replies: "I am that I am." We could take this to refer to a pure Being that is not constrained by time, and is in fact beyond all limits and definitions, including those imposed by illness. Similarly, in a non-dual mode which emphasizes the identity of self and Divine, *jnana yoga* teachers such as Ramana Maharshi (1988) remind us that we are too quick to surround the personal experience that *I am* with qualifiers: for example, I am 5′11″, I am 170 pounds, I am a professor, I am in Baltimore, I am a husband, and so on. All these qualifiers have, or will be, altered in time—sickness and aging bring this fact home with force. Yet for some, rather than invoking despair, this opens the door to a sense of a boundless "*I am*" that transcends our social, temporal, and physical limitations. What are we to make of these experiences of a healing not only *of* the body, but *from* the body? While I but introduce this theme here, it will be developed at greater length in the book's final chapter.

In starting off with this musical conceit of first, second, and third movements, I do not mean to imply that these are stages which unfold in a neat sequence. In fact, as the linguistic echoes are meant to suggest (*impossibility, I'm possibility, the "I am" possibility*), they can be deeply interpenetrating modalities. Someone dealing with a serious impairment—for example, an amputated limb—may experience in the same day, and perhaps even at the same time (1) frustration with their broken body, felt as something limited and freakish (*impossibility*); (2) a compensatory use of their other limbs to complete a task (*I'm possibility*); and (3) a sense that they are so much more than this formed and de-formed body (the *"I am" possibility*).

Coda

A musical coda draws on earlier themes, but it may do so in playfully improvisational ways. It is in this spirit that I finally turn my focus not to Perlman's busted string but to the man himself, his body, biography, even his name. The story of Perlman's three-stringed instrument, and his resilience in dealing with it, takes on added resonance in the light of his childhood polio. He writes:

> My parents were very supportive in a normal way. It was never: "Oh, we have a child who has polio!". . . . With my childhood friends, the abnormal thing about me was not that I walked with crutches—they got used to that. The abnormal thing about me was that I had to practice three hours a day. The other kids thought that was crazy. (J. Straus 2011, 143)

For a long time, Perlman did not want others to focus on his disability, or how it might have shaped him as a musician. He was angered with headlines like "Crippled Violinist Plays Concerto." He did not want to be so defined, pitied, or exalted. We can indeed see how a case like his can be used to feed the damaging mythology of the "supercrip" (Reynolds 2022, 73). That sort of narrative locates the source of disability solely in the individual—not in the larger society and its modes of possibly inadequate response—and then implies that the individual can and should overcome any obstacle.

Yet, though initially resistant, Perlman ultimately owned his disability as a not insignificant part of his identity. He came to speak on disability-rights issues such as removing architectural barriers to access. He even refused to play in some venues because of such accessibility issues, whether for himself or for his audience (J. Straus 2011, 143–45). As mentioned earlier, re-possibilizing the world involves social cooperation. Credit is due to Perlman's parents, childhood friends, teachers, impresarios, concert hall architects, and everyone else who helped make his genius possible, but also to Perlman himself and his inspiring resilience.

J. S. Bach chose to use his own name as a musical note sequence, B A C H (H is the German notation for what we would call B natural), in the last *contrapuntus* theme of the *Art of the Fugue,* the piece he was working on in his final days. I ask the reader's indulgence while I end this musical introduction with a brief theme based on Itzhak Perlman's name. First, Itzhak, the Hebrew version of the English "Isaac," comes from the biblical story of Sarah and Abraham. When they were both quite old, such that Sarah had "stopped having the periods of women," a divine emissary tells her that she is to have a child . . . and she laughs! "'Now that I am withered, am I to have enjoyment—with my husband so old?'. . . . The Lord asked, 'Why did Sarah laugh . . . Is anything too wondrous for the Lord?'" (Gen. 18:10–14). When Sarah does in fact bear a child, she names him Itzhak, which in Hebrew means "to laugh." Sarah says, "God has brought me laughter; everyone who hears will laugh with me" (Gen. 21:6). Itzhak (Isaac) is viewed as the progenitor of the Jews, a people who have suffered much, but were thus born of laughter.

We see in this tale the themes we have been treating, now all woven together There is a seeming physical *impossibility*—new birth from old and withered bodies? Yet Sarah and Abraham claim the stance that "*I'm possibility.*" In later life they take on new names, move to a new land, and even miraculously have a child. Finally, and obviously, the story speaks to a transcendent dimension, which I have termed the *"I am" possibility.* Sarah and Abraham hear a call of the Divine, the "I am that I am" (Ex. 3:14), summoning them to overleap their limitations. I will revisit this biblical story in chapter 7.

So much for the name "Itzhak," but what of "Perlman"? Well, our artist is something of a Pe(a)rl-man. A pearl is formed when a parasite or other irritant lodges in a shellfish, leading it to deposit concentric layers of mineral. This adaptation to irritation creates a thing of jewel-like beauty. So, too, can something comparable happen when we face serious illness, injury, or impairment. For Itzhak Perlman, as in the story of his violin string breaking—and perhaps earlier as a child when part of his body broke—his adaptive struggle helps birth a precious pearl.

Of course, there is a danger here of falling into what Reynolds (2022, 74) calls "inspiration porn." Few of us with illness and impairments can retune our violin as expertly as a Perlman can. In fact, the demand for high-performance recovery—that the person struggling with pain or disability be ever cheerful and resilient, making lemonade out of all of life's lemons—can create unneeded stress and suffering. When a string breaks, the most that many of us can do is grieve our loss, then pick up the fiddle and saw away as best we can. There are likely to be many dissonant notes, but we may hit upon unexpected harmonies, ones we will be exploring throughout this book.

Part 1

Twenty Healing Strategies

2

Escaping and Embracing the Body

Illness and Healing

We have suggested that universal to the human experience are encounters with bodily adversity. These may include chronic pain, illness, disability, and the changes that come with age. In the biomedical model these are often modeled as machine breakdown. As such they can be treated by appropriate medicines, surgeries, dietary changes, physical therapy, and the like. This disease model, with its associated diagnosis, prognosis, and treatment protocols, can be of great use in relieving various modes of dysfunction and prolonging life. However, this model can also fail to treat human suffering, or make it worse, because of a lack of investigation into the very nature of illness.

For we have seen that severe or chronic illnesses are not just biophysical but existential events. The term "illness," rather than "disease," is often used in medical phenomenology to refer to the sickness-as-experienced, insofar as it disruptively reverberates across many of life's dimensions. Excellent work on the phenomenology of illness and its treatment has been conducted by sociologists (Frank 1991), literary figures (Broyard 1992), medical anthropologists (Kleinman 1988), scientists and clinicians (Cassell 1985; Sacks 1994), and many philosophers whose writings inform my own (Aho 2018, 2019; Aho and Aho 2009; Benner 1994; Carel 2014; Carel and Cooper 2013; Dahl et al. 2019; Svenaeus 2001, 2011, 2015, 2017; Toombs 1992, 2001; Zaner 1981; Zeiler and Käll 2014). I will try here to just outline some key elements in the experience of illness, but a bit more systematically than was done in the prior "musical overture." Then I will pivot to the primary focus of this and the following chapters: the healing strategies that we are able to employ in response to illness.

First, illness can bring about a contraction and disordering of our lived spatiality. A flight of stairs no longer beckons upward but becomes an impassible barrier. A half-mile walk to the store may simply lie beyond our capacities. We may even remain confined to our bed, separated from the wider world (van den Berg 1966), which has now come to feel alien, "unhomelike" (Svenaeus 2015).

This is not only brought about by an alteration in our lived space, but in our temporal sense. Ordinarily, human beings live largely in relation to the future, directing their activity toward desired goals (Heidegger 1962, 95–107), but in the midst of suffering, time can narrow its compass. Our previous life ambitions may now seem unrealizable. Even getting through a single day or hour can be a struggle, especially in the face of chronic pain. The aching, limited, or worrisome present is aversive, pushing us away, but paradoxically also pulling us inescapably inward.

Sometimes we speak of serious illness as an event of "gravity" that has befallen an individual. In fact, the contemporary scientific notion of gravity can provide an interesting metaphor for these experiences. As Einstein discovered through his work on general relativity, gravity does not operate according to the Newtonian notion of attraction-at-a-distance between two bodies (how this could happen was mysterious even to Newton and his contemporaries), but rather through the fact that a massive object warps or curves the space-time around it, thus determining the path that other objects travel. As a bowling ball lying on a trampoline makes the latter sag and bend around it, so a massive body bends the space-time grid such that, for example, when we accidentally drop a pen, its most direct path is downward to the massive earth.

In this sense, a bodily breakdown is indeed a matter of existential "gravity." Lived space and time begin to bend inwards around the ill or injured body, becoming inhibited and constricted. The body now exerts a "massive presence" as a center of concern and limitation. That is, our lifeworld has been warped in an analogue of the way mass warps the physical spatiotemporal field.

Or let me substitute a different metaphor. Sometimes I look back through the many photos I have taken over recent years with my phone. I see the streets of Amsterdam from an enjoyable academic trip, or a beautiful spring morning where I paused to take a picture of flowers in bloom or trees swaying under an azure sky. Such happy, such expansive moments! And then suddenly I come upon a sequence of photos I took of some body part of mine in case I needed to show my doctor how it looked—perhaps a weird bump or rash on my leg that might be a precursor of Lyme disease. The sudden and unexpected contrast between the beauty of the larger world and such photos of small body-splotches is a bit shocking; with a shudder I delete the latter when they're no longer needed. But the ill person, whose perspective may be similarly collapsed to a small disfigured or dysfunctional body part, cannot delete it from their life so easily.

Such changes effect a multidimensional dis-integration of one's lifeworld. In health I usually live out my capabilities seamlessly, but illness can fragment the self–body relation, making the latter feel alien, uncanny. (I will say more on this shortly.) Then too, the body itself seems to fragment into different parts and functions, each heir to its own disorders and medical specialty.

The self–other relations that structure our social world may similarly dis-integrate. Pain and illness can be profoundly isolating: our preoccupation with bodily discomforts can bring about an introversion of our attention. Rare is the person with a severe toothache who is filled with expansive, compassionate attention toward others. Moreover, these others can neither share nor relieve our painful sensations, which themselves may prove resistant to linguistic expression (Scarry 1985). Nor, as previously said, do others necessarily want to hear of our sufferings—their own feelings of being unable to help, and fears of their own vulnerability, may lead them to subconsciously distance themselves. Moreover, on the practical level, our incapacities may make it simply impossible for us to share in others' life-routines.

The chronically ill and disabled may thus wrestle with chronic loneliness, and perhaps a sense of being stigmatized. This can be exacerbated by private financial worries if chronic illness endangers one's livelihood or triggers the need for expensive drugs and medical care. In my country, the lack of guaranteed universal health care and, more generally, of a strong social safety net leaves individuals feeling even more overwhelmed by their afflictions.

This can reach the point where questions drill down to the heart of one's very identity and place in the cosmos. Who am I, after all? Why did this happen to me? Where is God in all this? Am I being abandoned or punished? A sense of existential homelessness can be as painful as our physical sensations, and together these reverberate in a self-reinforcing cycle.

So how does one heal from all this? Here I would identify "healing," which is derived from the same root as the word "whole," with a reintegration of the various dimensions of life that have been torn asunder by bodily breakdown (Leder and Jacobson 2014). This can happen independent of any medical cure. So "healing" must be distinguished from clinical improvement, though the latter may assist the former, and vice versa.

Sometimes healing is facilitated by contact with the health-care system and sensitive treaters. At times, though, the medical system can be dehumanizing and alienating, and simply reinforce the modes of disruption described above (Toombs 1992). Just as there are studies done on "iatrogenic disease" (disease caused by medical interventions), so we might refer to this as "iatrogenic illness," with the patient's world further dis-integrated by its medicalization.

For the most part, in this and the following three chapters I will focus on *the healing strategies employed by ill persons themselves*, not on the efficacy, or lack thereof, of clinical interventions. The "patient"—a word drawn from the same root as the word "passive"—is very much an *agent* whose coping skills deserve study and respect. Here, practitioners have as much to learn from their clients as vice versa.

There is already a significant literature on the adaptive coping strategies employed by patients, speaking to their frequency of use and effectiveness. One article identifies more than two hundred previous longitudinal reports on predictors of adjustment to cancer alone (Stanton et al. 2007). However, this is a somewhat amorphous research area, with many different studies conducted on different illnesses and patient populations, conceptualizing coping strategies in different ways, and therefore arriving at differing results.

The best attempts can run into difficulty even when trying to systematize through meta-analysis. For example, a recent paper examined 106 qualitative and quantitative studies on how individuals cope with chronic disease, all conducted between 1976 and 2016 (White et al. 2018). The paper's authors arrived at the "THRIVE model," which breaks down adaptive strategies into five basic categories: "therapeutic interventions," "habit and behavioral factors," "relational/social factors," "individual differences," and "values and beliefs." While admirable in this attempt to order a vast literature, the classificatory problems here seem to me far from resolved. For example, a tendency toward *acceptance, benefit finding,* and *positive reinterpretation* is characterized as on the "values and beliefs" spectrum. But then *hope* is considered an "emotional factor," while *dispositional optimism* is counted as an "individual difference." A classificatory system that divides into separate categories what are so organically blended—positivity, benefit-finding, hope, and optimism—remains problematic.

If conceptual categories may separate traits that in life are interwoven, they can also lump together things that deserve to be distinguished. For example, a prominent questionnaire on adaptive coping tracks six modalities of internal and external control, one of which is labeled "*Positive Attitudes.*" This is said to refer to "internal cognitive and behavioural strategies (i.e., realization of shelved dreams and wishes; resolving cumbering situations of the past; take life in own hands; doing all that what pleases; positive thinking; avoiding thinking at illness)" (Büssing et al. 2010). But aren't these factors rather different from one another? This one category combines diverse actions and thought patterns involving past, present, and future respectively.

In this chapter, and the three that follow, I take a different approach, one informed not only by my medical schooling and personal illness experiences, but by my philosophical training. I begin with the basics of the phenomenological understanding of the embodied self. The nature of lived embodiment lays out, so to speak, the chessboard of possible moves we can make when responding to bodily challenges. This provides a way to understand the wide range of adaptive strategies that are available at times of bodily distress—ways of actualizing the sense of *I'm possibility* that I described in the first chapter.

The structure of human embodiment thus provides a foundation upon which to build our analysis of healing. Of course, no single system can capture the diversity of illness experiences and individual responses. Nonetheless, the usefulness of this approach will, I hope, be demonstrated by the way it helps us understand aspects of our responses when under duress, while providing an overview of possibilities for those struggling with chronic challenges, or seeking to offer others therapeutic help. These strategies can help us fulfill, as Perlman said, "the artist's task to find out how much music you can still make with what you have left."

The healing strategies examined in this chapter are broadly divided into those that involve "*escaping the body*" versus those "*embracing the body.*" Within each category I take up four subcategory variants, each itself a different shade of the tendency being examined. In addition to the eight healing strategies discussed here, in succeeding chapters I will go on to examine another twelve more, twenty in all (and if you make it to the end of the book you may find a twenty-first).

At the front of this book, a "wheel" diagram (figure 1) visually represents these twenty strategies, grouped into five categories, each with its four subvariants, in the order of presentation as one goes clockwise starting from the top. Figure 2 represents the same strategies regrouped into a visual "chessboard," another metaphor I use throughout the book. This is meant to suggest how core features of embodiment create a number of possibility spaces that someone can move to in the face of bodily breakdown. Turning to these diagrams from time to time will help the reader keep the developing picture in mind. Also, as I mentioned in the introduction, someone reading this book, whether an ill person or a clinician working with a patient, *may want to use these diagrams in a workbook fashion, turning this text into a tool to assist healing.* Following the figures, I supply a list of "Six Questions" to help someone assess which strategies they most rely on, how those strategies are helpful or limiting, and which other ones might prove beneficial in the future.

Among these twenty healing strategies, I will not seek to define any one modality as better or worse, more or less effective. This is not a clinical trial that evaluates and ranks therapies. On the contrary, I would suggest that each strategy has its own benefits and may prove appropriate at different times, according to differences in condition and personality type. Each of these strategies also has its shadow-side if employed excessively or inappropriately. Nonetheless, for many, the more coping strategies one has at one's disposal, probably the better—what works in the morning may not work in the evening, and flexibility of response is an asset when dealing with chronic challenges.

As I said earlier, I make no claim that this book is the essential and transcultural "final word" on healing. One might suggest I have neglected certain strategies that certain individuals, or entire societies, employ. If this book provokes that kind of critique and supplementation, then it will have served a purpose. Nonetheless, I would also suggest that the "chessboard of healing" here outlined is non-arbitrary. Just as a game takes place on a configured board or field, and has rules defining allowable moves, so does the nature of lived embodiment limit and vector our possible responses.

The *I Am* and the *I Have*

This structure of embodiment has been explored extensively in twentieth and twenty-first-century phenomenology. The lived body (Husserl's *Leib* in German, or Merleau-Ponty's *corps propre*) is understood as something quite different in kind from a nonliving material body (*Körper* in German). The living body is not just a physical object with size and weight, but a set of powers and receptivities from which our experience derives its form (Husserl 1989; Merleau-Ponty 2012). For example, wherever I am physically stationed I discover to be the *here* around which my world is arranged. What is to my right or left, above or below, stands so in relation to my body. The perceived characteristics of surrounding objects, their shape, color, sound, tactile qualities, all are so in relation to my body's sensorium. Moreover, these objects have a practical significance that refers back to the *I can* structure of the lived body which has developed over time through the cultivation of habit-patterns (Merleau-Ponty 2012, 139). *I can* reach that cup of tea and drink it; *I can* type this chapter on my keyboard, my fingers remembering where the letters are though my intellect has long forgotten. The experienced world we inhabit embodies forth our sensorimotor and expressive abilities. Our body also has a plethora of desires and aversions—for example, in relation to other bodies, material goods, natural environments, all pulling us hither and yon.

Thus, we should not think of the body as an isolated physical object. Again, to use a scientific analogy, this would be akin to an outmoded Newtonian description of the universe as composed of separate objects moving through the fundamentally empty container of space and time. Contemporary physics uses more of a unified "field" model, whether it is analyzing gravity, quantum interactions, or electromagnetism.

The lived body is analogously embedded in a field often referred to as the "lifeworld" (in German, the *Lebenswelt*) by phenomenologists. The body is a product of that world—it is born, nurtured, and conditioned by parents, caregivers, and social norms—but it also produces that lifeworld by virtue of its own sensorimotor, cognitive, and affective affiliations. For example, a shift in mood can change one's perceived world from *welcoming* in the morning to *sinister* later the same day, even if only because one is worried or has drunk too much coffee. How much more so may pain or illness shift one's experienced world. But the "good news" is that one can also shift this lifeworld in a healing direction, for example by listening to soothing music, laughing at a favorite comedy, or spending a relaxing day at the beach.

What we have said up until now suggests the degree to which *I am* my body. Putting aside (insofar as we can) a cultural history that overidentifies the self with a disembodied mind or soul, we see how central to our personhood are our embodied desires, perceptions, and actions. Someone would not say, for example, that "my hand picked up the cup" but that "I picked it up." It would seem strange to declare "my eyes are reading this book," rather than simply "I am reading it." In such ways, as I ordinarily go through my day *I am* my body, its powers none other than my own.

Nevertheless, I am so ambiguously, for I also experience my body as something *I have*—that is, non-identical to the self, and showing its independence in many ways. There always remains some awareness of my body as a physical thing in the world, visible to others (Slatman 2014, 53–83). This can be understood as inaugurated when the child first sees her "specular image" in the mirror, commencing a split between her somewhat inchoate interoceptive experiences of her own body and what others see from outside (Lacan 1989, 1–6). As Merleau-Ponty writes, referring to Lacan, "I am torn from myself, and the image in the mirror prepares me for another still more serious alienation, which will be the alienation by others. For others have only an exterior image of me, which is analogous to the one seen in the mirror" (1964, 136).

This gaze of another can indeed be alienating. Sartre gives the famous example of someone catching you while you are looking through a keyhole—suddenly one is no longer the seer but the seen, trapped as an object of shameful visibility (Sartre 1956, 322, 340–400). This objectification, moreover one that can emphasize the *deficiencies* of one's body, is vectored and intensified for people caught in modes of structural oppression. Women in a sexist society are often conditioned to experience their body as an object to be judged by others according to its appearance. The result is an internal alienation, and limitations on the exercise of one's full subjective freedom. One learns to be an object as much as subject, to take up less social space and use one's body in constrained ways, for example, by "throwing like a girl" rather than with full-bodied force (Young 2005; Weiss 1998). In a racist society, people of color also find themselves associated with a body-object, and one that is viewed as inherently deficient or dangerous (Fanon 2008; Gordon 1997; Alcoff 2006; Yancy 2017; Lee 2014; Sekimoto and Brown 2020). If one is nonwhite, for example Pakistani or Black, one may experience discomfort in largely "white spaces," being stopped, questioned, avoided, or surveilled (Ahmed 2007; Yancy 2017). Then too, persons with "disabilities" are often viewed as aberrant and lesser simply by virtue of their non-normative body type (Kafer 2013; Clare 2017). In our later years we may discover the dismissive gaze of an ageist society which views older bodies and lives as being "over the hill" (Aho 2021).

Paradoxically, while this is a way one can feel the body as that which "*I have*" (split in two, objectified by the other's look), it can also seem to reinforce that inescapably "*I am*" this body. One's social identity is reduced by the public gaze to a body or even body parts (a woman's breasts, Black skin, a "hunchback," etc.). Anything that lies outside such physical characteristics—one's intellect, character, experience, accomplishments—is overlooked or dismissed. I will return to these themes in more depth in the treatment of "embodied injustice" in chapter 6.

Whether the body is something that *I am* or *have* is not an either-or question but an essential existential ambiguity. I am always and ever both (Toombs 1992, 51–87). Different experiences can swing us toward, or seem to subsume us in, one of these polarities, or make us more or less attentive to their tension. For example, we may be swimming in the ocean, lost in its wild pleasures (*I am* my body), and then as we emerge onto the beach become aware of someone staring at our exposed flesh (*I have* a body).

These swings can also be affected by changes within our own body. Good health often allows us to take our physical capacities for granted (Leder and Jacobson 2014). One wakes up, walks the dog, drives to work, and so on. At such times, self and body are lived as an unthematized unity such that *I am* my body. However, when pain, illness, or physical limitation arise, their problematic nature disrupts the flow of life and calls for reflexive interpretation. As Wehrle (2019) writes: "To *have* one's body thus presupposes a temporal distance from our ongoing and operative embodiment in which our bodily or functioning intentionality must be (at least in part) interrupted."

This is analogous to Heidegger's famous discussion of the tool, an instrument we need not thematize as long as it is working well. Our attention then remains on the task we are engaged in, and the tool is simply "ready to hand" (in Heidegger's terminology). We pick up the hammer and hold it properly according to the habits of usage we have cultivated, but we focus our attention on the nail we are pounding. However, if the hammer were to break or not function properly it becomes "present at hand," that is, something we must reflexively thematize as an object (Heidegger 1962, 102–7). We begin to engage in a hermeneutical process: What has happened, why has this tool broken down, how can I repair or replace it? This can happen in the same way when our body breaks down. It then transitions from the taken-for-granted backdrop of action to a thing we must attend to and interpret. Reynolds refers to this as the "bioreckoning" (2022, 47) inaugurated by injury or illness. This makes me become aware of my body as that which *I have*, just as a broken tool makes me focus on it as problematic.

However, just as when we are subject to social discrimination, it may be said that *both* sides of the self–body ambiguity are highlighted by illness. Waking up weak and nauseated by the flu, I am reminded, somewhat rudely, how much *I am* inescapably embodied. In fact, we do not usually say "my stomach has a flu," but that "*I* have a flu," this is *my* condition. At the same time, our bodily processes are revealed as something alien—I *have* a flu (the same phrase, but now with different italicized emphasis), and it *has me* in its grip.

In the many cases where pain, illness, or impairment are chronic, what healing strategies become available to help the sufferer cope with long-term challenges? I will start here with strategies that focus on viewing the body as that which *I have*—but which need not *have me*—that is, these strategies accentuate one's capacity to *free oneself from the body*. If illness creates a sense of self–body separation, one can actually lean into this, and through various modes of distancing, regain one's autonomy. Then I will turn to a series of strategies at the other end of the spectrum that involve *embracing the body*. Even when the body surfaces as alien, one can move toward it, rather than away, with a newfound sensitivity to its needs and calls. The body becomes not exactly that which unproblematically *I am* prior to illness, but which now *I am-with* in the mode of a friend or ally.

I will keep to relatively brief treatments of each of these strategies, knowing that over the course of four chapters I will be surveying no less than twenty. While necessarily providing only a sketch of each one, hopefully these will prove descriptively useful, and also open up possibilities for future research programs. For example, one might take a single strategy and devote a chapter, or even a book, to its elements and applications.

Conversely, one might focus on a single disease, such as multiple sclerosis, and ask which of these twenty strategies seems most helpful, and for which symptoms, personality types, and at which stages of the disease's progression. Or one could focus on clinical work with a single individual—which strategies have they employed so far, and to what effect; and what other ones might prove helpful? The language and examples provided here are intentionally simple, but are in service to a phenomenological approach that can be rich, complex, and useful.

Escaping the Body

Ignoring. One approach people often use when their body causes problems is to simply ignore them. A woman with an arthritic knee wants to garden—pain and stiffness threaten to block her, but she chooses to pay them little mind. Her focus shifts to pulling weeds, watering vegetables, and enjoying the sun and breeze. Her illness recedes to the background of her attentional field, and consequently its associated distress and dysfunction diminish. This continues when, later in the day, she becomes absorbed in a conversation with friends. Even if the pain is present, she has found a way to minimize its aversive and disruptive power through modes of distraction.

Ignoring, as through the use of distraction, may seem like a primitive healing strategy. After all, the related word "ignorance" has pejorative overtones, and dictionary definitions of "distracted" include "unable to concentrate" and "bewildered." Ignoring a problem can indeed shade into a maladaptive distraction or denial. Perhaps this knee pain is a biological message to stay off it and, if this is ignored, the gardener risks aggravating the condition. Then too, there are aches or impairments so significant that they simply *can't* be ignored. As mentioned, each healing strategy has limitations and a shadow-side if applied inappropriately.

But *ignoring* the problematic body remains not only one of the most frequently used but often one of the most valuable of healing strategies. Our perceptual field tends toward a gestalt structure with a foregrounded focus that stands out from a contextualizing horizon. For example, while we're sitting in a café, a conversation two tables over leaps out from the background noise because it has captured our attention. This has the effect of "turning up the volume," not as would be registered by a neutral recording device, but as experienced by the lived body. What we focus on tends to grow in amplitude and intensity, while that which we ignore comparably recedes. This can be the case with pain, illness, and impairment, whose level of significance and consequent distress may be proportional to the amount of attention they consume.

Neuroscientific understandings, such as the breakthrough "gate-control" theory, and Melzack's somewhat more sophisticated "neuromatrix" theory, suggest that pain experience is not simply the result of a peripheral stimulus but is filtered and modulated by multiple spinal and cerebral centers of the central nervous system (Melzack and Wall 1996; Melzack and Katz 2004). Focusing on the pain can "turn up the signal" at the level of the central nervous system, making suffering more intense and chronic, even when the peripheral stimulus is in fact no longer present. In the words of the Harvard Medical School's Dr. Haider Warraich, a specialist on chronic pain:

> Almost everything we know about pain and how we treat it is wrong. Both patients and physicians have been taught that chronic pain is essentially acute pain prolonged. But while acute pain rises up the spinal cord to the brain, chronic pain can often descend down from the brain, often without any trigger from below. (DuLong 2022)

Hence *ignoring* chronic pain, using cognitive strategies of minimization and distraction, may block it from entering into conscious experience, and might even begin to rewire our neural circuitry. Experientially, I have sometimes suffered from a painful peripheral neuropathy, but not during those hours when I was totally absorbed in teaching classes. Sometimes *ignore-ance* is bliss.

Refusing. Even if pain or limitation reach the level where they simply cannot be ignored, many individuals will *refuse* to give in to their body as a controlling factor in their social, emotional, or professional life. This is another effective strategy that can be employed to "escape the body."

Refusing may be a response to an immediate and limited challenge. For example, someone decides to embark on a trip despite a severe cold; the self asserts its prerogatives. But it can also be an effective life strategy in the face of ongoing challenges. One might have been born with a birth defect or suffer from a chronic injury or illness, but simply refuses to see oneself as its unfortunate victim. We mentioned the story of Dawn Halfaker, who had her right arm blown off in an explosion in Iraq and then underwent a long and painful recovery period (Sherman 2011, 196–201). Nonetheless, she displayed an overarching spirit of refusal to give in to self-pity and limitation, and eventually emerged as a CEO and a left-handed tennis-player. We saw this similarly in the parable with which we opened the book: though it seems impossible to play a symphonic work with just three strings, Riemer writes, "Itzhak Perlman refused to know that." There are conditions, and personality types, for whom *refusing* forms a highly effective strategy. The word "refuse" comes from the Latin word *refundere*, meaning to "give back, restore, return," and this approach can help restore a sense of positive autonomy (from *auto-nomos*, "self-rule") in the face of bodily assault.

As always, though, there is a shadow-side to this healing strategy. After all, our English term "refuse" can have negative connotations, both as a verb (signifying "unwillingness") and, when putting the accent on the first syllable, as a noun (meaning "matter rejected as worthless, trash"). Insofar as we reject reality and what our body is telling us we may be unable to make adaptive adjustments. This can lead to refusing needed precautions, treatments, or lifestyle changes.

Speaking personally, when I recently had a case of Covid-19, my tendency was to try for a quick comeback, resuming long walks with my dog and tracking on my phone what I hoped would be ever-increasing step counts. By *refusing* to be a victim of post-Covid fatigue, I thought to will myself back to my accustomed activity levels. It didn't work. I soon rebounded from testing negative to positive again for the virus, and throughout my tortuous two-month recovery, any attempt of mine to beat post-Covid fatigue through sheer willpower only made it worse. It was like trying to speed the growth of a plant by pulling at it from above, which only risked dislodging the root system. *Refusing* limitation, which had worked well for me in relation to other physical problems, proved counterproductive in this case.

Objectifying. When the body manifests pain, illness, or limitation, there is a natural thrust toward interpretive objectification (Leder 1990, 69–92). A stomachache may suddenly grab our attention. We become conscious of where it hurts, consider its possible causes (something I ate; work-related tension; a stomach virus?), and therefore what to do about it. We can no longer take the functioning of our digestive system for granted, and our stomach now becomes an object of our scrutiny in the manner of Heidegger's "broken tool." This *objectifying* may be furthered by the aversive element of pain. After all, biologically, pain is meant to be unpleasant, and to motivate us to attend to it in an effort to stop or alleviate it. This attention and aversion both contribute to the distancing that is characteristic of the strategy of objectification.

Many people struggling with physical challenges do regard their problematic body or body part as an "it," something *I have, not am*, something in need of repair as if it were a defective car part. Of course, this attitude is fostered in our culture by a pervasive scientific materialism.

Well before the sick person lies down on an examining table he or she may have guessed at provisional diagnoses, discussed symptoms with friends, or surfed internet health web pages. I earlier introduced the terminological distinction used in the medical humanities between "disease," a term categorized by third-person biomedical logic, and "illness," the dysfunction as actually experienced by the sufferer (Cassell 1985; Toombs 1982). Yet, insofar as our collective experience has been increasingly influenced by the objectifying model of disease, this distinction between third- and first-person perspectives has progressively blurred. Someone's experience of "illness" may, from the beginning, be vectored through the disease model. (In chapter 4 I will examine the pros and cons of undergoing objectifying modes of clinical treatment, but here I focus on the person's own earlier self-objectifying.)

The strategy of objectifying, like any other, has its shadow-sides. Adopting a biomedical perspective can further the feelings of alienation from our own body inaugurated by pain and dysfunction themselves (Frank 1991, 50–63). Our body can feel like an "it," a machine foreign to our own intentions. Moreover, taking a biomedical perspective can tilt us away from a sense of our lived body as a psychophysical whole, and from the consideration of holistic lifestyle changes that might repair the sources of our distress. (In chapter 8 I will speak more on the value of "inside insights"—messages arising within our own body that direct us toward healthy practices.)

Finally, *objectifying* can also increase our distress as we worry about the panoply of diseases that might be causing a symptom or test result. I experienced this recently when a significantly elevated PSA (prostate-specific antigen) was concerning enough to trigger a biopsy. Before that took place my internal fears, combined with internet searches, had convinced me that I was suffering from an extremely aggressive form of prostate cancer. I was actively investigating different treatment protocols when my biopsy came back negative. The prostate cancer had never been real, but my emotional suffering was.

Still, *objectifying* remains a crucial strategy for healing. Emotionally, it can give the afflicted person more sense of distance and control (for example, if it had turned out that I did have aggressive prostate cancer, I was already "prepared for the worst"). Moreover, if investigation can assist with diagnostic naming, that in itself often brings a measure of relief. The patient understands *objectively* what is causing an experience or condition that until now has been subjective, private, and inchoate.

Then too, objectification is often a stage on the way to clarifying what therapeutic approach is the most appropriate one. The biological imperative already implicit in pain or disability—that is, to recognize, interpret, and remedy a body problem—may be brought to a resolution. It is fashionable in phenomenology to critique *objectifying* the body, but we should not lose sight of its immense value when used well.

Transcending. I mentioned Havi Carel's case in chapter 1: an energetic young woman was startled by a diagnosis of LAM, a progressive and usually fatal disease severely affecting her respiratory functions. Needless to say, the shock was enormous, and afterward came the struggle to heal—not to find a cure, which simply wasn't available—but to live well in the face of this bodily assault. Carel writes:

> Against the objective horror of my illness I cultivated an inner state of peacefulness and joy. . . . I don't know what caused this response but I thought about it like this: I have no control over this illness, but I have full control over my emotions and inner state. I cannot choose to be healthy, but I can choose to enjoy the present, embrace the joyful aspects of my life and train myself to observe neutrally my sadness, envy, grief, fear and anger. (Carel 2014, 76–77)

There are a number of strategies implicit in this quotation, but chief among them is what I will term *transcending*. Rather than being subsumed by suffering and limitation, the individual asserts dimensions of self that transcend her body. For Carel, this included her emotions and inner states over which she retained control, an emphasis of ancient Stoicism. Intellectual figures such as Stephen Hawking, one of the great physicists of our time despite a motor neuron disease that left his body almost entirely paralyzed, exemplify this capacity for mental transcendence. So does someone bedridden with a flu who immerses themself in a historical novel: they mentally inhabit another time and place, free from the confines of their sick body. In my own case, I spent a good deal of time *transcending*, or attempting to, during my two-month-long post-Covid fatigue; I meditated and studied non-dualistic teachings on my porch, read poetry, listened to audio novels, and even immersed myself in an eight-season fantasy show (*Game of Thrones*, if you must know).

The use of humor can also be a way to transcend our physical or emotional suffering. In a workshop for elders I conducted, I remember a man whose T-shirt read "Better to be over the hill than under it!" He was prone to illness-related falls but he had learned to make a game of it and laugh, rather than rage or hang his head in shame. In fact, there are many people who find ways to joke about their injury or impairment. A sense of humor need not be just an emotional defense mechanism, but a positive way of transmuting pain into joy and communion with others.

Our departmental project assistant, Lisa Flaherty, had to have a complicated surgery involving the insertion of nine screws to stabilize her wrist following a fall and serious injury. And yet she, and we, spent the next few weeks cracking jokes, from "I'm really screwed" to "No more screwing around," and . . . well, you can imagine. I remember Ram Dass saying that humor was very close to spirituality: both give us a certain freedom, an escape from the heaviness of our predicament.

Indeed, as mentioned in the chapter 1 discussion of the *"I am" possibility*, for many with serious illnesses, transcending is implicitly or explicitly spiritual in nature. *Who am* I, if I am not just this limited, damaged, or aging body? What will remain of me after death? When dealing with serious or even terminal illness, or simply with getting older and seeing our temporal horizon shrink, these are no longer theoretical questions. For many, religiously based answers play a crucial role in making it all bearable and meaningful. Someone may be participating in the sacrificial suffering of Christ; in the Buddha's confrontation with aging, illness, and death; in preparing for a joyful afterlife; or being cradled in the arms of the Goddess. Physical events are thus situated in a metaphysically healing context. I will return to and deepen this theme in the book's final chapter.

Yet like any other strategy, that of *transcending* has its shadow-side. For example, it may impose upon the ill person the belief that he or she should be able to overcome any adversity—by manifesting the meditative detachment of a Buddha or the self-sacrifice and faith that Christ exemplified. Not surprisingly, we are likely to "fail" if these are our criteria for successful healing, and this can compound the sense of painful inadequacy that bodily impairment itself often triggers. Moreover, an undue focus on metaphysical transcendence may lead to a hazardous neglect of the physical. We earlier saw Ram Dass talk about how his stroke helped connect him to an Essence far beyond his body. Yet by his own account, the stroke might have been prevented if he had been paying greater attention to his "incarnation," and taken blood pressure medication.

* * *

In closing this discussion of "escaping the body," it should be noted that these four modes—*ignoring, refusing, objectifying, transcending*—often intertwine. A colleague at my university recently, and very sadly, died of complications following an unusual liver disease and transplant. This involved, for example, regurgitating material that was damaging to his lungs, leading to trips to the ICU and hospital stays of many months. A friend who visited him in the hospital over successive days told me, "John [name changed] does what he calls 'poos in his bed' but has no shame around it. When I asked him if he was concerned about his favorite nurse having to clean it up, he said, 'No, she's quite used to it.'"

This might seem consoling, but my friend actually found it disturbing: John seemed to have become so very distant from his own bodily functions. Our sick colleague had not only been an accomplished intellectual, professor, and administrator, but a bon vivant and celebrated wine-writer, that is, fully involved with sensuous life. Now he lay all day half-watching a cable channel with the sound turned off. My friend forthrightly asked this sick colleague whether he'd be able to reengage with bodily existence in the way necessary to achieve at least partial recovery. He replied, "I don't know. I guess we'll see." Alas, he recently died in the hospital.

Here we can infer multiple strategies of disengagement at play. Experiencing severe setbacks and long-term hospital confinement, my colleague seems to have *objectified* his body, even *ignored* it—if he "pooed," it was simply something *it*, the body which he *had*, rather than *was*, did. He *refused* to be embarrassed. To some degree, he may have been *transcending* his very identification with corporeal existence.

On the one hand, all this had an adaptive and therefore healing function. John was not weighed down by shame about his lack of bodily control, nor did he let it affect his positive relationship with his nurse. But on the other hand, we may sense a shadow-side here. Perhaps this level of disengagement was a form of giving up that made it difficult for John to commit to physical recovery. Whether his move toward "escaping his body" in any way accelerated his downturn, or simply was a register and acceptance of his impending death, remains an open question.

Here it is worth noting that there may be a "healing" dimension even to life-ending decisions. If bodily existence has become a source of insupportable and perhaps irreversible suffering, then the choice to *refuse* that life—and maybe *transcend* it—is understandable. An individual may come to feel that death is the best or only source of healing for their suffering, and may also wish not to be a burden to others. Unfortunately, the modern medical system is often geared more to defeating death at any cost rather than helping people to come to terms with it in a healing fashion.

That said, a premature choice of death has a deep shadow-side for self and loved ones. I know this, having had two family members who chose suicide. Was "escaping the body" at a moment when life felt intolerable for them a form of healing, or its very opposite? Perhaps both.

Embracing the Body

Earlier, I wrote that the self stands in an ambiguous relationship with embodiment. On the one hand, especially at times of unproblematic health, the body seems like something *I am*, with my own powers and preferences lived out in action. On the other hand, the body is also something *I have*, a material object in the world, and a power that can turn against my wishes. We have seen that illness and impairment can exaggerate the self–body split. We have explored a series of healing strategies that lean into, or even deliberately widen, that rift in order to create zones of freedom for the self. These I called modes of "escaping the body." I now turn to countervailing strategies that seek to lessen the distance and dissonance between the self and the body; these are various ways of "embracing the body."

For the body is not only something *I have* and *I am*, but is also a being *I am-with*. This is not quite the same as the *I am* experience wherein we live unproblematically, and often unreflectively, through our bodies. This sort of pre-thematic union may return if the impaired person fully recovers or develops effective compensatory functions. But in many cases, chronic illness and impairment, and consequently some sense of self–body duality, persist or linger. Nonetheless, this body need not be any more alien than another person to whom I am closely bonded. In the case of a good friend, we do more than simply coexist side by side; *I am-with* them in a deep way. For example, when going on a trip together we see the same sights, share experiences and confidences, and surmount challenges together with one another. Similarly, we can experience *being-with* our ill or impaired body, traversing in tandem our challenging life journey. Rather than seeking to detach from my body, I choose to hold it close, embracing it from within.

This is not to say that the *I am-with* relation always needs to take a positive form any more than it does with other people. For example, a sufferer from anorexia nervosa writes: "Somehow I learned before I could articulate it that the body—my body—was dangerous . . . *I did not trust it.* It seemed *treacherous.* I watched it with a wary eye" (Hornbacher 1999, 14). Osler (2021) suggests that anorexia should not be viewed primarily as a perceptual distortion of body-image or an obsession with thinness per se, so much as an experience of a renegade body which the anorexic seeks to subdue through self-starvation. Unfortunately, this is a failed "healing strategy" insofar as it only leads to more hunger and body/food obsession, intensifying warfare between the hostile parties of self and body.

Given my focus on healing, I will stress more positive modes of the *I am-with* relation wherein the ill person embraces his or her body, again discussing four variations on this theme: *accepting, listening, befriending,* and *witnessing.*

Accepting. The Serenity Prayer, written by the Protestant theologian Reinhold Niebuhr, and used in Alcoholics Anonymous and other such programs, famously says, *"God grant me the serenity to accept the things I cannot change, courage to change the things I can, and wisdom to know the difference."* Bodily dysfunction may alert us to things that we can and should change through treatment or lifestyle alterations. However, there are often elements of physical dysfunction that we simply need the serenity to *accept,* and this can serve as a helpful healing strategy. It is not always easy to accomplish. The prayer suggests that some will need a sense of divine help to overcome resistance. *Transcending* and *accepting* can thus be strategies that work together synergistically.

The word "accept" comes from the Latin *acceptare,* meaning "to receive willingly." Acceptance is a form of saying "yes" to reality, and is thus somewhat opposite in spirit to *ignoring* and *refusing.* For some, this might be the "yes" of full-bodied welcoming. "This cancer was the best thing that ever happened to me." People often speak of serious illnesses as helping them reorder their priorities, bringing them closer to loved ones or God, or simply awakening them to the small joys of the ordinary that had been overlooked. In this sense, an illness is not only something we "heal from" but something that can be *healing in and of itself,* if we embrace its life-teachings.

For others, the "yes" is not filled with positivity but just the acknowledgment of difficult truths: "I may not like it, but *it is what it is.*" I myself had to struggle to arrive at acceptance during my post-Covid fatigue, when at the time I didn't know if it would ever end. My tendency was to become very vigilant—"Am I any better today?"—frustrated—"No, I feel just as weak as yesterday"—and at times deeply worried—"Is this turning into truly long Covid?" Needless to say, this was hardly the best way to rest up and heal emotionally and physically. I did remind myself of the Serenity Prayer; accepting what I could not change helped me to also focus on what I could change (my own resistance and restlessness), and may have accelerated my recovery.

The notion that acceptance can be of clinical use is also highlighted by newer models of chronic pain. Individuals often fear that chronic pain, like acute pain, is indicative of something dangerously wrong with their bodies, but this is often not the case. Treatments like cognitive-behavioral and pain-reprocessing therapy can help lessen the distress that forms a large emotional component of the pain experience. One randomized clinical trial studying the efficacy of pain-reprocessing therapy concluded: "Psychological treatment focused on changing beliefs about the causes and threat value of primary chronic back pain may provide substantial and durable pain relief" (Ashar et al. 2022, 14).

Sometimes we benefit from *accepting* not only our internal body state, but also its social consequences and others' reactions to it. In chapter 1 I referenced Susan Wendell, author of *The Rejected Body*, a classic in disability studies, who fell victim to myalgic encephalitis with its disturbing set of symptoms—muscle pain and weakness, profound fatigue, dizziness, headaches, and short-term memory problems. No magic bullet presented itself. She had to learn to accept this new condition, and its ramifications:

> Recognizing myself as disabled certainly required that I change my self-identity and adopt a radically new way of thinking about myself. This included accepting the reality (though not the justice) of the stigma of being chronically ill, especially the shame of being unable to do many things that people still expected me to do. It also required reimagining my life with a new, much more limited and perpetually uncomfortable body, and then reorganizing my work, home, and relationships to make this different life possible. (Wendell 1996, 26)

Acceptance is an existential attitude. Wendell still recognizes the limitations imposed by her illness, and the injustice of her treatment by others—and yet accepting enables her to drop unnecessary denial, tension, self-pity, and anger. This in turn brings about a psychophysical relaxation, and an ability to face and solve problems head-on. With chronic conditions such is not a one-time achievement, but something that may need renewal on a daily basis. Can I accept that my pain is worse this morning? That I have to cancel an evening engagement? With a progressive condition such as multiple sclerosis, can I accept the latest worsening of my symptoms, and the prospect that I will now be wheelchair-bound? Through acceptance I more *am-with* my body in positive ways, rather than tethered to an implacable enemy.

Acceptance may be one of the more difficult strategies for which to find a shadow-side. What could be wrong with accepting reality rather than battling against it? But perhaps a hint of shadow may be found in the title of the Serenity Prayer mentioned earlier. On closer examination, it could equally be called the "Courage Prayer" or the "Wisdom Prayer," but its emphasis on action and discernment can be forgotten if we over-focus on serene acceptance—which is meant to apply only to elements that are truly unchangeable. Sometimes it is the patient who demands change, who *refuses* to accept the limitations of their condition, who ends up doing the best. Premature or excessive acceptance may thus at times be deleterious, leading to an overly passive approach to healing.

Listening. Friedrich Nietzsche, the nineteenth-century German philosopher, wrote: "Behind your thoughts and feelings, my brother, there stands a mighty ruler, an unknown sage—whose name is self. In your body he dwells; he is your body. There is more reason in your body than in your best wisdom" (1954, 146–47). Nietzsche's point is deliberately countercultural. It has been customary in Western philosophy and theology to ascribe wisdom to the intellect or soul, while associating the body with unreasoning passion, or with a mindless machine. And yet, experientially, we discover that the lived body has access to many layers of knowledge unavailable to the conscious intellect. The skilled pianist's hands fly across the keyboard in a way no longer guided by the reasoning mind. The driver of a car cannot recall just where to take a left, but her body "knows"—there is a feeling that arises from the whole gestalt as she approaches an intersection that *this is the place.*

Embodied knowingness stretches down into the "interoceptive" realm, that is, the realm of stimuli arising from within the body and its internal organs. Someone with low blood sugar may not remember when they last ate, but the gnawing in their stomach, their increased irritability and difficulty thinking, all combine so that their body summons them toward a glass of orange juice. Yet, for one prone to acid indigestion—like me—their body might direct them elsewhere, as toward a glass of milk. In fact, I experience a bit of anticipatory stomach upset or reflux when so much as *thinking* about a glass of orange juice. My body warns me in advance.

Of course, much depends on whether one is *listening* to such messages. As I discuss at greater length in chapter 8, our culture has done a poor job of preparing us to hear and value these signals. With the goal of what Michel Foucault characterizes as "disciplining" the body (1979, 135–308)—a pervasive power strategy used to enhance docility and efficiency in institutions such as schools, factories, prisons, and the army, not to mention the professional world—we are taught to ignore or override many of our bodily messages. The ideal is a "self-disciplining" person who places duty ahead of physiological signals, for example, by putting in long hours of work despite fatigue, while liberally applying caffeine as needed. (Yes, I write this as I am drinking a cup of coffee.) A lack of *listening* to the body skews not only our organization of time but of space. Poorly ventilated classrooms and cubicles, harsh fluorescent lighting, and dehumanized factory spaces can be the sources of existential and even medical "dis-ease."

Then, too, we increasingly dwell in that virtual environment constituted by our smartphones, computers, and other screens. Excessive (which is now typical) levels of smartphone use can contribute to anxiety, depression, loneliness, and low self-esteem (Turkle 2011; Price 2018), in addition to physical problems. "By chronically raising levels of cortisol, the body's main stress hormone, our phones may be threatening our health and shortening our lives" (Price 2019).

Since our body is intimately connected to its lifeworld, to *listen* to our body thus also means *listening for what environments it will find most depleting, or conversely, most healing*. For example, we may choose to surround ourselves with objects of beauty or inspiration: works of art, perhaps, or treasured photos, or an altar of sacred symbols. As John Keats famously begins the poem *Endymion*:

> A thing of beauty is a joy for ever:
> Its loveliness increases; it will never
> Pass into nothingness; but still will keep
> A bower quiet for us, and a sleep
> Full of sweet dreams, and health, and quiet breathing. (Cox 2009, 148–49)

Of course, issues of health and quiet breathing had particular significance for Keats, a doctor-in-training turned poet, who had nursed a brother dying of tuberculosis—and was himself to die shortly afterwards of that disease.

Later in that stanza Keats suggests that a "thing of beauty" may not only be an artistic production, but something in the natural world:

> Such the sun, the moon,
> Trees old and young, sprouting a shady boon
> For simple sheep; and such are daffodils
> With the green world they live in . . . (Cox 2009, 149)

For many people connections with nature, if only through a daily walk, caring for a plant, or keeping windows open, is experienced as an important element of healing. Nor is this merely a matter of subjective impressions. As a *New York Times* article asserts:

> It's a medical fact: Spending time outdoors, especially in green spaces, is good for you. A wealth of research indicates that escaping to a neighborhood park, hiking through the woods, or spending a weekend by the lake can lower a person's stress levels, decrease blood pressure and reduce the

> risk of asthma, allergies, diabetes and cardiovascular disease, while boosting mental health and increasing life expectancy. Doctors around the world have begun prescribing time in nature as a way of improving their patients' health. (Sheikh 2019)

Simply *listening* to our body, as well as for the healing environments it seeks, can serve as an inexpensive, preventive health strategy. Moreover, this approach is available independent of the vagaries of health insurance, and sometimes obviates the need for expensive end-stage treatments. The more sensitive we are to bodily messages, the more we can forestall developing certain diseases. Again, I will return to this topic in depth in chapter 8.

Listening may be a particularly important strategy for groups that for reasons of gender, race, or sexual orientation have been systematically neglected or underserved by the clinical establishment. For example, Maya Dusenbery comments on how women's symptoms are often misdiagnosed or misbelieved. When she asked her interviewees what they recommended:

> I often heard *Listen to your body. Trust that you know when something is wrong. Don't second-guess yourself: get a second opinion instead.* This is very good advice, but we should be clear about why it is necessary advice: because all too often, when women enter the medical system, they encounter health care providers who do *not* listen to them, who do *not* trust that they know when something is wrong, who make them second-guess themselves and doubt the very reality of what they're feeling in their own bodies. (Dusenbery 2018, 317)

Often, listening to your own body is not only crucial in diagnosing an illness, but in its ongoing management as well. For example, Parkinson's disease, a progressive neurological disease, can yield a complex symptomatology giving rise to uncontrollable tremors of the limbs, slowed movement and mentation, difficulties with swallowing and bowel and bladder functions, muscular rigidity, and so on. Living well with such an illness, whose manifestations shift from day to day and year to year, can be assisted by sensitive listening. "What patterns of rest and exercise work for my body? What diet? How much sleep do I need? How much time in a natural setting? How am I responding to this new medication regimen, or does it still need to be tweaked?" Simply *ignoring* or *refusing* the body may lead to a dysfunctional slide into ever-worsening symptoms.

For myself, that bout with Covid-19 presented quite an education in the benefits of listening to my body. For several weeks, shading into months, I experienced fatigue and heat sensitivity which at times were quite debilitating. As previously mentioned, when I would attempt prematurely to reassert my own strength by long walks, or preparing dinner and cleaning up, it would often lead to a setback. I had to listen carefully to what my body was able to do, or not do, at each stage of recovery and modify my regimen accordingly. I also had to cultivate my awareness of which environments would be healing ones. I spent a lot of time sitting on my porch with a lovely view of trees and garden, and when inside I would occasionally watch on my TV a live webcam of a windswept Hawaiian beach. Unable to travel due to Covid, I would imagine myself on that beach (in the next chapter we will address "*imagining*" as a healing strategy), going so far as to pull up a chair and drape a towel around my bare shoulders, while pretending my air conditioning was a Hawaiian breeze. This helped me access the sense of peace, and being out in nature, that my lived body so craved.

Not only bouts of illness, but the natural process of aging often calls us to become better listeners. When we're younger there are many things we can get away with—heavy drinking, bad diet, lack of sleep, and so on—even though we are disregarding or punishing our body. The recovery capability of a youthful body can be quite astonishing. But as we get older the aches and pains, the modes of limitation and vulnerability, increase and so must our capacity to listen carefully to our body's need for rest, exercise, proper food, healthy breathing patterns, and care around our points of chronic injury or weakness. In chapter 7 I will turn in greater depth to the experience of aging, which can be both grim and filled with grace.

Listening may seem like a healing strategy without a shadow-side, but again that would not be quite right. For example, the Parkinsonian patient—and I here draw on discussions with Joan Boor, a close friend who has lived with the disease for some twenty years—must cope with times when the body's messages are confusing: "Is this anxiety I'm feeling a function of Parkinsonian neurology, emotional stress, or my medications?" Sometimes the Parkinsonian body's messages may be downright misleading. Joan has found that when her body suggests that certain forms of movement are impossible, choosing to override that by force of will may work. At such times, *ignoring* and *refusing* the body's messages proves more beneficial than *listening*; or at least one needs a sophisticated way to blend these modalities, like that of a parent who knows to listen and respond to a crying child, but won't necessarily acquiesce to their every wish. In such ways, I *am-with* my body constructively.

Then too, with a variety of conditions, recourse to a professionally informed opinion may trump all. Someone might, for example, have dangerously high blood pressure without receiving any direct bodily messages of distress. Here, the strategy of *objectifying* (a blood pressure measurement at the doctor's office) provides more crucial information than just *listening*. As I will shortly discuss, different healing strategies can often complement each other. For example, once informed of having high blood pressure, one may then listen more carefully for what elevates it (such as rooting, as I do, for chronically hapless sports teams), and what keeps it in check.

Befriending. As mentioned, pain and disability can trigger the sense of our body as alien, something attacking us from within. As the philosopher Jean-Luc Nancy put it, a part of his body was revealed as an "intruder." Suffering from heart failure, he writes: "My heart was becoming my own foreigner—a stranger precisely because it was inside" (Nancy 2002, 4). "It became strange to me; intruding by defection: almost by rejection, if not by dejection" (Nancy 2002, 3). The sense of alienation is only increased in his case by a heart transplant, yielding another's organ inside his own body, along with the immunosuppressants he must take to forestall graft rejection, but which cause their own modes of bodily distress.

In the face of such challenges, *befriending* the body—not only *accepting* what is happening and *listening* to the body's messages, but actively demonstrating an attitude of care, like one might offer to a friend who *I am-with*, can be important to healing. We may discover that the injured or painful body part "likes" being cared for. Just as an infant or animal responds pre-linguistically to the experience of being nurtured, so bodily parts and functions may be primordially responsive to care (Leder 2016a, 42–55). Perhaps a muscle relaxes as we rub it with tenderness, or our stress hormones decrease, our immune functioning improves, and so on. As mentioned above, befriending our body may also involve seeking life-world elements that assist healing, whether it is time spent in nature or, as in Jewish lore, having a nice bowl of chicken soup whose soothing heat and odors caress both the inner and outer body.

Strange as it may sound, I find myself occasionally speaking to my stomach (which I said was prone to acid reflux), warning it when a challenge is coming or thanking it for dealing with a spicy meal. Similarly, Lisa Flaherty, whose broken wrist I mentioned earlier, told me: "I talk to my left hand before going into work. I tell it 'I know you want to do all the right hand is able to, but not yet. Be patient!'" Sometimes befriending our body involves some stern instruction, coupled with compassion, just as we might use with a child or a companion animal.

More generally, research data confirms what seems intuitively correct: self-compassionate individuals make better use of a variety of adaptive coping strategies for chronic illness than do those who are preoccupied with self-blame (Sirois et al. 2015). Yet compassion for self and body is not always an easy attitude to adopt. Bodily breakdown may be accompanied by feelings of failure, shame, and guilt, as if we must have done something wrong to merit this punishment. The word "pain" in fact derives from the Latin word, *poena*, for "punishment." The body seems both the agent of this retribution as well as its object, that upon which the punishment is carried out.

Yet to befriend the body, and thereby oneself, helps to reintegrate what the illness has existentially disrupted. Arthur Frank, previously mentioned as recovering from a heart attack and testicular cancer, writes of the moment when he reclaimed his body from the objectification rendered by both illness itself and its medicalization: "That day I stopped resenting 'it' for the pain I had felt and began to appreciate my body, in some ways for the first time in my life. I stopped evaluating my body and began to draw strength from it. And I recognized this body was me" (Frank 1991, 60–61). The body thus becomes not simply what *I have*, but what *I am*, and *am-with*: the friendship is bidirectional as Frank feels both supportive of, and supported by, his body.

Again, this might seem like a healing strategy without a downside, but it is not optimal for everyone in all situations. We have explored how deliberately estranging ourselves from our body can also be adaptive, as we choose to *ignore, refuse*, or *transcend* corporeal limitation. Then too, some people when dealing with physical illness thrive better in a "battle posture," for example, summoning all their combative energy to take on and defeat enemy cancer cells.

Witnessing. The last strategy whereby I "embrace" my body so that *I am-with* it in a positive mode is what I will call *witnessing*. Unlike *befriending*, here we adopt a more dispassionate awareness of our bodily sensations. The goal is not exactly *listening* so that we may respond to our body's requests, but rather a state of "mindful" observation. Generally, the process taught in mindfulness training precludes any attempt to alter or judge what we are witnessing. Yet mindfulness training has been shown by many studies to be effective in diminishing anxiety, depression, and often physical pain, in the latter case enhancing our sense of increased cognitive and emotional control (Zeidan et al. 2012).

Again, a fair amount of the "painfulness" of pain—and by extrapolation, illness, disability, and aging—is not simply the result of immediate bodily sensations. Rather, our present experience of pain serves to trigger painful memories from the past, forebodings about the future, and feelings of fear, anger, sadness, and frustration. Much of the suffering connected with bodily pain and limitations arises through our emotional reactivity. But through dispassionate *witnessing* we can lessen our suffering, and maybe even the problematic symptoms themselves.

There are many protocols for learning mindful witnessing, including Kabat-Zinn's Mindfulness-Based Stress Reduction (MBSR) trainings used in medical centers around the country (Kabat-Zinn 2013). In general, witnessing involves paying careful attention to what is occurring in our body, perhaps starting with the breath, or with a progressive body-scan, which in time focuses on the area of discomfort. Steven Levine recounts the experience of a woman who was dying, and tortured by chronic pain:

> She began to investigate: What is the texture of this sensation. Is it hot? Or cold? Does it stay in one place? Is it moving? Does it vibrate? . . . What actually is the experience that mind so quickly calcifies with labels of pain and emergency? . . . Later she related back to this moment of moving into, instead of pulling back from, her pain, and said, "There was a spaciousness, a gentleness involved in this investigation that I never associated with my condition." The direct experience of her pain was quite different from what she had imagined. She said that indeed most of what she had called pain was actually resistance. . . . Her aversion to the pain had become a hell-realm for her, reinforcing and intensifying each day's discomfort. (Levine 1982, 116)

So, *witnessing* involves a pivot in the direction of gentle awareness. Though a distinct strategy, it can certainly be blended with the other forms of embracing the body discussed previously. We can *accept* whatever we discover upon investigation, *befriending* rather than rejecting our problematic body. Mindful awareness can also then facilitate *listening* for what will best assist the healing process.

Yet the potential for suboptimal results should be acknowledged for this, as for all healing strategies. To again draw on personal experience, I prefer to *ignore* my flare-ups of chronic nerve pain rather than deliberately *witness* them. Perhaps I am "doing it wrong," but I often find that applying focused attention to the pain site tends to tune up the signal, increasing rather than diminishing its sharp sting. Different strategies work—or don't work—for different individuals at different times, and experientially derived self-knowledge is key to using them well.

The Keyboard of Possibilities

These last reflections suggest the need for a more explicit discussion of how healing strategies are chosen and interrelate. Under the heading of "escaping the body," I have discussed *ignoring, refusing, objectifying,* and *transcending.* As modes of "embracing the body," I have treated *accepting, listening, befriending,* and *witnessing.* Should a sick individual choose a single favorite among these, combine several of them simultaneously, or alternate between them? Is there a logic that dictates which modes are simply opposed to one another and which ones can be used in tandem?

Earlier I mentioned how the phenomenology of embodiment—for example, how I both *have* my body and *am* my body—creates a kind of "chessboard" of possible healing strategies; that is, places on the board to which we can move our own chess pieces. This is represented in figure 2 at the beginning of the book. I will complement that here with a related image, that of a musical keyboard. In chapter 1 we reflected on Itzhak Perlman's creative playing of a three-stringed violin, but let us now switch instrumental metaphors.

Just as a keyboard, such as a piano or harpsichord, has notes ranging from high to low, so the strategies laid out so far constitute a spectrum. At one end of the spectrum are those that involve escaping the body, for example, by refusing and ignoring it. At the other end are strategies of embracing the body, for example, by listening to and befriending it. Certain "notes" on this keyboard simply don't harmonize with each other, or cannot be played simultaneously. One can't *ignore* the body while at the same time *listening* to it. One can, though, create an alternating trill. For example, one might choose to ignore an arthritic condition while running errands in the morning, but later listen to the need for a restorative hot bath and rest.

Certain notes, even high and low ones, when played together yield resonant chords. For example, to *objectify* the body through biomedical approaches can combine with *befriending* it in holistic ways. Sometimes these approaches are almost one and the same: undergoing surgery for my painful and limiting neuropathy was my way of *objectifying my body in service to befriending my body,* since all other efforts at pain management had failed.

Just as a musical note, like C, can be played in different octaves, or incorporated into distinctive keys, so can certain healing strategies be played in different registers. For example, *transcending* often involves "escaping the body," finding an intellectual or spiritual dimension of self that outruns the purely physical. But there are also modes of transcendence that "embrace the body": for instance, the notion of incarnation is central to Christianity, even unto a belief in the resurrection of the body after death. In the context of Asian traditions, *witnessing* physical sensations can be a way to clarify that you are *not* your body (as in Hindu Advaita teachings), or as a way of realizing the import of physical sensations (as in Buddhist *vipassana* practice). That is, *transcending* and *witnessing* could either be played in the key of "escaping the body" or "embracing the body," depending on how each is employed.

As discussed in chapter 1, the healing process can be compared to composing and playing a musical piece. This unfolds on a limited keyboard, but one that allows for great personal creativity. There are improvisatory elements; as pain and limitation fluctuate or progress, we seek the appropriate notes of response. There are dissonances that need to be integrated, and somehow harmonized as part of a greater whole. Living well with illness and impairment is less a science than a work of art, albeit one filled with wrong notes and failed strategies. Since chronic illness manifests in diverse ways and may progress through a series of stages, it is good to have at our disposal a versatile keyboard of responses and understand the full range of our instruments.

3

Chronic Healing: Repairing Time

In the previous chapter I focused on healing strategies derived from our ambiguous *I am/I have* relation to the body. In this chapter I will concentrate particularly on strategies that relate to issues of ability and temporality. To suffer from a "chronic" pain or illness (from the Greek *khronos*, meaning "time") is not only to indicate that this problem lasts a long time, but that the condition *disrupts our experience of time itself.* It is not necessarily true that "time heals all wounds," but serious wounds do demand a healing of time.

The *I Can('t)*

I previously introduced the lived body as not only something *I am/I have*, but as supporting what Husserl and Merleau-Ponty refer to as the "*I can.*" For example, as dinnertime approaches, *I can* walk down the stairs, make a pot of spaghetti, and grab a chair and watch TV. The lifeworld I inhabit is organized around all these things *I can* do as an embodied person. The rooms of my house, the appliances in my kitchen, the magazine I read, all exist in relation to my bodily organs—arms, legs, mouth, digestive system, eyes, ears, nose, cerebral cortex, and so on. Yet these organs, and their biological potentialities, had to be developed through long social training. As a child I laboriously learned to assume an upright posture and walk, to climb stairs, to use a toaster without risking electrocution, to spell out the alphabet for reading, and so on. Over time these habits of perception and action became sedimented within my body (Merleau-Ponty 2012, 143–55) so that little if any conscious reflection is needed during performance. For instance, by adulthood my habits of driving allow me to hurtle down the road at high speed while also listening to music, sipping on coffee, occasionally admiring the scenery, checking my rearview mirror, passing a slow driver, and engaging in conversation with a passenger. The body has learned to organize its diverse organs and functional groupings, interweaving complex action patterns. Yet woe to the driver-in-training who tries to do too many things at once and too early before such sedimented habits are formed.

Since the development of habits is so central, instead of simply noting that *I am* or *have* a body, it could be said that *I inhabit* my body. This in turn enables me to *inhabit* my lifeworld in a rich variety of ways (Merleau-Ponty 2012, 153–55). As we develop new habits—for example, those of an apprentice bird-watcher who learns to discern different calls and telltale flashes of color—the world we experience expands correspondingly. Body and world summon forth one another, with a relational primacy not captured by emphasizing either pole of the subject–object dichotomy. Birds exert a fascination on earthbound beings, perhaps leading someone to learn about bird-watching; this training then reveals a rich new world of observations, which provokes interest to learn more, and so on, in a cycle.

At times of bodily dysfunction, the way I *inhabit* both body and world are correlatively altered. I then particularly experience my body as the foundation not simply of the *I can* but of the *I can't.* Returning to my dinnertime example, due to illness, injury, or the incapacities of old age, I may lose the ability to cook for myself, or even my stomach's ability to digest certain foods. That body and world which I *inhabit* may now begin to feel *uninhabitable.* As mentioned, this tends to provoke a transition from the sense that *I am* my body to the body as something *I have,* and moreover which *has me.* That is, it burdens and limits me, asserting an obstructive, or even a malevolent presence (Leder 1990, 69–99). "The experience of illness is always the experience of both 'having' and 'being had,'" writes Toombs (1995, 99), whose own multiple sclerosis played a key part in triggering her phenomenological explorations.

This sense of alienation from the problematic body is not only characteristic of illness, but of those who endure oppressive discrimination. A Black person entering a "white space," a woman under an objectifying gaze, and a gay person in a homophobic environment may also have a sense of bodily inhibition. The tilt from feeling that *I am* my body freely, to feeling that *I have* a body that is being watched and evaluated, often correlates with a shift toward the *I can't.* Fanon (2008), Gordon (1997), and Yancy (2017) discuss the disempowering sense of having a Black body that is suspected, surveilled, avoided, or constrained within a white-dominated culture. For Young (2005), learning to "throw like a girl," cross one's legs, and walk only with restraint are modes of inhibition that accompany objectification. In such ways, those wounded by discrimination can be said to be suffering something like a socially caused illness. Here the most important healing strategies involve not just inner adjustments, but sociopolitical change. I will discuss this theme of "embodied injustice" further in chapter 6.

It would, however, be incorrect to presume that the *I can't* surfaces only during modes of disruption like illness and injustice. In human development, the *I can* and *I can't* are equally fundamental. Given this balance between them, I will refer to this dimension of embodied existence as the *I can('t)*. From early life we practice bodily abilities—for example, to track faces, suck, cry out, and crawl—but we also experience limitations, such as the inability to access our own food, grab things out of reach, or satisfy other desires. This balance between the *I can* and *I can't* continues throughout life. I can walk to the grocery store but, alas, I can't transport myself there instantaneously. Still, it is true that when illness or injury intervene, the seesaw of ability/inability is tipped in the direction of the *I can't*. When I'm feeling dizzy or am suffering from vision trouble, driving or even walking to the grocery store may become impossible. The lifeworld I inhabit correspondingly contracts.

For these reasons, structural dichotomies of the lived body such as the *I am/I have* or the *I can('t)* must be temporalized. The body is constantly in flux. I can take an energetic walk in the cool of the early morning, but perhaps not when dragging through the heat of late afternoon. Of course, more dramatic changes occur over the course of years as illness or old age bring limitation. In the fullness of time we likely discover that we all are only "temporarily abled." Moreover, this alters the rhythms of daily life. We may now need to take medications at certain times, monitor our sleep and energy levels, visit practitioners, manage pain during the day, and so on, thus changing the way we experience the flow of time (Jowsey 2016; Leder 2016a, 28–32).

With any injury or illness that dislodges us from the customary flow of time, there is also what Wyllie (2005) and Fuchs (2005) term a "desynchronization." While most of us pursue our work and social life organized by long-range goals and the rhythms of a busy day, the ill person desynchronizes from this shared time, as well as that which structured her previous life. (This desynchronization can also be brought about by unemployment, addiction, incarceration, and other modes of social rather than physical distress.) From "crip theory," a way of doing disability studies in conversation with queer theory, has come the notion of *crip time*: certain people may simply need more time to process language, complete physical tasks, or prepare for, travel to, and arrive at events. This presents "a challenge to normative and normalizing expectations of pace and scheduling. Rather than bend disabled bodies and minds to meet the clock, crip time bends the clock to meet disabled bodies and minds" (Kafer 2013, 27). The disabled person, as well as those around them, needs a sense of temporal flexibility.

Yet sometimes time can be disrupted by serious illness. In chapter 1 we mentioned Paul Kalanithi, a top Stanford neurosurgeon, and his unexpected encounter with metastatic lung cancer. Suddenly he was unable to run a marathon, perform surgery, advance in his career, and feel a full husband to his wife. Kalanithi was thus desynchronized from his past identity; from his present, which was no longer organized by timed patient visits and surgeries; and from the bright future that had beckoned him, a pleasing blend of professional advancement and open-ended possibility. He was also desynchronized from his fellows as he stared into his private abyss.

Of course, the body's changeability can be a blessing, rather than a curse: one can alter in positive ways. I will now turn our attention to healing strategies which render central the body's temporal flow. As in the last chapter, I will present eight strategies, which again can be divided into two groups of four.

The first grouping is focused on transmutations of the *I can('t)*; I will call this the process of "remaking the body." In response to illness and incapacity, we can seek to *restore* former abilities; *transform* the body by developing new habits and uses; *incorporate* external aids; or use our *imagining* internally as a healing force. Later, I will turn to strategies designed to "re-time" the body; that is, more explicitly alter its relation to time itself, including past, present, future, and their narrative continuity.

This time around I will go further and subdivide each grouping of four strategies into two pairs. Each pairing highlights how strategies can exhibit opposing, but also complementary, ways of dealing with physical problems.

Remaking the Body

Restoring and Transforming. Jill Bolte Taylor (2009), a 37-year-old Harvard-trained neuroanatomist, underwent a catastrophic stroke, with a left-side brain bleed caused by an arteriovenous malformation. Because of her professional training she was able with unusual acuity to observe, and later write about, her progressive loss of function. The stroke affected her language centers, memory, cognition, affect, perception, and movement in ways that took eight years to rebuild. It also opened up a great sense of joy and empathy as the right hemisphere of her brain gained prominence—but I will first focus on the rehabilitation of her analytic left-brain functions. This will help introduce healing strategies which I respectively call *restoring* and *transforming*.

I call *restoring* the attempt to reclaim what was but no longer is. The *I can('t)* presents itself as part of a temporal continuum. In the immediate aftermath of the stroke, Taylor discovers that she can no longer do what she was formerly able to do. Nonetheless, she envisions that she will be able to do again what she once did if she works hard at *restoring* function. A temporal diagram would be structured as a loop—her present inability leads her to focus on a future when she may reclaim capacities from the past. We find this looping structure implicit in the word "rehabilitate"—that is, to again (*re*)claim habits that we once possessed. In Taylor's case, this work is slow and painstaking:

> Essentially, I had to completely inhabit the level of ability that I could achieve before it was time to take the next step. In order to attain a new ability, I had to be able to repeat that effort with grace and control before taking the next step . . . How to walk. How to talk. How to read. How to write. How to put a puzzle together. The process of physical recovery was just like stages of normal development. I had to go through each stage, master that level of ability, and then the next step unfolded naturally. (Taylor 2009, 90–93)

The effort to *restore* lost abilities and capacities often serves as a primary temporal orientation for the ill person and their treaters alike. In practice this may unfold through the use of surgeries, medications, exercises to increase strength and flexibility, and so on. Increasing mobility after a shoulder injury; allowing a bone to reknit after fracture; strengthening a leg after a torn ligament; resuming normal activities after a sustained bout of the flu; or in Taylor's case, coming back from a devastating stroke—in all these examples, the temporarily dis-abled person, and their caregivers, are focused on *restoring* the *I can.*

Like other strategies, the one we are examining has its shadow-side. For example, the quest for *restoration* can be the source of wishful thinking, inappropriate treatments, and significant disappointments. Kafer refers to a *curative imaginary* for those with disabilities: "Within this frame of curative time, then, the only appropriate disabled mind/body is one cured or moving toward cure" (Kafer 2013, 28). Restoration of function, or achieving the cultural image of an ideal body, is not always possible in cases of significant injury, illness, or impairment. Even the "miracles" of modern medicine, such as organ transplantation, can delay our deterioration and death, but never defeat it.

Contrary, and at times complementary, to *restoring* is the strategy of *transforming*. The lived body may recover the *I can* by developing new usage patterns, abilities, and habits. We saw a metaphorical example of this in the chapter 1 story of Perlman adapting to a broken string, as he found creative ways to still complete the piece by transforming his fingering and bowing. "You know, sometimes it is the artist's task to find out how much music you can still make with what you have left."

The *Oxford Handbook of Rehabilitation Medicine* describes rehabilitation as employing three fundamental approaches: not only the "restoration of previous abilities," which we have treated, but also "acquiring new skills and strategies" and "altering the physical and social environment to optimize participation" (Sivan et al. 2019, 10). That is, the body–world relationship can be healed not only by reduplicating a previous status quo but by *transforming* one's body and/or one's world.

As an example, the *Oxford Handbook* discusses the case of a middle-aged man with multiple sclerosis who suffered from walking difficulties secondary to partial nerve paralysis complicated by spasticity. While attempts can be made to restore his function by the use of medications, and treatment of his spasticity, he can also learn to transform his bodily use-habits. During the day he might master a new walking pattern, a different pace or length of stride which helps compensate for his losses. At night, he might use his arms and upper body strength to help lift his legs into bed. Then too, external assists might come into play; for example, a walking stick to help support his standing and movement, or even a wheelchair when needed. I will shortly say more about how such tools are *incorporated* into the lived body (Leder 1990, 30–35), over time becoming part of one's own body schema.

Transforming the body–world relation can involve modifying not only the former but the latter—or as the *Oxford Handbook* says, "altering the physical and social environment to optimize participation." For example, the gentleman with multiple sclerosis may use a perching stool or grab rails. Social support may also be key, including that of family, coworkers, and health care providers. Even temporal patterns may need rearranging; for example, his employer may be asked "to change or reduce his hours if prolonged periods of standing are leading to increasing fatigue" (Sivan et al. 2019, 11). Who is functionally "able" or "disabled" is influenced by the pace of life and its demands, architectural features, the level of health care and assisting resources, and other socially constructed elements (Wendell 1996, 35–56). In chapters 4 and 5 I will discuss in greater depth these interpersonal dimensions of healing.

Having contrasted the strategies of *restoring* (reclaiming what one did in the past) and *transforming* (embracing a new way of doing things), it should be recognized that in practice these interblend. For example, my contact lenses, compensating for a lifelong condition called keratoconus, *restore* my 20/20 vision but only by *transforming* my body to now include this plastic addition. Or to choose another example, due to chronic back problems that led to surgery, for years even holding a book open and tilting my head to read has triggered pain. This is a problem when you are both a professional academic and an avid reader. But I have found that new technologies, including electronic reading devices (easy to balance on your lap, no need to hold pages open) and listening to audiobooks on my phone, have *restored* my capacity to read, while also *transforming* it.

I'll always prefer the pleasure of having a physical book in my hands to scanning an electronic screen. But I find that the audiobook is one of the few areas where a technological advance has actually taken us back to the more originary pleasures (in cultural and childhood development) of oral storytelling. I teach a class on Jane Austen and positively encourage my students to "read" by listening to a great narrator voice the different characters, often bringing out comic moments that a contemporary reader would miss.

Incorporating and Imagining. Though I have alluded to them previously, it is useful to discuss in a more detailed way two complementary strategies I will call *incorporating* and *imagining*. These help us to restore or transform our body over time and so are inherently temporal—while also opening onto another axis we might call that of the *exterior/interior* of the lived body. As I will discuss in chapter 8, this distinction is not meant to be conceived of as a metaphysical dualism, like Descartes's division of body and mind, and yet it has provisional uses.

Etymologically, the term *incorporating* captures the notion that something exterior has been brought into our body (*corpus* in Latin). Sometimes this incorporation may be quite literal; for example, someone suffering from abnormal cardiac fibrillations may receive an implanted pacemaker (Leder 2016a, 80–83). However, I use the term *incorporating* more broadly to refer to the way external objects can be assimilated into our habits of bodily usage such that they no longer function as fully "outside" us even if they remain physically distinct (Leder 1990, 30–35). Though the blind person's stick is an external object, it can be assimilated into the way she *inhabits* her lived body; the stick literally and metaphorically amplifies her reach. Her "length" of touch is increased such that it can better take the place of a distance-sense like sight. The blind person's motility is also improved because the stick provides some orientation and stability when she is moving through an uneven, and sometimes unexpected, world.

De Preester (2011) makes a useful distinction between tools and prostheses which are *incorporated*, that is, they are eventually regarded as part of our own body schema; and other tools that *extend* our bodily capacities—for example, a wheelchair—while still remaining clearly outside our body schema. However, I will continue to use the term *incorporation* more broadly to include at least some, though not all, of what De Preester would consider "extensions." While the wheelchair remains a machine exterior to the body, when employing it we learn how to meld our body's perceptual-motor attention, gestures, and skills with the structure of the technology. This is similar to my previous example of learning to drive a car: at first, it remains something quite separate from the *I can*. Pressing down on the brake and accelerator, or turning the steering wheel, starts as a herky-jerky process that is filled with uncertainty. In time, though, we learn how to navigate even tricky roads with what has essentially become a car-body blend. We lean into curves and brake with ease, often with no need to pay explicit attention to what we're doing. Similarly, the wheelchair can be incorporated so that it becomes part of the bodily *I can*, a new form of motility when our legs give out.

The healing strategy of *incorporating* may include a wide array of things that support or supplement our body function. In my own case, I use a flexible knee brace which, after my meniscal surgery, steadies me on a long walk; a dental appliance for moderate sleep apnea which assists my breathing through the night; and, as mentioned, contact lenses for my severe astigmatism, as well as reading glasses. As Slatman writes, "we may think of bodily aids and adjustments as exceptions to a 'normal' situation, but it has actually become more normal to meet somebody with a prosthesis than without one" (2014, 58).

This should make us hesitant to identify the "lived body" exclusively with a skin-bound biological entity. Prostheses and other tools and technologies can modify and extend our bodily use-patterns. These appliances often help those suffering from illness and incapacity to function more effectively in the world, even when, or *especially* when, they are taken for granted, since this may indicate that they've been assimilated into the pre-thematic structure of the *I can*.

For example, after so many years of wearing contact lenses, I tend to forget how bad my unaided vision actually is. (I would have been legally blind in one eye for most of my life without them.) I only notice my contact lenses when I put them in or take them out, when I can't find them (which is distressingly often), or if they are hurting my eyes. Like Heidegger's broken tool, the lenses surface at such times of challenge and dysfunction. When unproblematic they experientially disappear, simply incorporated into my power of vision.

Of course, as with all healing strategies, *incorporating* has its shadow-side. We may become so overreliant on an external technology that we cease to develop our own abilities. For example, the wheelchair may provide a too-easy way to avoid the hard work of strengthening muscles and relieving spasticities that would help someone regain the ability to walk. A helpful technology overused could thus contribute to physical deterioration. Technologies can also be cumbersome and intrusive—for example, many people are uncomfortable wearing the CPAP—continuous positive air pressure—mask all night even though it is the preferred treatment for serious sleep apnea. (Note: I have recently transitioned to this treatment and love it.) Moreover, prostheses can malfunction, wear out, or simply be expensive, and thus unevenly available to the public in ways dependent on income and insurance coverage. There are benefits to relying, when possible, on one's own "natural body."

If *incorporating* is nonetheless a valuable healing strategy wherein we "interiorize" an external object, *imagining* moves in the opposite direction: we gradually "exteriorize" into bodily performance what starts as internal imagery. This use of *imagining* as a healing modality sometimes comes in for criticism as unsubstantiated "New Age" nonsense. However, both scientific studies and personal experience suggest the power of our imagination in improving bodily health and performance. Certainly, this is attested to by many top athletes and sports psychologists, who find that pre-visualizing a game situation, and the desired outcome, helps one to achieve success.

As to the clinical value of *imagining* we can look for confirmation not only to specific studies but to the structure of medical research at large. The "gold-standard" double-blind study must control for the placebo effect (Moerman 2002) in order to evaluate the efficacy of any new drug or surgery. Patients simply *imagining* that they are receiving a helpful treatment has so much healing efficacy that this must be controlled for to determine if the medicine or surgery in itself has any benefits. For example, if the group receiving a placebo (in a double-blind study neither patients nor treaters/researchers know which group this is) has a 30 percent improvement rate, and the group receiving a trial medication has a 40 percent improvement rate, assuming the study is large enough and statistical significance is achieved, this is taken to confirm the efficacy of the drug, which may then move to market. But what remains unthematized is the power of *imagining the effects of the medication*, which in this case might have had three times the efficacy as the medication itself (30 percent placebo effect, versus the added 10 percent from the drug itself). Of course, since it is free, *imagining* generates no income for the pharmaceutical companies, and in fact it can liberate us from participation in the medical-industrial complex. Needless to say, it is under-investigated by those who would pay for such studies.

As an example of the restorative power of imagining, let's return to the case of Jill Bolte Taylor (2009), the 37-year-old trained neuroanatomist trying to recover from the effects of a devastating stroke. I will pick up from an earlier quote:

> Imagery has been an effective tool for regaining physical functions. I am convinced that focusing on how it feels to perform specific tasks has

> helped me recover them more quickly. I had dreamed of skipping up steps every day since the stroke. I held the memory of what it felt like to race up the steps with abandon. By replaying this scene over and over in my mind, I kept that circuitry alive until I could get my body and mind coordinated enough to make it a reality. (Taylor 2009, 127)

I take it that Taylor's own account is not best served by her dualistic language of "body and mind." Through perceptual and kinesthetic imagery, she elicits her body's own habit-memory, thus helping to restore motor function.

As another reference point I'll turn to personal experience. I have already mentioned how imagining I was on a restful Hawaiian beach (assisted by watching a live webcam) helped in my recovery from Covid-19. Something similar was crucial in my healing from the chronic intractable pain of a peripheral neuropathy in my ankle. For many years I was on a high-dose medicine that helped relieve much, but not all, of sometimes excruciating pain. Using a book on self-hypnosis for pain relief (Elmer 2008) which emphasized visualization, I found I could lessen the pain a bit. I might imagine my leg surrounded by ice to cool the burning nerve, or else filled with golden light. The pain relief seemed real but limited, and I went on to have a beneficial neurosurgery that I will discuss later in the book.

Some two years after the surgery, though, walking on uneven snow and ice triggered a serious resurgence of nerve pain that limited my mobility for several months. I was contemplating a new surgery which this time would involve cutting the nerve entirely, numbing out a large region of my leg. However, I started using a Chinese qigong technique called *la qi* that invites visualization. In the Chinese perspective, "qi" (or ch'i) is a universal psychophysical energy that is in all things, including our body, and is responsive to mental direction. We can open up to the energizing and health-giving qi around us through gentle movements, and the power of attention and visualization. In this case, again drawn to the beach environment, I would imagine myself breathing in cooling and expansive energy from the ocean, sand, winds, and sky. The practice yielded powerful and rapid relief. (I will explore this experience at greater depth in this book's last chapter.)

Part of the practice also involved visualizing my body as whole and well, and capable of all of its customary activities. My teacher, who had studied this particular mode of qigong in China, said in a Zoom tape I listened to over and over: "The body does not know the difference between imagination and reality." The practice involved visualizing the healing process as happening in one's body *right now*, not at some time in the future. To think of healing in futural terms can reinforce the sense of the present as deficient—and all the more so if one imagines that an injury or illness will never get better. This can become a self-fulfilling prophecy as the body settles into what seems a permanent *I can't.* The healing strategy of *imagining* instead emphasizes the rehearsal of the bodily *I can* sometimes even in the face of current evidence to the contrary.

That said, a reliance on *imagining,* while free, holistic, ever-available, and safe, can still have a shadow-side. The notion that everything can be healed through the power of thought, prayer, or imagery may lead us to overlook or refuse a valuable medical treatment or lifestyle change. I have chronic acid indigestion, which so far has not been relieved very much by *la qi* practice, probably because I continue to consume too much caffeine and acidic foods.

Also, the New Age notion of the unlimited power of the mind to heal illness can lead to feelings of guilt or shame when our recovery is incomplete or nonexistent. Perhaps a checkup shows a recurrence of cancer; our viewing this as a personal failure (my thoughts brought this on!) will only grievously compound our suffering. Many of those challenged by pain and illness already have a tendency to harsh self-blame, as if they could punish themselves into recovery, or they believe that the affliction is itself a punishment for some wrongdoing. We must make sure that a potentially healing method, like *imagining,* is not used to support a self-attack that serves the opposite of healing.

Re-timeing the Body

The previous discussions have focused on rehabilitative methods which seek to *restore* or *transform* bodily abilities and the body–world relation, along with complementary methods such as *incorporating* and *imagining.* However, not everything is fixable; coping well with illness and aging also means living with the reality that the body is ever impermanent, and is transforming and deforming at every moment, year, and decade.

Ultimately, the embodied self should not be conceived of as an entity "moving through time" so much as one that *is time.* If *I'm possibility,* a focus of chapter 1, it is because, more generally, we could say that *I'm time.* (I use this abbreviation, "*I'm,*" for two reasons; first to distinguish it from my earlier discussion of the unqualified "*I am,*" a realm of pure Being that may transcend temporal limits; and secondly, because by a pleasing trick of spelling, the letters *I'm* are central to the word *time.*) In saying "*I'm time*" I am alluding not only to Heidegger's masterwork on the internal relation of *Being and Time* (1962) but to the notion of *uji* employed by Dōgen, a thirteenth-century Zen priest and founder of the Soto school. This Japanese term, *uji,* is sometimes translated as "being-time." As Tetsu'un Loy writes of Dōgen: "Like everything else I am not in time because I am time. What I do and what happens to me are not events that occur in time; they are the forms that my being-time takes, when my activities are no longer situated within a clock-time understood as a container external to me" (Loy 2017, 87).

In other words, when we proceed phenomenologically, putting aside the Newtonian notion of absolute space and time as container, we discover that we always *are* time unfolding. We are always here and now in the present, and yet this includes within it the unfolding of all temporal dimensions. As Stambaugh (1990, 50) comments on Dōgen: "My body-mind incorporates now how I was raised and nurtured as a child, how I have taken care of myself as an adult, how my parents, grandparents and so on lived their lives, whether I have trained as an athlete or sat in an armchair all my life." My here-and-now body thus contains my past, as well as all the future possibilities that beckon from afar motivating my actions.

For these reasons I will now turn to healing strategies that work most directly with issues of our past, present, and future, as well as their interweaving into a life narrative. Illness alters and disrupts our temporal flow. I will consider these strategies as modes of "re-timeing" the body; that is, using the temporal dimensions as a reservoir for healing responses.

Remembering and Anticipating. Imagine that one day you slip on an unseen patch of ice, sustaining a compound fracture and ligament tear (this happened to a friend of mine). Time itself is suddenly torn into the before and after of the accident. In many other cases, distressing bodily changes are more incremental. For example, we may simply age out of things we were once able to do. The normal diminution of muscle strength and energy, the accumulation of small injuries, and the onset of chronic conditions such as arthritis or heart disease gradually shift the *I can('t)* balance toward various incapacities.

In the face of a somewhat frustrating present and future, one healing strategy is *remembering* our past. This need not be seen as a trivial or escapist focus. For example, Robert Butler (1974) formulated what is now a widely accepted concept in gerontology, that "life review" is a natural and potentially healthy part of aging. Recalling all that we were able to do may help us feel that we have already lived a rich and fulfilling life. The friend I mentioned earlier who has Parkinson's disease, Joan Boor, is quite reduced in her current motor capacity. But recently she told me: "I don't want to climb Mount Washington anymore . . . but remembering I once did that makes me feel so much better about my life." Schachter-Shalomi and Miller (1995) suggest that much death anxiety is really a matter of "unlived life," a sense that our own potentialities are still unfulfilled, leading to fear and sadness as the end approaches. However, remembering in a positive way all that we have explored and accomplished can lessen such feelings. There is much pleasure and meaning to be had in recollecting the past, going through photo collections, reminiscing with family and old friends, and recalling one's "glory days."

Moreover, as the phenomenologist (and my valued mentor) Edward Casey writes, it is not only the "mind" that remembers, but the lived body itself (2000, 146–80). The trained pianist's body knows how to play a rehearsed sonata; the smell of suntan lotion can trigger a body-memory of previous visits to the sea; we remember how to ride a bicycle even though it's been years since we rode one; I could go on and on with such examples. Sometimes this body-memory can be restorative. Joan, with Parkinson's, recently got in a pool to do water exercises and found the body-memory returning of when she had been a competitive swimmer. This was emotionally and even physically strengthening; her body started to reclaim a bit of confidence and strength from reaccessing the *I can*. Similarly, we have seen Jill Bolte Taylor, in her recovery from a stroke, call on the body-memory of racing up steps in order to recover her capacity for movement.

As with any healing strategy, *remembering* has its shadow-side when used excessively or inappropriately. It can become an instrument for our denial of present realities. In *The Coming of Age*, Simone de Beauvoir's (perhaps overly negative) treatment of aging, she sees resistance to change as fundamentally characteristic of older people: "They refuse time because they do not wish to decline; they define their former I as that which they still are—they assert solidarity with their youth" (Beauvoir 1996, 362).

Even when we're not in denial, memory can trigger a sense of all that we have lost. In remembering previous experiences and capacities that have disappeared, a sense of the *I can't* may overwhelm any awareness of what *I can* still do (sit on the porch, chat with my neighbors, enjoy the sunshine, take a slow stroll). We become immersed in painful "nostalgia," a word derived from the Greek *nostos* or "homecoming," combined with *algia*, "pain." Excessive remembering may accentuate the painful sense that we cannot recover our previous body and world (Svenaeus 2011). Remembering can thus be a source of either life-negation or life-appreciation, depending on whether it leads us to accept and work with, or resist and regret, our body's inherent changeability.

The strategy of *anticipating* represents the complementary opposite to *remembering*, one focused primarily on the future. To use the previous example of a sudden ankle fracture, we may anticipate the time when the leg will heal fully, the pain will disappear, and we can resume hiking. As Wyllie notes, an orientation to the future is built right into our bodily structure:

> The eyes are forward-looking, the arms of able-bodied individuals function toward that which is in front of one, and walking is generally easier in a forward direction . . . In short, the embodied subject is itself a spatio-temporal field orientated to what is in front and directed toward the things yet to come. (Wyllie 2005, 175)

This anticipatory hope may provide energy for the rehabilitative processes discussed earlier. After an injury, we may need physical therapy and a regimen of home exercises, including some that are fatiguing and painful. When afflicted with a chronic disease, we may have to tolerate dietary restrictions and other lifestyle changes; medications with side effects; surgical interventions followed by a long recovery period; chemotherapy or radiation treatments; and so on. Patience (from the Latin *patientia*, "the quality of suffering or enduring") is needed to bear not only the illness itself but the accompanying medical interventions. Otherwise we can lapse into melancholic suffering: "then one no longer has the possibility of 'things getting better,' nor does one have any possibility of relinquishing or escaping from the past because a static future does not allow openness to change and movement" (Wyllie 2005, 173). Given all this, the anticipation of better days to come can be crucially sustaining, an insulation against despair.

This can be particularly important for those dealing with serious impairments. With burn scars, gnarled hands, and a wheelchair, Alison Kafer received many grim predictions of how damaged and limiting her future would be. Yet she writes:

> Those who have been most vocal in imagining my future as ripe with opportunities have been other disabled people, who are themselves resisting negative interpretations of their futures. They tell stories of lives lived fully, and the future, according to them, involves not isolation and pathos but community and possibility. (Kafer 2013, 2)

As with all healing strategies, there is a shadow-side to *anticipation*. Our orientation toward the future is not always so positive; we may in fact anticipate the worst. (That is often my modus operandi.) An extensive literature suggests that "catastrophizing"—including fear of the future, the sense that something terrible may happen, that pain may never diminish or may even get worse—is associated with increased physical pain, disability, and depression (Quartana et al. 2009).

Moreover, *anticipating*, just like *remembering*, has the downside of potentially devaluing the present, overlooking the current *I can* as we focus on our future hopes. This can cause a stasis and reversal of time-consciousness, one that the French philosophical psychiatrist Eugene Minkowski refers to as a state of "expectation" (*attente*). Ordinarily we move purposefully toward a desired future, with our goals organizing our present activities. But when stuck in expectation, "we see the future come toward us and wait for that (expected) future to become present" (Minkowski 1970, 87). That is, we are trapped in passivity while awaiting the expected event. For the patient who anticipates that a specialist visit will prove diagnostically determinative, or finally provide the needed treatment, waiting for the appointment may seem to take forever as one day slowly follows another, though on the calendar it is but a couple of weeks.

In his philosophical novel *The Magic Mountain*, Thomas Mann examines the life of tubercular patients in an Alpine sanatorium, with particular attention to the alterations of time consciousness which accompany their repetitive days, weeks, months, and sometimes decade-long stays. Here he describes the weeklong waits for postal delivery, which offers our hero, Hans Castorp, the opportunity for brief encounters with his love interest, Clavdia Chauchat:

> One can say that he consumed one whole week waiting for the return of that single hour every seven days—and waiting means racing ahead, means seeing time and the present not as a gift, but as a barrier, denying and negating their value, vaulting over them in your mind. Waiting, people say, is boring. But in actuality, it can just as easily be diverting, because it devours quantities of time without our ever experiencing or using them for their own sake. One could say that someone who does nothing but wait is like a glutton whose digestive system processes great masses of food without extracting any useful nourishment. (Mann 2005, 285)

I have observed this process of expectant waiting among incarcerated individuals whom I have taught over the years (a focus of chapter 6). The prisoner serving a long-term sentence often fervently anticipates the day of release. This can supply sustaining hope, but it can also deaden the present, so that the prisoner ends up processing "great masses of food without extracting any useful nourishment." With the inmate stuck in expectation, his prison time becomes an endless *I can't*. In such cases, you truly "serve time" rather than having time serve you (Leder 2000,

86). This can equally be the fate of those with chronic illnesses who are trapped in expectation by their very desire for a future cure.

Our expectations can be fed by the *curative imaginary* (Kafer 2013, 27), a cultural fantasy of medicine's mission and ability to create the able body. This can affect not only patients but physicians themselves, who are dedicated to defeating disease, disability, and death with every weapon in their arsenal. The curative fantasy can come with great financial and personal costs associated with overtreatment, its painful side effects, and unnecessary end-of-life suffering.

Presencing and Re-envisioning. This brings us to the temporal orientation I will call *presencing*. Earlier we discussed Havi Carel, who at age 37 discovered she had LAM, a rare, progressive, and at the time, uniformly fatal pulmonary disease. At that moment the timeline of her life fragmented. Since she was relatively young, there was little solace to be found in *remembering* what was, nor was it realistic for her to *anticipate* medical salvation in the future:

> When I walked through the park I would look at the young mothers playing happily with their children and a wave of envy would wash over me. You will never have this, I would tell myself over and over: the sense of security, the naive belief in the goodness of life, long lazy afternoons in the park, mundane concerns about redecorating and scraped knees. (Carel 2014, 38)

This brings about *desynchronization*, as Carel felt thoroughly out of sync with others, as well as her prior self and the future she had anticipated. Though the temptation to collapse into self-pity and depression was strong, she learned to refocus her attention on the present—what she could do and be right now. The illness thus began to open a zone of liberation:

> Time did change for me. I began to take it much more seriously. I began to make a point of enjoying things thoroughly: memorizing sensations, views, moments. I wanted to feel that I am living life to the full in the present. That I *am* now.
>
> By focusing on the present I learned to discount the future, while it seemed to me that so many of my friends were doing the opposite. They seemed to be always waiting for something to happen: the promotion, the birth, the trip. I had nothing to wait for but bad news. . . . Yes, Really Bad Things could happen to me at any minute. But not now. And now is where reality is: liquid time solidified into a crystal drop of Now. I grasped that drop with both hands, clutching, savouring, enjoying. Now became the place for me, too, to be. (Carel 2014, 144–45)

Thus, illness and disability may challenge any customary task-oriented use of time. In the strategy of *presencing* we choose to plant our feet firmly in the present, and realize that the now is in fact a present; that is, a gift best opened by giving it our full attention. The curtailment of *anticipation* by serious impairment, or by the aging process which ever shortens our future, or even by learning that we have a fatal illness, invites us to plunge more deeply into our present life. Heidegger (1962), among many other spiritual and philosophical teachers, notes that "being-unto-death"—owning our mortality—can deepen our authentic existence. This is similarly stressed in Buddhist teachings on the impermanence, and therefore the incalculable value, of each moment. A study of individuals with life-threatening illnesses found that the ability to find significance and peace in the present moment was an important contributor to their quality of life (Mount et al. 2007).

In this regard, the lived body itself provides an anchoring presence. As much as our mind might drift toward *remembering* or *anticipating*, the body often pulls us back to the immediacy of current reality, including the need to go to the bathroom quickly, get something to eat when our blood sugar is low, catch up on sleep when fatigued, or stay off an injured leg. In my earlier book *The Absent Body*, I stressed these modes of what I termed *dys-appearance*: the body's tendency to appear to explicit awareness especially at times of dys-function or dis-tress. In that book I examined the phenomenological roots of the Western tendency to see the body as something alien, problematic, and dangerous. However, there are many cultures, including our own at times, that encourage what might be called *eu-appearance*: the body surfacing in ways that are pleasant or helpful, as Carel describes above. Body-awareness can also free us up from the endless and often distressing play of thought and emotion. One example is the use of the breath in many meditative techniques. Paying careful attention to our in-and-out breath keeps returning us over and over to the present when our worries are running away with us. (This and other features of breathing will be taken up in chapter 9.)

Of course, the strategy of *presencing*, like others, can have a downside if inappropriately applied. Prudence suggests that many people with chronic conditions should proceed with due concern for the future. For example, someone with a tendency to painful acid reflux had better not *presence* to the point of gorging on spicy foods, heedless of the sleepless night that will arrive later. More seriously, those with long-term conditions such as autoimmune disorders, cancer, degenerative arthritis, and heart disease, to name but a few, may need to undergo painful treatments, maintain disciplined exercise and dietary regimens, and generally approach the present with ample concern for their long-term well-being. To do so is also to take others into consideration: our well-being is intertwined with that of our loved ones, whose own horizons of temporality may extend beyond our own. For example, we may want to be "present" to see and care for our grandchildren. We might say that *presencing* well is not only about the "present present," but also about maintaining our awareness of other presents yet to come.

For some the experience of *presencing* can open onto a timeless realm. This *timeless presencing* is a form of the "*I am*" possibility (chapter 1) and a mode of *transcendence* (chapter 2). Again, Jill Bolte Taylor's writing about her stroke and recovery proves illuminating. As left-brain damage dislodged her customary analytic approach, she reflects on the different experiences that this opened up:

> To the right mind, no time exists other than the present moment, and each moment is vibrant with sensation. Life or death occurs in the present moment. The experience of joy happens in the present moment. Our perception and experience of connection with something that is greater than ourselves occurs in the present moment. To our right mind, the moment of now is timeless and abundant. (Taylor 2009, 30)

At first it may seem self-contradictory that Taylor experiences the now as a portal to something "timeless and abundant." We are used to thinking of the now in chronological terms as a vanishingly small unit of time, each one registered by the clock and immediately surpassed by the next. We ask, "What time is it?" but one could always accurately answer "it is now." That is, each moment of our life takes place in the present, even if we spend it ruminating on the past or the future. Hence, when freed up from our conventional way of conceptualizing and experiencing time (which Taylor associates with the left brain), there can be a sense of the now not as something fleeting, but quite the contrary, as abiding and limitless. This inaugurates a kind of reversal of perspective. Rather than the now being thought of as a small moment in time, Time reveals itself as an experience that unfolds within the ever-present Now. This profoundly healing sense of dwelling in, and as, a timeless realm—a realm anchored by and yet also transcending the body—will be explored at the book's end.

Having spoken of past, future, and presence, it may seem that our treatment of temporality is complete. Yet dividing up chronology in this conventional way can also be misleading about human experience. As Wyllie writes: "Lived time is a unity of the past, present, and future, and is more than simply a succession because the immediate 'no-more,' 'present,' and 'yet-to-come' are ordinarily never sharply separated" (2005, 174). I have a set of future goals or possibilities—conditioned by past experiences which made me "who I am"—which lead me to act in the present toward desired ends. Moreover, this movement toward the future, incorporating my past, often has a *narrative* structure; I am forever telling myself and others stories about who I am, and am living my life in accordance with those stories (Charon 2008; Frank 2013).

Yet our temporal life-narratives can be challenged by serious injury or illness (Svenaeus 2011). Bury (1982) coined the term "biographical disruption" to describe how serious illnesses can upend or redirect our sense of time and identity. His sociological study of rheumatoid arthritis patients, who were often encountering a serious and unexpected illness for the first time, suggests that "there are more profound disruptions in explanatory systems normally used by people, such that a fundamental re-thinking of the person's biography and self-concept is involved" (Bury 1982, 169). This disruption need not always be the case (Jowsey 2016); it may depend upon the timing of the illness and the character of the individual undergoing it. But in many instances, serious illness calls out for a healing strategy that I will name *re-envisioning.*

I return to the narrative of Kevin Aho, my relatively young, athletic philosopher-friend who, in the midst of a vigorous cycling journey, suffered a totally unexpected and massive heart attack. His account is worth quoting at length:

> Any meaningful identity that I could envision was now constrained by the illness. And I would have to work against the background of these constraints to create myself again. Again, this process of reopening the future has been gradual. I've had to slough off identities that no longer hold for me. The most obvious is letting go of the sense of myself as someone who is fit, athletic, and strong. . . . At least for the time being, I have to make-do with slowness and being patient, with walking, stretching and meditation, letting go of the past and acknowledging that there are many different ways to interpret the idea of strength. . . . But the heart attack cracked me open. I was suddenly overflowing, not just with anxiety but with love and compassion. I called my brothers weeping, shortly after the angioplasty, telling them how much I cared about them and how thankful I was to have them in my life. My girlfriend became my fiancée in the Intensive Care Unit after my blood clot. . . . As I struggle with the limitations (of) my altered body, let go of a former self that is no longer livable, and work to refashion a new identity in the face of a precarious and restricted future, I am grateful for what the heart attack has taught me. I recognize now that I am not, and never have been, a masterful and autonomous subject, that I am fundamentally defenseless and dependent on others. And the recognition of our shared vulnerability is healing

> insofar as it binds us together in the wake of pain and loss, reminding us that we are not alone in our suffering. (Aho 2019, 197–200)

This is a poignant example of what I call *re-envisioning*. Aho is not focused on *remembering* who he once was, which would likely bring feelings of regret and resistance to his physical downfall. Nor is he simply *anticipating* an ability to regain strength in the future, though that prospect is real and has since happened. Nor, though there are resonances, is this identical to Carel's focus on *presencing*, that is, living fully in the now. *Re-envisioning*, which entails a significant shift in the trajectory and meaning of one's life, can include a reinterpretation of past, present, and future alike. Aho is building or discovering an altered narrative about what is and should be central for him, and maybe for us all. This correlates with a different relationship with his own body, which is no longer associated primarily with fitness and capability, but with vulnerability and empathic relationships. The future, once an open realm, is now "precarious" and "restricted"—but also thereby expanded as a place for giving and receiving love. Though the heart attack reveals a frightening *I can't* with regard to Aho's athletic prowess, it also cracks open a deeper *I can* concerning intimacy with others.

In the face of serious illness or injury, and particularly for those without an easy medical remedy, *re-envisioning* can form a crucial healing strategy—one that overlaps with what the AKU adaptive coping questionnaire characterizes as "reappraisal" (Büssing et al. 2010). Our revised narratives often incorporate mythic elements, for example, that of the "hero's journey" into an underworld who emerges, like Aho, with saving revelations (Hawkins 1993; Frank 2013). More prosaically, a meta-article summarizing the findings of dozens of studies notes that "benefit-finding," that is, a patient's "beliefs about gains or positive outcomes as a result of *the chronic illness*" (White et al. 2018), does itself give rise to psychological benefits and positive outcomes as if it were a self-fulfilling prophecy (Büssing et al. 2010). Another meta-article, this one on chronic illness and temporality, reflects on how stories

> offer people an opportunity to knit together the split ends of time. For people living with chronic illness, narrative stories may be applied toward fitting the illness disruption into a temporal framework. That is, narrative stories can provide a context that encompasses both the illness event and surrounding life events and recreates a state of interrelatedness. (Jowsey 2016, 109)

Re-envisioning, like any healing strategy, is not a universal solution. As Behrendt writes about a school of authors associated with "narrative aversion," "doubt has been cast on the assumptions that we are all naturally self-narrators and that narratives are to our general advantage" (2017, 52). For some people, an illness may be simply a series of discrete, disruptive experiences and is best treated as such (Woods 2011). A clinician oriented toward "narrative medicine" might mistakenly attempt to situate a medical setback in the context of the patient's life story, when the patient simply wants symptom information and reduction.

Moreover, it must be recognized that even for sufferers who are narratively inclined, not all *re-envisionings* are to the good. Certainly, a prematurely cheery story thrust upon someone may violate their own pace and way of processing tragic events (Ehrenreich 2009; Behrendt 2017). And while many people feel that "any meaning of illness is better than none" (Broyard 1992, 65), this can give rise to stories that are overly thin or based in wishful thinking—"I've learned my lesson, now God will cure this disease"—and thus prone to collapse when one meets a setback. Finally, as mentioned, many people, when faced with serious accident, illness, or incapacity, stave off meaninglessness by concluding that their suffering is justified by their own sins; they "must have brought it on themselves" through offenses against God or nature. Then we reread the past through the lens of fault-finding, darkening our view of both present and future.

Here, the sensitive treater (Charon 2008) might seek to reshape the patient's narrative in a healing direction. This is not a matter of a doctor imposing his or her story on a passive patient; for example, "we're going to defeat this enemy with all the weapons we have." Rather, the caregiver can challenge negative elements, and assist the emergence of a *re-envisioning* that is appropriate to the individual. As Egnew writes: "By addressing the inevitable existential conflicts uncovered in patients' narratives and helping them edit their stories to promote acceptance and meaning, suffering can be transcended. This requires that clinicians be skilled in narrative medicine and open to engaging the patient's existential concerns" (2018, 160).

This appropriate *re-envisioning* may be tailored to a person's cultural background. For example, a study of Chinese individuals with HIV diagnosis at a time when this was considered uniformly fatal, emphasizes "the revision of life priorities in accordance with their perception of the importance of family obligations in the Chinese sociocultural context" (Zhou 2010, 322). For many of the study's subjects, although their personal hopes had been radically curtailed by disease, consolation came from knowing that they could use their remaining time to further their family's well-being. On the other hand, Sri Lankan nuns coping with chronic disease found assistance from Buddhist teachings on impermanence, and they focused on their responsibilities to their community (Wijesinghe and Parshall 2016).

Chronic Healing

In closing, since we've repeatedly referred to "chronic pain" and "chronic illness," perhaps we should also speak of *chronic healing*. With this term I have several meanings in mind. For one, the healing strategies that I have described unfold over time, rather than once and for all as settled positions. Just as a chronic illness has its ups and downs, its slow progressions, and its daily challenges, so the various healing strategies I've discussed may be combined or exchanged for one another. A focus on *remembering* what I was once able to do is perhaps coupled with *anticipation* for what I may do again, and this in turn supplements the daily work of *restoring* function or *transforming* my body and world to better cope with impairment. A *re-envisioning* of my life may also emphasize the importance of *presencing* to the here and now. A combination or rotation of strategies may help, insofar as flexibility is an asset in the face of chronic assaults. We have the freedom to move around the chessboard of possibility.

This freedom is not contextless—there are vectors of force that pull us in certain directions. We might find ourselves coping with a chronic pain syndrome, or a progressive neurodegenerative disease. Here, the metaphor of playing on an open chessboard might seem a mischaracterization of the harsh reality. But in chess, too, we deal with an opponent, or to choose more neutral language, another player, who makes moves of their own and may wreck our initial strategies. The body is such a partner, and is capable of placing us in "check" by discomfort or dysfunction. Still, the chess game is not over, at least until death. There remains the ability to choose optimizing strategies, making the most of our position from day to day, and year to year.

Yet the term *chronic healing* is meant to refer not only to the challenge of healing over time, but of *healing time itself*. Our customary sense of lived time is challenged and disrupted by serious illness, injury, and incapacity. To reclaim not necessarily the old life, but a new life still rich and meaningful, entails healing our relationship to a temporality which can threaten to stagnate, fragment, or slip away.

Lastly, it should be noted that *chronic healing* is not done alone. For the sake of simplicity, I have confined myself largely to references that emphasize a kind of individual work. The image of playing chess may also lend itself to the notion of the lone player. But in their accounts, figures like Taylor and Aho speak much about the loving assistance provided by others as they struggled to reconstitute their life. *Chronic healing* is thus often a collective work that is helped, or at times impeded, by the larger community, a theme which we will turn to in the next chapters. It is, in this sense, more a team sport than a solitary chess match.

Unfortunately, the medical system does not always produce ideal teammates. A physician who rushes through a rapid history and physical, never hearing the patient's narrative of suffering, may fail to assist *chronic healing*. This is not to hold the individual doctor responsible. He or she is probably under institutional pressures to see as many patients as possible, maximizing billable hours. But the upshot is that doctor and patient inhabit two different temporalities, and end up unable to communicate across them in healing ways. There are also ways in which medical norms can push patients in certain directions, limiting their autonomy. For example, Gunnarson (2016, 349) and Zeiler (2018) write about the "dominant orientation toward transplantation" that is imposed on patients with kidney dialysis, an orientation which may plunge them into a focus on a particular future, foreclosing other healing strategies.

This opens onto the question of whether the notion of *chronic healing* will prove relevant not only to sick individuals but to sick social structures. We in the United States incarcerate huge numbers of citizens, and in racialized ways, condemning them to "serve time" as punishment (again, taken up in chapter 6). We leave many others with little chance of meaningful employment, with time hanging heavy on their hands. We provide many lower-level employees with boring, repetitive tasks in "dead-end jobs," making Monday to Friday drag, and impeding any sense of life progression. We compel others to work under rushed conditions or for brutally long hours, driven by economic need, productivity demands, or the obliteration by electronic interfaces of any clear division between work and leisure time. One could go on and on here. To some extent, these social problems can be viewed as themselves "chronic dis-eases"—that is, we lose any sense of ease and meaning in relation to the flow of time. There is a deep need for chronic healing on the societal level, which in turn would profoundly impact the health and well-being of individuals.

4

Objectification and Communion

Intercorporeality

We have been examining the chessboard and the moves possible for a person who is responding to challenges arising from within their own body. We have started from features of embodiment like the ways *I am* or *I have* a body; the *I can('t)* of its habitual abilities; and the way *I'm time.* These have foregrounded the embodied "*I*." It is true that having a body individualizes us—it is a primary way we are marked with separate identity throughout our life. (For example, when taking attendance in class, I scan the individual faces in order to mark who is present or absent.) Moreover, illness and incapacity can highlight this feeling of being separate. I alone experience my own pain and limitation.

Nonetheless, to have a body is also the way we are deeply *connected* to others, not in an external or contingent way, but as something that inhabits us from within. This interpenetration of bodies is there from the very beginning of life. Biologically, our body only came into being (in most cases) because two other bodies mingled their genetic material—and their consensual passion, we hope—creating a form that then develops within the mother's body. Subsequently the infant may feed directly from the mother's breasts or be cradled while given a bottle. Body-to-body touch has been shown to be an important element of early development for both animal and human infants (Ardiel and Rankin 2010). As we grow up, we continue for a long time to rely on embodied nourishment and protection granted by parents and other caregivers.

But beyond this, our body has an intuitive and immediate way of reading and reacting to the gestures, actions, and emotions of other bodies. Merleau-Ponty systematically developed how intersubjectivity is not based on an intellectual inference of others' existence, but on a prepersonal synergy (Carman 2008, 135–50):

> Now it is precisely my body that perceives the other's body and finds there something of a miraculous extension of its own intentions, a familiar manner of handling the world. Henceforth, just as the parts of my body together form a system, the other's body and my own are a single whole, two sides of a single phenomenon, and the anonymous existence, of

> which my body is continuously the trace, henceforth inhabits these two bodies simultaneously. (Merleau-Ponty 2012, 370)

Again, this process begins immediately; for example, minutes after birth infants demonstrate an ability to attend to and imitate human faces (Meltzoff and Moore 1983). As we grow up we learn, by imitation as well as training, how to hold our body, codes of proper and improper behavior, how to dress ourselves, what foods to eat, and so on. Sometimes these bodily habits are rigidly enforced, while in other cases, we develop them simply by modeling our actions on parents, teachers, and our peers. For example, feminist theorists have examined how being "female" involves a transmitted performance, mastered through repetition, as to how girls and women are to hold and use their bodies (Young 2005; J. Butler 2006). In general, we also learn what body types are valued in our culture, and this shapes our self-image for good or ill—too often for ill if the race, gender, shape, or other aspects of one's body are devalued, thereby becoming a source of self-doubt and shame.

Language, though often associated with intellect, is another embodied mode of interconnection, as we learn to hear, speak, read, and write the words shared in a culture and perceive according to its categories. Then too, our desires are not only directed toward other bodies, but are influenced by them as we learn to crave the electronic devices or stylish clothing that others have or want, and which are peddled by the media. Yet embodiment is also at the root of empathic care. The word "compassion" derives from the Latin *com* (with) and *pati* (suffer, feel); we do feel within ourselves a resonance with others' sufferings. If we see a person or animal writhe in pain, we do not simply "infer" their suffering: it can send a shock wave through our own body.

These kinds of examples, which could be continued ad infinitum, make clear two things. (1) The "individual self" is something of an ideological construct because the "I" is always part of a "We," that is, nested collectivities of people, practices, technologies, natural environments, economic and political systems, and cultural traditions that shape us into who we are. And (2) this "We" is not best imagined as an amalgam of individual "minds" or "souls," but as involving an "intercorporeality" or "intercorporeity" (Merleau-Ponty 1968, 141) in which we participate from conception to death. As Diprose writes, building on Merleau-Ponty's work, "the self is produced, maintained, and transformed through the socially mediated intercorporeal 'transfer' of movements and gestures and body bits and pieces. . . . Bodies, as they are lived, are socially constituted, built from an intertwining with others who are already social beings" (2002, 54).

To express all this tersely, I'll simply say "*We inter-act.*" In discussing the bodily *I am, I have, I can('t)*, and so on, the pronoun "I" foregrounded the personalized self–body relation. Switching to the pronoun "We" now highlights how this "I" was never an isolated individual, but is always formed and defined through relations with others. ("We" is capitalized here so as not to seem lesser than, or derivative from, the always capitalized "I.") The word "interact" derives from the Latin *inter*, "between, among," and *actus*, "doing, impulse." To say "*We inter-act*" is to emphasize that our acting is always "inter"—it is always unfolding among and between us, such that our relationships with others are primary. The hyphen in "*inter-act*" helps us to register the significance of this embedded connectivity.

Though intersubjectivity was at play and sometimes explicitly discussed in relation to previous healing strategies, I now turn to our last four strategies, which explicitly foreground *inter-active* relations. Despite the fact that, as corporeal beings, we are never truly isolated, we can certainly feel this way. We have mentioned, and will later say more, about how much illness and impairment can restrict our spatial reach, "desynchronize" us from the flow of socially shared time, and impair our ability to be close with others. As a result, to heal we often have a need to reconnect with those around us, and to use that to help reintegrate our world. In this and the following chapter I will thus explore four styles of embodied *reconnecting*, completing our list of twenty healing strategies.

Since our body does manifest an objective, material presence, I will start by addressing a strategy I call *being-objectified*: we often turn to another, such as a health care practitioner, to analyze and treat problems in the body-object (*Körper*). Conversely, since the lived body (*Leib*) is inherently subjective, *communing* with other subjects who share similar embodied challenges can also prove healing. In the next chapter, I then turn to ways in which *receiving* help from other people can ameliorate our physical and psychic deficiencies. Finally, the challenged person can find purpose and self-esteem through *giving* to others despite, or sometimes through and because of, their bodily deficits. These are all healing forms through which *We inter-act* and *reconnect*. Since these strategies are so significant and multilayered, involving not just ourselves but others as key to the healing process, I will unfold my analysis more slowly, taking on only two modes per chapter. We will thereby complete our survey of twenty healing strategies—again, Figures 1 and 2 provide an overview of these.

Reconnecting with Others

Being-Objectified. Earlier I wrote on *objectifying* as a strategy. In that section the focus was on the way in which individuals objectify their *own* dysfunctional body patterns, thereby gaining a greater sense of distance from, and perhaps mastery over, distressing symptoms. I now turn to "*being-objectified*"—that is, how individuals seek to heal through being objectified *by others*. Of course, there are unpleasant forms of involuntary objectification, such as a woman subject to an unwanted sexualized male gaze. Yet at other times we willingly invite others to objectify us, as when we are ill and need expert help. Ultimately, the two healing strategies that involve objectification, self-regarding and other-mediated, often overlap. It is usually not until we have objectified aspects of our own body, viewing them to some degree as *other* (than it has been, should be, and *other* to the self), that we decide to take our body to a clinician. As mentioned, our self-regard has usually already been influenced by the pervasiveness of the objectifying "medical gaze" in our society. "Is this a cyst or a fibroma?" one wonders, skimming through website images. Or: "Shouldn't I be on that drug I just saw on TV?" The cultural zeitgeist already populates our own mind.

However, in discussing *being-objectified* as a healing strategy, I will mostly narrow the focus to direct *inter-actions* such as a visit to a healthcare practitioner. Perhaps a disfigurement, disability, or disturbing set of symptoms has provoked enough concern that we seek a professional. Since the practitioner is armed with medical knowledge, years of clinical experience, and various diagnostic technologies, we hope they can uncover whatever is happening in our body. This uncovering may at times be literal: we are willing to take off our clothing and expose our nude body parts, including ones we may feel ashamed of. As Diprose (2002, 107) writes, "our body and our life, that which is most intimate and private, is given to a stranger. It involves an offering that we would more usually reserve for a lover, a mother, or a friend." We consent to be palpated, poked, and prodded in sometimes painful ways, stuck with needles, and encased in diagnostic imaging machines. Sometimes we even allow our body to be absorbed into the totalizing world of the hospital where, as if a prisoner, we are stripped, banded with an identification number, consigned to a small room, and subject to unpredictably timed questionings by those in authority. (More will be said on the correlation between patients and prisoners in chapter 6.)

Already one can see a shadow-side to all this *being-objectified*. Many patients feel the process to be dehumanizing, even if they deem it necessary to access treatment. In the midst of suffering, when we are most vulnerable and yearning for sympathy, it can be painful to find ourselves reduced to an organ system, disease, and insurance code.

Oliver Sacks, the famous neurologist and author, himself suffered a severe neurological injury (an example I will return to later). Suddenly seeing life from the other side, he now experienced his condition as something

> "moral"—not quite an adequate word—associated with the reduced stationless status of a patient, and, in particular, conflict with and surrender to "them"—"them" being the surgeon, the whole system, the institution—a conflict with hateful and even paranoid tones, which added to the severe, yet neutral, physical affliction a far less tolerable, because irresoluble, moral affliction. I had felt not only physically but morally prostrate—unable to stand up, stand morally before "them," in particular, before the surgeon. (Sacks 1994, 129)

Even Dr. Sacks's knowledge and status as a physician, as well as his identity as a young, well-off white male, did not protect him when he was unable to stand up, physically and existentially, in the face of objectification. How much more can this take place for patients from groups that are discriminated against, and persons with lower levels of education, financial resources, or social support systems? Many such individuals—women in a sexist society; persons of color surrounded by racism; disabled or aged persons facing ableism and ageism—have already experienced disempowering objectification within the larger society insofar as their bodies are marginalized or devalued (Fanon 2008; Gordon 1997; Beauvoir 2011; Young 2005; Weiss 1998; Kafer 2013; Yancy 2017). This objectification can itself become a cause of disease; for example, experiencing racialized stress has been shown to elevate blood pressure, with all the consequent long-term problems that can ensue (Ngo 2017, 59–60).

In any case, a process of alienation begun by illness may be exacerbated by contact with a medical system that often reflects wider cultural prejudices. A survey of electronic records showed that Black patients were two and a half times as likely as white patients to have at least one negative descriptive term used in their electronic health record (Sun et al. 2022). In one study, 12.3 percent of Black respondents reported discrimination in their health care as compared with just 2.3 percent of White respondents (Stepanikova and Oates 2017). This explicit or implicit bias has very real consequences for health care. For example, as the chronic pain specialist Haider Warraich notes, "research has shown that people who've faced racial discrimination are more sensitive to pain. Despite that reality, studies reveal that doctors are actually less likely to prescribe pain medicines for Black people" (DuLong 2022; see Hoffman et al. 2016). Moreover, patients who perceived racial discrimination in health care were more prone to delay care, less likely to receive the appropriate chronic disease screening, and less likely to follow their doctor's recommendations (Blanchard and Lurie 2004).

It is also worth noting that "dominant" groups suffer as well from social prejudice: in his book *Dying of Whiteness*, Metzl [2020] shows how racism, and the movements with which it is associated, shorten many white lives through widespread opposition to gun control as well as to a variety of beneficial educational and social programs, including the Affordable Care Act.

Turning to sexual identity, Dusenbery (2018) makes a detailed and compelling argument that in a male-dominated medical system, women are disadvantaged by both a "knowledge gap" and a "trust gap." With regard to the former, disease research has often focused on the male body, whereas women's physiology and maladies are less well investigated. Then too, women's accounts of symptoms are more likely to be distrusted and lumped into the categories of "psychogenic illness" or simply "medically unexplained diseases."

To take another case of what I will term in chapter 6 "embodied injustice," rampant ageism in the health care system can lead to the undertreatment of pain, depression, and physical illness in the elderly because their problems are falsely attributed to their age. Alternatively, there is also dangerous overtreatment of the frail elderly because of doctors' relative lack of medical training in, and sensitivity to, the special needs of older patients (Ouchida and Lachs 2015).

In addition to the potential for dehumanizing and prejudicial treatment, *being-objectified* also generates great financial costs for the individual and society, given all the diagnostic tests, pharmaceuticals, and surgeries used. In contrast, Dr. Thanh Neville, a critical care physician, started a "Thanks and Wishes" program that humanized ICU treatment by reaching out to patients and families; for example, by writing a sympathy card after someone had died. She said, "I'm shocked at how much it means to people." Dr. Vivek Murthy (2020, 22), a past U.S. surgeon general, notes that the average cost of this healing program was just "$30 per patient. Not $30,000." Obviously, *being-objectified* is far more profitable for the health care industry. This capitalist incentive is a stressor not only for patients and the larger society, but also for medical providers who are pressured to meet productivity goals.

That said, *being-objecified* by practitioners can serve as a powerful healing strategy—as long as everyone is aware of the shadow-sides mentioned above and thus are better able to manage or avoid them. This is best assured by a framework for health care that I will characterize by the four "H's": that which is hermeneutic, humanistic, holistic, and (clinically) helpful. Though this book primarily focuses on healing strategies that individuals can and do access on their own, it would be a crucial omission to not consider in some depth how the medical system can best assist healing.

"Hermeneutics" refers to the practice or study of *interpretation*. First employed in a seventeenth-century context of biblical exegesis, hermeneutics has taken on a cross-disciplinary meaning, such that it can refer to the interpretation of a wide variety of texts, whether a legal code, a literary novel, or a set of scientific data (Palmer 1969). Many scholars have characterized medicine as an intrinsically hermeneutical art or science. As I explore elsewhere, the clinician in search of an integrative diagnosis and treatment plan interprets many things: the history and symptoms of the patient; the physical features of his/her body; the results of lab tests and diagnostic imaging; all in the light of medical categories, clinical experience, and the unique profile of this sick individual (Leder 2016a, 87–105).

Given interpretation's importance, an investigation of the object-body does not mean that a clinician arrives at a completely "objective" truth. In a hermeneutical enterprise there always remains ambiguity and subjectivity. It is rare that a numerical lab test will answer all questions—the numbers have to be contextualized in relation to the patient's symptoms and lifestyle. Nor is the physician an idealized scientist occupying a "view from nowhere." She herself, as interpreter, is influenced by her own social and medical training and experience. Recognizing all this helps the practitioner to step down from a pedestal and the patient to rise up from a prostrate position, to engage one another in a more productive dialogue.

This requires each participant to enter, to a certain degree, into the discursive world of the other. The clinician listens sensitively to the patient's account of symptoms, and later refrains from using "medicalese" while explaining, in a jargon-free fashion, her findings and recommendations. That practitioner also has to arrive at some understanding of the patient's own language and world—their history, lifestyle, cultural background, and beliefs—while responding thoughtfully to their questions and concerns. In the best of circumstances, then, *being-objectified* supports, rather than undercuts, the patient's subjectivity. (I will give a personal example of this later.) Unfortunately, this is often challenged by the financial incentives and layers of bureaucracy that can interfere with the time and space needed for a fully productive clinical encounter.

This sense of medicine as a shared hermeneutical enterprise ideally goes hand in hand with taking a *humanistic* and *holistic* approach to care.

The patient is not the "endocarditis in room 315" but a human being with an identity, job, family, and unique personality. Here I think the phenomenological notion of the "lived body" is a particularly useful concept. Usually, humanistic medicine has not sought holism through an enriched notion of embodiment, but instead has accepted the Cartesian dualism of a body-machine coupled with a mind, or perhaps uses the language of a triadic "mind-body-spirit." Yet this can bring about a conceptual, and sometimes a practical, fragmentation rather than true holism. A surgeon scrubs up before an operation (body); then a psychiatrist addresses any postoperative depression (mind); and a chaplain pays a brief visit to the patient and family to see that all is well (spirit). The "mind-body-spirit" paradigm may thus apportion tasks to different practitioners who do not necessarily communicate with each other or integrate the healing process.

Though "integrative medicine" (which combines traditional medicine with alternative practices) is frequently now the term of choice rather than "holistic," the field still often resorts to the same tripartite model of self, as in this overview statement: "[Integrated medicine] views patients as whole people with minds and spirits as well as bodies and includes these dimensions into diagnosis and treatment" (Rees and Weil 2001, 119). (To be fair, integrative medical practice includes treatments such as acupuncture, which itself is rooted in the Chinese notion of qi, a mode of energy that is simultaneously mental/physical/cosmological.) The tripartite model divides the self into different elements, which subtly undercut the "integrative" perspective. For example, the struggle to resume life activities after open-heart surgery is not best seen as a physical, plus a psychosocial and spiritual, problem; but as an existential challenge engaged in by the whole embodied person as illustrated by their posture, whether protectively slumped or erect; their quality of voice, whether clear or muted; their confidence in physical activity, whether energetic or guarded; their cardiac response to stressors; their desires and fears about returning to sexual activities; their anxiety in the face of mortality; and so on. A phenomenological approach to lived embodiment can assist, both through theory and practice, more genuinely holistic care.

Of course, medical objectification should be not only hermeneutic, humanistic, and holistic—ideally, the results also need to be clinically *helpful*. This is worth specifying because such is not always the case. Many a patient with lower back problems receives an MRI which images a herniated disk, perhaps then leading to surgical intervention. However, that herniation may not be the source of the pain: often similar anatomical abnormalities show up in the MRIs of asymptomatic individuals. The "objective" results of a test may thus prove irrelevant to the problem at hand, or even be actively misleading. Not everything that is measurable is clinically real.

Conversely, not everything that is real is measurable. Many patients are distressed by having "medically unexplained symptoms" although the suffering they experience, such as persistent fatigue, dizziness, or muscle pains, is very real to them. In the absence of measurable findings, there is a risk of their being told, whether explicitly or implicitly, that it is "all in your mind" (Nettleton et al. 2005). Within a materialistic worldview this is tantamount to saying their disease is imaginary, which of course can compound the patient's distress.

For patient care in general, it is a challenge to sift out just what tests to order; how to properly contextualize their results; and then just what would be the most helpful treatment recommendations. In certain societies, where medical care is financially incentivized by payments for tests and procedures, there is an *overuse* of the healing strategy of *being-objectified*. The result may be too many tests ordered, prescriptions written, and surgeries performed, with all the attendant expense and clinical side effects, including tragedies such as the opiate addiction fueled by "big pharma." This is often accompanied by neglect of the environmental and psychosocial factors which are so important in causing and treating diseases. Of course, the reverse can be true: for those who are disadvantaged even in an affluent society, and in many places around the world, there may be an *underuse* of *being-objectified* since there is a lack of needed resources for, and access to, optimal medical care.

Aristotle thinks of "virtue" in most human domains as involving a mean between vicious excess and deficiency—not a simple arithmetical mean, but feeling and behaving "as one ought and at the thing one ought, in relation to those people who one ought, for the sake and as one ought" (Aristotle 2011, 34). This is the challenge, not only for the individual but for society, regarding the use of *being-objectified*; how to do this at the right times, in relation to the right conditions, and in the right ways. Here I have suggested the value of the four "H's": hermeneutical, humanistic, holistic, and helpful. When used rightly, *being-objectified* can be healing whether or not it results in a medical cure. It can give us greater distance on potentially devastating bodily events; help validate and explain what up until now has been inchoate; lessen or forestall symptoms; and restore our confidence that there are others who can understand and help one's private suffering.

To bookend Oliver Sacks's story of his "moral" reduction through *being objectified*, I'll give an example from my own life of its positive use as a healing strategy. Having suffered for years from a strange but sharp and disabling pain in my lower ankle, I went to many specialists in search of relief. It was hard to even figure out who to see. Foot-focused orthopedists said the pain-site fell just above their region of expertise, while ankle specialists couldn't locate any structural problem. Might it be a vascular issue involving an enlarged vein pressing on a nerve? Vascular specialists disagreed—one said no, one yes—ultimately leading, somewhat at my insistence, to a rather fruitless surgery. Finally, though, I located a plastic surgeon who knew just what I had, having seen previous cases: it was an idiopathic peripheral neuropathy at the lower end of the saphenous nerve. It was a relief just to know what I was suffering from, receive a diagnostic label for it (even though "idiopathic" means "we don't really know what's causing it"), and then be given appropriate treatment options: if the pain proved uncontrollable by medication, nerve surgery was indicated.

Fortunately, my surgeon took the time (nearly an hour during one office visit, and we had a number of visits) to not only do various diagnostic maneuvers but to explain the results, converse about my lifestyle and what was most important to me (for example, walking miles each day in natural surroundings with my dog), and discuss with me the possible treatments, including the ins and outs (literally) of different surgeries. He could cut the nerve and bury it in muscle to try to stop it from regrowing, which would permanently numb my outer leg. However, there was also a chance he could sever but preserve the nerve, allowing its ends to regrow together inside an implanted cadaver-sourced protein nerve-sheath. Upon his recommendation I opted for the latter surgery if it proved achievable. This he wouldn't know until he was actually inside my leg. After he saw my nerve while I lay inert under general anesthesia, he did in fact choose this new form of surgery. It has since proven not perfect, but highly successful, allowing me to resume those lovely dog walks.

This was an example of the Aristotelian "virtuous" use of the strategy of *being-objectified*. The diagnosis and treatment were arrived at through a process that was hermeneutical, humanistic, holistic, and offered me genuinely helpful options. Given the experientially recessive nature of the body interior, I had to rely on someone else to open me up and render the nerve visible and treatable (Leder 1990, 36–68). Yet the total context left me comfortable enough to empower the surgeon to make a crucial decision while I lay unconscious.

In other words, I trusted the lived body of the surgeon to be discerning and skillful enough for me to place myself in his hands. Though at that crucial moment of choice I was reduced to being an object-body, in the larger context my subjectivity was thereby supported. Ultimately, one might ask, was the choice of which surgery to use his decision or mine? It seems most apt to say that "*We inter-acted*" such that it was *our* decision.

Communing. If intercorporeality allows one to *be-objectified* by another, it also makes space for the converse experience of *co-subjectivity*. In the words of Russon and Jacobson: "Your *understanding* of my expression of sympathy, enthusiasm, or disagreement is not the same as the simple pressure against your skin, the excitation of receptors within your retina . . . and so on: on the contrary, it is your *recognition* of what I *as a subject* am expressing to you *as a subject*" (2018, 194). This recognition allows for the emergence of deeply felt empathy. While sometimes thought of as a cognitive/emotive function, empathy finds its roots in our intercorporeality:

> Not only is another embodied being different from other objects, particularly in terms of a caring response, but because of the continuity of the flesh . . . I know about being cut and bleeding. I know about a comforting hug. I know about hunger . . . The whole of this knowledge cannot be quantified or easily described in words, but my body knows these things. (Hamington 2004, 55)

Within this context I now turn to a strategy I call *communing*, one involving embodied healing co-subjectivity.

As discussed earlier, disease and incapacity can trigger a sense of isolation. We are pulled away from the mainstream of life-activity as others proceed with their routines. We may also experience internal discomforts that are nearly impossible to communicate (Scarry 1985). Then too, others may not wish to hear of our woes. Our own distress may prove upsetting to them insofar as it makes them feel powerless to help, or triggers concerns for their own vulnerability.

Moreover, certain types of bodily challenges, which may limit or disfigure a body compared to the idealized norm, can lead to what the sociologist Erving Goffman (1969, 11–12) called "stigmatization." Many with *visible* disabilities have bodies that are stigmatized in society, even when this takes the form of a well-meaning desire to offer "help to the handicapped." Then too, as previously mentioned, there are individuals who feel isolated precisely because their chronic distress is *invisible*.

A good friend and colleague, Sr. Missy Gugerty, has long suffered from the effects of chronic Lyme disease which in her case has led to fatigue, cognitive deficits, and other disabling symptoms. Yet for the most part these are not obvious to others. There is a disjunction between her outward-facing surface-body and what she experiences from within. As she explained to me, many individuals, including those aware of her condition, start by saying "you look great!" (She did, by the way, when I recently saw her.) While well-intentioned, this proclamation makes her feel even more alone with bodily struggles neither perceived nor acknowledged by others. She told me, "Don't start by telling me 'You look great!' because that just shuts me up. I'm not going to then say, 'But I feel awful.' I assume you don't want to hear that. Start instead by asking '*How are you feeling?*'" Yet for the reasons mentioned above, people often shy away from this inquiry, leaving the ill person to manage alone.

Having to bear with loneliness is not only the cause of psychosocial distress, including increased depression, suicidality, anxiety, and aggression, but has been implicated as a risk factor for many physical problems. It can play a role in increased inflammatory response, diminished immune function, elevated blood pressure, the possibility of recurrent stroke, and the progression of Alzheimer's disease (Holt-Lunstad et al. 2010, 2015). The medical risks arising from feeling or being alone are thus akin to those associated with smoking, low exercise, obesity, or substance abuse.

The experience of *communing* can serve as an antidote for these reverberating effects of isolation. In this section on intersubjectivity, it seems particularly apt that voices other than my own be featured—hence my mention of Missy Gugerty, and now a turn to personal communications with that longtime friend with Parkinson's, Joan Boor, as well as with Michelle Burack, a Parkinson's clinician who, familiar with my writings, had reached out to me independently. Starting with their accounts, I will categorize some different forms that the healing strategy of *communing* can take.

Communing with Others Who Share the Same Condition

While illness and incapacity can isolate, they can also form an intercorporeal bridge with others who share similar problems. Dr. Burack, an assistant professor in the Department of Neurology at the University of Rochester, has helped organize the "Parkinson's Café," which runs group exercise programs and activities for PD patients, while also providing a venue to share useful information. My friend Joan has participated in a similar group created by a pharmacist who was moved to do so one day after watching her burst into tears when she would pick up her medications. (Note: This strong emotion, an expression both of Joan's distress about her PD symptoms and of her struggle to obtain and pay for appropriate meds, can also relate, as Burack writes, to a neurologically caused "pseudobulbar affect, a change in the way the brain regulates expression of emotion, [which] leads to tearfulness/crying with minimal provocation. I think it is important that PD really makes clear how arbitrary the boundary is between 'bodily incapacity' and things we might be inclined to label 'mind' or 'emotion.'")

Joan told me of the healing from isolation provided by her Parkinson's support group. The group gathered once a month, and it was comforting to meet others with the same sorts of bodily challenges—for example, the muscle wasting, and the flattened, mask-like facial features (*hypomimia*) characteristic of PD—and feel that she was not alone with them. Somewhat surprisingly, Joan found that her experience of these commonalities also enabled her to see more clearly the individuality of each person she met in the group. "This person was so intelligent. That person so imaginative. It made me feel like I must have those special features too." *Communing* thus helped Joan to discover the particularities of each person, and herself, that transcended the disease.

That PD patients often feel stigmatized by the larger society makes these gatherings even more valuable. Joan describes how

> we would go out to eat, go shopping. In society, people do not always understand the possibility of spilling a drink. [Note: Fatigue, tremor and muscle dyscoordination are common features of PD.] But in this group people would understand and be supportive. It was really important for me to be physically with the other people. Empathy is a very physical thing. You see things, notice things, feel something different.

Burack independently wrote to me about the same phenomenon:

> If you have tremor and spill a little bit of food, when you are in a group of people with PD, it is no big deal, whereas in a group of non-disabled people this "messiness" will stick out and cause a subtle shift in social attitude and treatment of you (because your behavior resembles that of a less-developed person)—a range of body language signals from overt avoidance to more subtle facial expressions (e.g., disdain), avoidance of eye contact.

Burack also provided another example of social stigmatization, in this case due to the tendency of those with PD to have a quiet voice, slurred words, and difficulty with word-finding:

> Most commonly, people smile and nod despite not understanding, rather than asking someone to repeat themselves with greater clarity; this leads to not being understood, not being included in conversation, not having needs met. This often evolves to people being *spoken-over* (e.g., a prolonged pause in conversation would simply be filled by another speaker) or *spoken-for* (e.g., the doctor turns to the care partner rather than waiting for the person with PD to speak for him/herself).

In a gathering of those who share in PD, there tends to be more understanding, more willingness to wait through pauses, more honoring of each person's individual voice.

There are many other benefits to the *communing* that happens when people meet face-to-face in this way. Abilities, rather than dis-abilities, are emphasized and reclaimed through shared exercise or other activities. There is the possibility of physical touch, that most intimate of embodied exchanges (Leder 2016a, 42–55), for example through hugs. There is also *communion* when sitting down to a common meal, which evokes the religious usage of this word. At the Last Supper, the sharing of bread and wine was a way of symbolizing/actualizing the interpenetration of Jesus's own flesh with that of his followers: "Take, eat; this is my body" (Matt. 26:26). Sharing food and drink with others in a mall café, distant as it may seem from a Eucharistic context, is a way bodies feed into one another, including the possibility of shared laughter and tears.

The philosopher Helmuth Plessner (1970, 138) wrote: "We laugh and cry only in situations for which there is no other answer." In his view, there are times when we reach our limits of personal response and instead give over to our body a physical process which "compulsively runs its course"—and yet is also deeply meaningful. When *communing* with others, such actions infectiously transmit from body to body, akin to the resonance of vibrating strings: "Laughter is one of the most contagious, universal, and instinctive connectors" (Murthy 2020, 211). I know from public speaking that the best way to knit an audience together with me and with one another, forming a communal body, is to get people laughing. How wonderful, then, that in PD gatherings people can laugh together over a food spillage rather than dreading a stranger's stare; and if someone bursts into tears, they need not fear the stigmatizing stare of strangers.

In this context, Burack feels a deep concern that a national Parkinson's organization is shifting its focus to virtual programming, featuring online informational and chat sessions. One can grasp the benefits of such an approach. It will give homebound or movement-restricted individuals an opportunity to participate when they might have been unable to attend in-person gatherings. Complex organizational and transportation issues will be significantly diminished. Individuals will no longer be limited to communicating only with those in their immediate area. Valuable treatment tips, and caring words, can now be shared across the world. The Parkinsonian body is thus extended by *incorporating* a computer or smartphone.

Yet there are also inevitable losses. Don Ihde (1979) writes of the amplification/reduction structure of any incorporated technology. For example, while the telephone *amplifies* the capacity of voice and hearing across long distances, at the same time there are *reductions* compared to unmediated encounters. We can no longer see or touch one another; even the gestural background that enriches verbal communication is lost. Ihde notes that technologies are non-neutral, pushing us in certain directions—for example, texts often favor brief, elliptical, and therefore sometimes ambiguous or tone-deaf communications—not a great medium to work through thorny emotional issues or complex decisions. Similarly, we run into various limits in the *communing* that is possible across a computerized interface. We lose the capacity for hugs, a common meal, shared activities, and the small nuances of expression that enrich face-to-face encounters. All too often, virtual PD meetings may take the form of information delivery, followed by questions and answers, while most "participants" sit passively before their devices.

That said, videoconference platforms do still allow people to see and hear each other and sometimes to bond across a distance. Many during the Covid-19 pandemic have been surprised by the rich conversations they have had with friends and loved ones, including people they might not have contacted except as a remedy to their isolation. Similarly, technological interfaces can serve to relieve the loneliness of someone with any serious affliction. Burack mentions, with regard to chat rooms and texting, that she thinks emoticons are a great invention: pseudo-facial expressions such as or or or can, with a single mouse click, do something to pictorialize embodied emotion.

Of course, much of this depends on our ability to afford, understand, and access these technologies. Given PD dyskinesias, struggling with the small interface and complex applications of a smartphone has been a source of deep despair and low self-esteem for Joan. Well-designed assistive technologies might help relieve such burdens, but again issues of access and affordability are key.

Whether mediated through personal meetings, or larger impersonal organizations, *communing* with others can also help with healing consequent to coordinated political action. Unfair as it may seem, certain diseases and not others benefit from advocacy and lobbying groups that help direct funding toward research relevant to that disease's causes and treatments, and to providing resources for ill persons. Similarly, those with "disabilities," whether congenital or the result of injury or disease, have often had to band together to battle on behalf of their rights. Sometimes this is a very local struggle; for example, to build wheelchair ramps in a town's public buildings. In other cases, it is a national issue like passing the U.S. Americans with Disabilities Act.

It might seem as if the healing strategy of *communing with others who share a similar condition* has no shadow-side—but it can. For example, Goffman in his work on stigmatization quotes from a blind girl who was released from the hospital to "The Lighthouse," an organization designed to assist blind people. "I was to spend the rest of my life making mops with other blind people; eating with other blind people, dancing with other blind people. I became nauseated with fear, as the picture grew in my mind. Never had I come upon such destructive segregation" (Goffman 1969, 37). While this approach has since been critiqued and surpassed, it illustrates the danger of an overfocus on gathering only with those who share a condition. One can feel separated off and defined by the disease. Burack also points to another potential downside in illness-based gatherings: "If someone newly diagnosed and relatively mild has their first experience in a support group with people with advanced-stage disease, it can provoke horror and despair. This is why we tried to have some dedicated groups for the newly diagnosed, in order to avoid having people assume that what they see is what will become their guaranteed future." As Aristotle might say, *communing* is best done through a careful and "virtuous" application, that is, in the right way and time, and with the right people.

Communing with Friends, Loved Ones, and Treaters

While I have hitherto focused on connecting with those who share the same condition, the healing strategy of *communing* has much broader applications. We can experience embodied co-subjectivity with caring family and friends, and this is indeed where people often find the most support. While those close to us usually don't share our specific illness (though Joan Boor's husband also has developed Parkinson's!), they *know us,* often through long years of shared experience and a depth of connection. For example, having a caring sister may make all the difference in dealing with the blow of an unexpected cancer diagnosis, the ups and downs of biopsies, chemotherapy or surgery, checkups, and so on, as hard emotions and decisions accrue over the years.

Here, though, I would distinguish, as others have, between "empathy"—a true sharing in someone's experience—and "sympathy" or "pity"—which may connote suffering recognized or felt from a distance. Though pitying concern and actions may be genuine, the healing strategy of *communing* involves a more powerful experiential resonance. Though others may not share the selfsame illness or incapacity, they have often undergone their own forms of affliction, giving them an enhanced ability to identify. For example, though there is so much I don't understand about Joan's PD, the fact that I have struggled with the distresses of chronic back and nerve pain lends me a greater capacity to feel for her, and to build a shared story in our conversations. So, to some extent, we are "in it together" when we talk (which we do frequently, having known each other now for thirty years). Paradoxically, this also involves admitting all that we cannot grasp about the other's hardships, a necessary humility in the face of our embodied differences.

It is not just our own illness history that can make us a *communion* partner for someone else in distress. A certain quality of embodied and emotional presence is also called for, and this is not always easy to summon up in the face of great suffering. After the Last Supper, the prototype of the Eucharistic ritual referred to previously, Jesus goes into the garden of Gethsemane. The Gospels quote him as saying to those gathered, "My heart is ready to break with grief. Stop here and stay awake with me" (Matt. 26:38). Yet one by one, through the dark night, his disciples fall asleep. Similarly, it is easy to "fall asleep"—that is, not be fully present—with someone who is in anguish from chronic pain or a progressive or fatal disease. It is so hard to witness and yet be unable to help. Yet "staying awake" helps make genuine *communion* possible. With Joan I sometimes feel more successful, and sometimes less so, in being fully awake to our conversations and her emotional and spiritual needs.

Simone Weil, the French philosopher and mystic, wrote of "affliction" (*malheur*) as "an uprooting of life, a more or less attenuated equivalent of death, made irresistibly present to the soul by the attack of immediate apprehension of physical pain. . . . There is no real affliction unless there is social degradation or the fear of it in some form or other" (Weil 1951, 118–19). What is most needed in the face of soul-deadening affliction, she writes, is for another to pay *attention*. "Attention consists of suspending our thought, leaving it detached, empty and ready to be penetrated by the object" (Weil 1951, 111). Giving attention to someone in anguish need not involve bustling about to make things better, but is simply a quality of presence which helps to restore their full humanity. Weil (1951, 115) tells us that in the original legend of the Holy Grail, "it belongs to the first comer who asks the guardian of the vessel, a king three-quarters paralyzed by the most painful wound, 'What are you going through?'" When in distress we are more likely to feel *communion* with the one who asks that question and stays awake for the answer, whether this interaction unfolds in a moment or over the course of many years. In the words of Henri Nouwen, "The friend who can be silent with us in a moment of despair or confusion, who can stay with us in an hour of grief and bereavement, who can tolerate not knowing, not curing, not healing, and face with us the reality of our powerlessness, that is a friend who cares" (Nowen 2014, 38).

Though we may find this kind of closeness only with a select few, the potential for *communing* remains far more expansive. There is a story in Buddhism of a woman who lost her only son and, suffering implacable grief, is finally directed to ask help from the Buddha himself. He tells her he has a curative medicine, but first she needs to come back with a handful of mustard seed—and it "must be taken from a house where no one has lost a child, husband, parent, or friend." She goes from house to house and though all want to give her mustard seed, "there was no house but some beloved one had died in it" (Carus 1916, 210). This leads her to realize that "the darkness of night reigned everywhere"—affliction was not hers alone but connected her to all vulnerable, mortal, sentient creatures. She then receives wisdom teachings (*prajna*) which can truly relieve her suffering, as well as enhancing her *karuna* (compassion, the other great Buddhist virtue). We can potentially *commune* with all sentient creatures—victims of a distant tragedy, an injured animal, a distressed colleague—knowing that we share in common this vulnerability to affliction, and yet that this is also transformed by our togetherness.

Though I started by contrasting *communing* with its medical opposite, *being-objectified*, I will close by noting that these strategies can be blended in a single encounter. Many health care practitioners, whether mainstream or "alternative," incorporate real empathy (not just professionalized "sympathy") in their interactions with patients. I am old enough to remember as a child going on house calls in mid-Manhattan with my father, an internist—and I came to know, especially after his premature death, that his patients viewed him as not only a skillful doctor but a deeply caring man.

Nor should these attributes of skill and caring be divided from one another. While a practitioner cannot internalize all the distress they may encounter even in a single day, a compassionate clinician can help alleviate loneliness, improve communication and compliance, and probably potentiate the placebo effect involved in the clinical encounter. We often speak of "health care" without pausing to consider how important "care" is as an ingredient in healing.

5

Receiving and Giving

In this and the previous chapter we explore modes through which our embodied selves *reconnect* with others. As I said earlier, we are never truly isolated: from birth to death we are caught up in a circuit of intercorporeality whereby *We inter-act* and are reliant on each other. In this chapter I will turn to the dyad of *receiving* and *giving* as crucial ways we deal with illness, incapacity, and aging. With this we will complete our survey of twenty healing strategies. Again, the figures at the front of the book may help to keep all these straight, as well as their governing principles of organization.

Receiving. In the strategy of *receiving*, the individual makes up for a physical challenge by relying on others' help to compensate for his or her own deficits. In practice, this can be blended with other intersubjective modalities that have already been discussed. For example, some modes of *receiving* are directly connected to *being-objectified.* A visiting nurse may help an incapacitated patient by monitoring their vital signs and administering medication. Other modes of *receiving* participate more in *communing.* Someone who is bed-bound after a bad fall may have a friend who empathically prepares a daily meal. Nonetheless, *receiving* remains a strategy that is distinct from these other two. As I define it here, *receiving* involves relying on another person's abilities in our own areas of incapacity, and this requires neither medical objectification nor loving communion.

At times, *receiving* takes the form of help with a physical action we can no longer perform. Someone may shop for a homebound person or wheel a recumbent patient through hospital corridors. Then too, choosing how or when to *receive* help can be key for the impaired person. The gerontologists Paul and Margret Baltes write of "selective optimization with compensation"—elders give over a domain of self-care that has become hard for them, such as bathing, so that they can reserve their energies for activities they view as higher life priorities (Baltes 1995). At a far extreme, the body may be quite immobilized by disease or end-of-life struggles such that others, supplemented by technologies, effectively take over the person's own survival functions. This is most marked during a lapse into coma when the living body becomes more *Körper* than *Leib* and is reliant on machine-maintenance. In less dramatic cases, *receiving* may play out in an emotional register. Someone struggling with severe depression may need a caring presence, assistance with daily functioning, and encouragement to reengage with life. Afterwards, the sufferer might say, "I couldn't have made it without your help."

Though brought to the fore by illness, old age, and other modes of affliction, our state of mutual dependence is a general fact of embodied existence. As Kittay (2006, 333) writes: "The person with an impairment who requires the assistance of a caregiver is not the exception, the special case, but a person occupying what is surely a moment in each of our lives, and also a possibility that is inherent in being human, that is, the possibility of inevitable dependence." We have seen that from the moment we are born we depend, directly or indirectly, on being fed and cared for by others, or we don't survive. Nor does this dependence cease even when it recedes to an unthematized background at times of adult health. When we get something to eat from the refrigerator we may not think of all those who contributed to its arrival there: the farmers who grew the food, the workers who processed, transported, and set it out on the supermarket shelves—not to mention the sun, rain, earth, and so on. As the Buddhist monk Thich Nhat Hanh points out, to look deeply into anything is actually to see how the whole universe, now 13.8 billion years old, went into its production. He invents the word "interbeing" (1991, 95–96) to translate the Buddhist term *pratītyasamutpāda*, which is often rendered in English as "dependent arising." This interdependence of all upon all is recognized too by developments in modern science, such as the primacy of field theories in physics, quantum "nonlocality," and ecological studies in biology.

Yet times of illness and incapacity particularly illuminate our (inter)-dependence, our need to *receive* help from others, in ways that may be difficult to accept. Being "independent" is valued highly in many Western countries. Our self-esteem often rests on seeing ourselves as both self-reliant and contributors; therein we feel a sense of agency and value. Conversely, when *receiving* we may feel weak, or fear incurring a debt that we can never repay, one that "gnaws at our pride and sense of equal worth" (Kittay 2019, 155).

Hence, we often prefer the role of being the "helper" rather than the "helped," though this preference may be vectored differently by social training around gender. For example, the "real man" may derive his self-worth from physical strength and being a financial provider; while the "true woman" has often been valued as a caregiver, whether of children, her spouse or partner, aged relatives, or strangers. These gender stereotypes are progressively being challenged, and hopefully left behind, but they still have a psychosocial effect on many men and women, as well as those with a fluid or nonstandard sexual identity.

Yet no matter what one's gender and life-orientation, learning not only to help but to *receive* well is a vital healing strategy. We simply cannot and need not face all life's challenges alone, at least if this can be avoided. In addition to accessing crucial help in dealing with our physical limitations due to injury, illness, disability, or aging, there are also existential benefits in our reliance on others. In accepting our own vulnerability and dependency, we may come to honest terms with the human condition and let go of a proud, isolating self-reliance. Our connection to others may deepen. The comedian Richard Pryor said that multiple sclerosis was the best thing that ever happened to him because he learned, in his need for assistance even to walk across a room, how to really *trust* other people (Kittay 2006, 337). We may form special emotional bonds with those from whom we receive help, not only family and loved ones, but also paid caregivers. The latter relationships can be one-sided or exploitative, yet it would be wrong to deny that deep bonds of affection can develop between caregivers and the cared-for—as long as a sense of dignity and equality is observed on both sides. (I will say more on this shortly.)

In a different way, reciprocal bonds can develop between humans and animals, for example, with a beloved pet or service dog. Those who are blind sometimes feel great affection and gratitude for the dogs they *receive* help from; many of these are highly trained animals who supplement their person's sensorimotor capacities, for example, by guiding them through busy streets. In this case, instead of a cyborglike human-technology blending, we have an interspecies cooperation. This demonstrates both the human-dog co-evolutionary partnership and the deep connection that can develop between creatures with different, but overlapping and complementary modes of embodiment, allowing for an exchange of giving and receiving (Haraway 2007; Abram 2011). I write this having just returned from a lovely walk during which my dogs gave me, and I them, our needed exercise.

I will shortly say more about the healing strategy of *giving*, but it is worth noting here that it often goes hand in hand with *receiving*, as we assist one another. Because of a ruptured disk leading to emergency surgery on my back, I remain severely limited in what I can lift, making it hard to do many household tasks like bringing in groceries or unloading the washing machine. My wife has kindly taken up the slack for me, and I have learned to *receive* from her rather than risk triggering a flare-up of pain and limitation. Conversely, she herself suffers from eye issues, and is dealing with the beginnings of glaucoma that has permanently affected her peripheral vision—we have recently agreed that I do almost all the night-driving. Our daughter, Sarah, who was home for much of the initial wave of Covid-19, often shopped for us because as "elders"—we are both in our mid-sixties—our risk of serious infection in grocery stores was greater than hers. In turn, we took parental care of many things for her. In ways like this, the whole is greater than the sum of the parts as loved ones supplement one another's capacities.

Complementary giving and receiving can also unfold sequentially instead of contemporaneously. As a parent, we might have raised our own children, wiped their bottoms, assisted them with early walking, and nursed them through illness. But especially if we reach what has been called "old old age," this relation may reverse. Our children, or perhaps the assistants they help provide, may now be wiping our bottoms, helping us to walk, and so on. If we *receive* help willingly, we give others the opportunity to give back what we ourselves once gave. This brings life full circle. Conversely, if we are overly resistant to dependency, we may rob someone else of the opportunity to complete their act of care, whether it is a professional or a loved one trying to be of service.

We might say that *receiving graciously* involves an Aristotelian mean whereby we avoid the vice of unwillingness-to-be-helped, as well as the other extreme of overreliance-on-help when it is not really needed. The latter can keep us stuck in the "sick role" (Parsons 1951) which can encourage dependent behavior when we might recover better by reclaiming our own agency. Well-recognized is the phenomenon of the ill or weak person who becomes too enamored of others doing for them what they could do for themselves, thereby frustrating their caregivers and retarding their own healing. This takes a particularly pernicious form when someone wrestling with addiction is surrounded by "enablers" and "rescuers." Thus, we begin to see that the healing strategy of *receiving* has its shadow-sides.

There can also be a shadow-side to *receiving* when the giver does not perform the act rightly. For example, one's helper may be fundamentally unreliable. Or it could take the form of incompetence or exploitation; for example, a family member simply seeking to be included in the will, or a paid caregiver who is not good at their job and behaves in a disrespectful and infantilizing way. As Kittay writes: "I cannot feel better off than I was before if I feel humiliated or frustrated by what you do, supposedly on my behalf. Care not administered in a way that preserves and respects the person's dignity is not a care most of us would desire. Indeed, it is a form of care we fear" (Kittay 2019, 211). It is important that the one *receiv-*

ing feels that their wishes and individuality are respected. As Inagaki et al. write (2016), summarizing a series of empirical psychological studies, "receiving support sometimes backfires because it mismatches one's personal preferences for support, leaves one feeling indebted, and signals that something distressing or negative has happened."

It is also important to address the potential downside for the other person involved, the caregiver. A family member, driven by a sense of guilt and hyper-responsibility, may come to feel overwhelmed by looking after an elderly relative. The helper may sacrifice too much of his or her own life, and even damage the helping relationship as feelings of martyrdom and resentment grow. The caregiver must thus care for self as well as the other. Appropriate self-protection should not be misconstrued as selfishness.

Even more evident is the way our *receiving* from paid caregivers can render the caregivers themselves vulnerable to exploitation. In our society these caregivers, who not infrequently are people of color or recent immigrants, are often both underpaid and underappreciated for the labors they perform. Caregiving is treated as a "lower-end job." This also has a gender component: because it has traditionally been viewed as "women's work," whether in the form of unpaid family labor or paid employment, caregiving has often been undervalued.

Without taking on here the rich literature in the field of feminist care ethics, it is important to note that this question of giving and receiving has both moral and political dimensions, involving not only the dyadic relation between helper and helped, but a series of nested dependencies and social commitments. As Kittay writes:

> We see that we need to structure our societies so that such inevitable dependence is met with the care, resources and dignity required for a flourishing life. We again recognize that we need social arrangements enabling those who provide care to be similarly provided with the care, resources and dignity they require for their own flourishing and for the possibility of doing the work of caring well. (Kittay 2006, 333)

For *receiving* to be optimally available as a healing strategy, there needs to be a widespread recognition of our mutual dependence; of the likelihood that all of us, at times, may need such help, whether because of illness and injury, or at the end of life; and that economic and physical resources must be provided for both those receiving and giving care. These resources might take the form of wheelchair ramps; braille and sign language for the sight- or hearing-impaired; nationally guaranteed health insurance;

good training, living wages, relief time, and respect for caregivers, and so on. *Receiving* is a crucial healing strategy, and one that needs strong support not only in our own lives, but within the larger society.

Giving. While mention has already been made of giving as complementary to receiving, it is important to thematize the former in its own special role as a healing strategy for those struggling with impairment. To find that we can still *give*, despite our embodied limitations, restabilizes a positive sense of self.

We have seen how bodily breakdown can shake one's world and identity, rendering primary the "*I can't*" dimension of embodiment. This frequently leads to feelings of personal deficiency. This last word derives from the Latin *deficio*, meaning to "disappoint, abandon, let down, fail." The disabled person may struggle with a pervasive sense of failure in the face of everything they can no longer do. For example, when I am hobbling on my nerve-pained ankle, unable to walk the dogs, make dinner, or clean up the dishes, it can trigger a sense of inadequacy. I have "disappointed, let down, failed" my family, or so it feels, though my wife kindly assures me otherwise. Perhaps feeling let down by one's own body plays a part; psychologically, *being-disappointed* can feed the sense of *being-a-disappointment.*

Moreover, since our experience of self is rooted in our body schema and body image (Gallagher 1986), once those are altered, we can lose our balance in the world. I mentioned that I wear contact lenses for an eye disease called keratoconus which has stabilized over the years, but left me legally blind in one eye and with poor vision in the other, yet well-corrected by contacts, though not by glasses. If I lose or break a lens the blurring in that eye, and the subliminal difficulties I have in synthesizing visual fields, leave me feeling weak, introverted, and a little emotionally and physically unstable.

In discussing her progressive multiple sclerosis, Toombs provides a vivid example of how bodily diminishment, as well as the treatment this invokes from others, can affect one's self-image. Erwin Straus (1952a), in an early article on the philosophy of the body, explored the multi-dimensional importance of the upright posture, and this is validated by Toombs's own experience:

> The loss of upright posture engenders feelings of helplessness and dependency. Moreover, it causes others to treat one as dependent. I have noticed, for example, that on those occasions when I use a wheelchair, strangers invariably address themselves to my husband and refer to me in

> the third person. . . . Consequently, this particular change in one's bodily way of being incorporates a profound transformation in one's sense of self. (Toombs 1992, 132)

One might say that Toombs lost her *standing* in the world when she could no longer stand up. People also seemed to feel that she could no longer *under-stand,* since they spoke only to her husband. A partial disability was falsely globalized into an overarching personal deficiency.

In this challenging context, the ability of the ill or disabled person to still *give* to others is an important healing strategy, one that can help reestablish a sense of agency and worth. The ability to be of service demonstrates to self and others that this life still has concrete value, that one's body still exhibits an *I can* and is not defined only by what it *can't* do. There is also a relief in "getting out of oneself" when giving. Cassell writes about the potential for solipsism in the afflicted: "The focus becomes entirely directed on the self. All purpose becomes directed at the relief of pain, sickness and suffering" (Cassell 2001, 387). Paradoxically, this can exacerbate rather than relieve suffering as one's world becomes increasingly involuted and concentrated on the negative. *Giving* expands the circle of concern and connection, relieving the temptation to self-centered brooding.

What kind of *giving* shall we engage in? Of course, that depends on the personality and interests of the challenged person; what their current bodily *I can('t)* permits; as well as what the needs of their family and friends, and of the larger world, seem to cry out for. As Murthy writes, summarizing his discussions with Dr. Steven Cole, a medical specialist on the effects of loneliness, and the relief afforded through service:

> There's no "best" or "one size fits all" way to help others. The goal doesn't even have to focus on people. When we're lonely, we may feel too intimidated to join a group that works directly with underprivileged kids or seniors, but our love of animals might lead us to a rescue shelter. Our concern for the environment might inspire us to pitch in when groups clean up the beach or forest. Our love of literature might draw us to the public library where we can volunteer shelving books. Any form of service will do, as long as it feels genuinely and personally meaningful. (Murthy 2020, 166)

There is even a neurological dimension to the personal benefits of this healing strategy; for example, *giving* to others lowers activity in the brain's stress and threat centers, including the amygdala, dorsal anterior cingulate cortex, and anterior insula. The same article that cites these findings summarizes a series of psychological studies which show that "giving support . . . can lead to a greater sense of autonomy and self-efficacy, [and] is associated with increased feelings of social connection, and increased happiness" (Inagaki et al. 2016).

It should be recognized that most effective *giving* isn't motivated solely by our awareness of our own need for healing, but of others' need for it as well. As Levinas (1969) famously explored, the very face of the Other inaugurates an ethical, even ontological, summons to move beyond the self and take up moral and political responsibilities. Diprose looks at how a "generous" relation to the world is always already present within multiple dimensions of lived embodiment:

> It is because bodies are opened onto others, rather than being distinct, that we can act, be affected, have an identity, and remain open to change without conscious direction. The generosity of intercorporeal existence is not governed by choice but is where agency, perception, affectivity and, combining all of these, identity, are born. (Diprose 2002, 69)

But do not severe pain and limitation limit our capacity for generous feeling and action? They can but need not. Jane Thibault, a friend and leading gerontologist, told me a story about a pastoral counselor summoned to the nursing home of a woman bed-bound by cancer (Leder 1997, 231–32). The woman was ill-tempered, and even nasty to the staff. The counselor, at a loss for how to help, finally hit on the idea of redirecting her attention to an unfortunate couple in the same facility, the husband suffering from Hodgkin's disease, and the wife from multiple sclerosis. He suggested that she take her own pain and offer it up as a form of prayer for the other couple. Though not religious, the patient overcame her skepticism. Later in the day the pastoral counselor was surprised to see her cheered up, and her pain diminished along with her self-centeredness. She didn't begin with her customary litany of complaints but with a single question: "How is the couple down the hall doing?" Dr. Thibault calls this strategy "dedicated suffering," the offering up of one's pain to God, and to the welfare of others, transmuting the leaden nature of personal pain into the gold of spiritual compassion. In the Hindu *Bhagavad Gita,* Krishna (a form of God) says, "Whatever you do, make it an offering to me—the food you eat, the sacrifices you make, the help you give, even your suffering" (Easwaran 2007, 176).

This brings us to a distinction between two modes of *giving*: that *in spite of* one's bodily problems, and that which opens up *because of one's bodily problems.* Dr. Thibault's example is interestingly ambiguous. Taken as an example of the first, the woman with cancer is able to offer well-wishes to the couple *in spite of* her own pain and limitation. One can imagine many other examples of service that proceed despite physical limitations. Someone politically committed used to go door-to-door before an election—but when rheumatoid arthritis makes that impossible, she still can donate money and make campaign phone calls. A mother with fibromyalgia is unable to help her son move into his new apartment—but she can help him understand the terms of the lease he is about to sign. Two grandparents don't feel they have the energy and mobility to take their second granddaughter on overnight stays as they did with their first—but they can still spell the exhausted parents by having the grandkids over for a day-visit. We all make readjustments according to the changing *I can('t)* of our altered body, and *giving* thus proceeds *in spite of* our new limitations.

Yet there are also modes of giving that open up *because of one's bodily problems*. Returning to Dr. Thibault's example, perhaps the grumpy cancer sufferer prayed for the other couple because her own illness gave her a heightened sense of empathy. She could thus offer up her own pain in "dedicated suffering," making of it a link between her, God, and the other troubled couple. Affliction can awaken our compassion for the distress of the world; a heightened desire to be of use; and new modes of strength, resilience, and understanding that make our service that much richer.

As an example of this "*because of*," I revisit a quote from philosopher Kevin Aho who, as a young, vigorous, and accomplished exerciser and author, suddenly suffered a serious heart attack while cycling:

> But the heart attack cracked me open. I was suddenly overflowing, not just with anxiety but with love and compassion. I called my brothers weeping, shortly after the angioplasty, telling them how much I cared about them and how thankful I was to have them in my life. My girlfriend became my fiancée in the Intensive Care Unit after my blood clot. . . . I recognize now that I am not, and never have been, a masterful and autonomous subject, that I am fundamentally defenseless and dependent on others. And the recognition of our shared vulnerability is healing insofar as it binds us together in the wake of pain and loss, reminding us that we are not alone in our suffering. (Aho 2019, 197–200)

This alchemy of suffering transformed into loving connection and service does not always come as quickly as it did in Aho's case. The physician Rachel Naomi Remen tells of a patient who survived bone cancer but needed years to work through his rage and despair, using painting, imagery, and therapy. After that, he finally felt able to help others who had also suffered physical losses, sharing his own experiences of struggle and healing. Meeting again with Dr. Remen:

> He showed me one of his earliest drawings. I had suggested to him that he draw a picture of his body. He had drawn a picture of a vase, and running though the vase was a deep black crack. . . . It was very, very painful because it seemed to him that this vase could never function as a vase again. It could never hold water . . . Now, several years later, he came to this picture and looked at it and said, "Ooh this one isn't finished. . . . He picked a yellow crayon and putting his finger on the crack he said, "you see here—where it is broken—this is where the light comes through." And with the yellow crayon he drew light streaming through the crack in his body. (Remen 1991, 29–30)

Admittedly, not all cracks cause light to shine through. An invalid can become compulsively self-absorbed and chronically bitter, taking their frustrations out on others, including relatives or paid staff. Whether illness closes or opens the heart is multi-factorial: it may be the consequence of a long-standing personality type; the facts of the clinical situation; one's religious background and beliefs, or lack thereof; whether or not there is a supportive environment; and also whether the person is willing to do inner work, as had the man with bone cancer that Remen describes.

Surely we should not condemn the patient who fails to rise to a heroic standard of patience, good cheer, and helpfulness to others. Chronic pain, for example, is very difficult to bear and simply wears one down. A certain amount of self-absorption and gloom is perfectly understandable. Still, if Buddhism is right, compassion for others is not something we are simply born with or not, like red hair, but something we can systematically cultivate no matter our circumstances—for example, by practicing generosity even when difficult; by doing *metta* (loving-kindness) meditation wherein we send well-wishes to all, even our "enemies"; or, in Tibetan Buddhism, by doing *tonglen* (giving-and-receiving) meditation, deliberately breathing in the suffering of others and breathing out for them whatever spaciousness and relief we can offer. This is not unlike, in a Christian register, Dr. Thibault's reference to a practice of "dedicated suffering."

Yet, as always, there is a shadow-side even to the healing strategy of *giving*. Not only may others expect too much of an ill or disabled person, but that person may expect too much of themself. He or she can try to *give* overmuch or in ways that simply don't fit with their bodily capabilities, thereby bringing about self-harm. For example, someone with a chronic illness may take on too many responsibilities and suffer a relapse into worsened symptomatology. Or someone may literally work himself or herself to death trying to provide for the welfare of the family. Again, gender training can come into play here; for example, the tough guy who is afraid to look weak and inadequate, or the woman who trudges on, trying to care for everybody except herself.

Once again, the Aristotelian notion of the virtuous mean is relevant here; ideally, we should *give* in the right way, at the right time, to the right degree, and to the right people or causes, in ways appropriate to our own passions and abilities. Of course, such advice may seem rather imprecise. As Aristotle states in the *Nicomachean Ethics*, ethical discernment is not an exact science; we must exercise *phronesis* (prudence, practical wisdom) in order to seek the mean between vicious extremes. It may be the work of years, or even of a lifetime, to cultivate *phronesis* in the application of all the healing strategies we have surveyed, including how best to *give* to others.

* * *

In these last two chapters we have explored four modes of intercorporeality. I have treated them as distinct from one another, but I will close by emphasizing their intertwining. The two most clearly in opposition seem to be the stance of *being-objectified* versus *communing* through co-subjectivity. Yet even here we have seen that these can be productively combined; for example, the health care practitioner who applies objective medical diagnostics and treatment, but as guided by genuine compassion. Also important is the patient's skill in *receiving*. For example, he or she needs to be receptive to the physician's concern and treatment plan, or if visiting an alternative bodywork practitioner, the patient may need to relax and *receive*, on a deep corporeal level, the treatment—for example, a massage or acupuncture needles which open the body's capacity for self-healing. Moreover, to foster healing we need to *give* not only to others, but to ourselves—in the form of rest, emotional support, a hot bath, whatever—and be able to graciously *receive* this self-care, feeling that it's deserved. Self-care, then, is a kind of *giving/receiving* wherein the two modalities blend.

This blend is also found in our *inter-actions* with others. In many rich relationships, over time the very roles of "helper" and "helped" seem to reverse themselves, or fall away entirely (Ram Dass and Gorman 2003). Ram Dass spent a long time thinking he was doing karma yoga (the spiritual path of selfless service) by helping to care for his elderly and largely incapacitated father. Ultimately, though, he found that he himself was equally the one being helped—by slowing down and growing in closeness, compassion, and attention. Was he then the "giver" or the "receiver," or both?

These lessons helped Ram Dass when he himself had an incapacitating stroke and had to readjust to *receiving* much care in his later years (Ram Dass 2001, 183–204). This in turn deepened the spiritual teachings he was able to *give* to others (including myself). We are helped by helping; we give by receiving graciously; and thus we commune with each other, sharing both the afflictions of our human existence and our capacity for love and wholeness.

Part 2

The Marginalized Body

6

Embodied Injustice: Incarceration and/as Illness

Embodied Injustice

The first half of this book treated twenty different healing strategies we can use in the face of bodily breakdown. From here on we will take up specialized but related topics. Initially, we can ask the question: Does our analysis of illness and other modes of affliction—and the strategies of healing that people utilize—apply only to conditions of physical breakdown? Or are they more broadly applicable to those dealing with socially imposed limits and setbacks, which could include poverty, being a refugee, growing old in an ageist country, struggling with racism, sexism, and homophobia, and so on? And how does being subject to these modes of discrimination exacerbate, or even mimic, the experience of illness, and also influence our modes of healing?

While we touched on such areas in earlier discussions, part 2 turns more directly to what I will call "embodied injustice" (with thanks to Rae Johnson's 2017 book, *Embodied Social Justice*). To speak of "embodied injustice" is to recognize that discriminatory treatment is not simply manifested through a wealth and power gap, and difficulty in accessing a good education, job opportunities, health care, housing, and such. All this is true. But these modes of injustice are often correlated with and "justified" by a devaluation of certain kinds of *bodies* (Fanon 2008; Alcoff 2006; Yancy 2017; Lee 2014). Moreover, being discriminated against, for example by sexism or racism, alters our embodied ways of feeling, perceiving, and acting in the world. This is one of the foci of a "critical phenomenology" which does not postulate a transcendental subjectivity separate from the world, but a self whose ways of perceiving and acting are profoundly shaped by sociohistorical conditions (Weiss et al. 2020).

In a feminist context, Karen Warren lays out what she takes to be a general logic of oppression used over and over again to solidify the power of a dominating group. The logic is said to depend on "value-hierarchical thinking" based on "oppositional value dualisms" (Warren 2000, 43–71). That is, the world is perceived as split into two elements (dualism), one of which is thought by nature, or divine decree, to be superior to the other (hence, "value-hierarchical"). Men in patriarchal cultures are thus thought to be superior in rationality and capability to women; similarly, "whites" are held superior to "blacks"; colonialists to the "primitive people" they civilized; humans to animals; and so on.

Warren notes that these modes of social oppression are often correlated with the metaphysical dualism that distinguishes "soul" and "body." Just as the soul is deemed superior and destined to rule over the unruly flesh, so those groups particularly associated with "soul" or "mind"—men, white people, colonizers—are meant to rule over (for everyone's benefit) those less rational, who are more associated with the body and nature.

Of course, the stark dualisms at the core of value-hierarchical thinking have been repeatedly challenged by those working in social justice-oriented theory. For example, the very notion and significance of racial differences has been thoroughly undermined by the study of human genetics, as well as work in the humanities and social sciences. Though a society may assert a clear opposition between the traits of those who are "black" and those who are "white," this is scientifically unfounded, denies the complexity of our genetic blending, and is contingent insofar as these racial categories shift between and within cultures. "Seeing" racial dualities is a historically conditioned perceptual habit that develops in oppressive societies, not a simple natural fact. However, the sense that we are seeing bodily markers tends to "naturalize" racism, making it seem an element of biology rather than of ideology (Alcoff 2006, 179–204).

Feminist and queer theorists have similarly undercut stark gender, sex, and sexuality dualisms. Restrictive roles and rules falsely accentuate the difference between "female" and "male" attributes; to be feminine is an issue of gender performance as dictated within a given society, not something inscribed in the natural order (J. Butler 2006; Prosser 1998, 30–31). Or as Simone de Beauvoir famously put it: "one is not born, but rather becomes, woman" (2011, 283). Even though one's biological sex may seem more scientifically real than one's "race," sex and sexual orientation are far from fixed. One may be bisexual, asexual, or of fluid sexuality, and identify as transgender or as transsexual, in the latter cases potentially using hormonal or surgical means of transition (Prosser 1998; Kafer 2013).

Nor, as many in disability studies have pointed out, is there a simple distinction between the "disabled" and the normal body. Much depends on how we define each category and the social assists or impediments constructed for different embodiments (Reynolds 2022). Moreover, even insofar as one is considered "able-bodied," most of us are so only for a period of time.

Though these strict dualisms are false, they still exert great social power. To speak of *embodied injustice* is to recognize not only that the "inferior group" is often identified particularly with the body as such—Warren's point—but also that it is labeled as *having the wrong kind of body*. These deviant bodies—be they Black, Latino, Asian, gay, female, Jewish, disabled, old, transgender, transsexual, and so on—are seen as in need of control and surveillance, and are in many cases subject to scorn or punishment. And once established, hierarchical binaries have cascading repercussions. In a short treatment I cannot do justice to the ever-expanding literature on these themes in critical race studies, feminism, queer theory, disability studies, and other related fields. I will just briefly drill down to some common elements that are relevant to our discussion of health and illness.

First, embodied injustice operates through *reductionism* and *objectification*. The problematic person not only *has* a body, but essentially *is* that body. Moreover, this person/body, in all their complexity, is reduced to particular attributes—for example, those of skin color, sexual orientation, or a certain disability—which are taken to define them in some essential fashion.

Second, this identity is labeled as *deviant* from a norm. As Isabel Wilkerson writes: "A caste system centers the dominant caste as the sun around which all other castes revolve and defines it as the default-setting standard of normalcy, of intellect, of beauty, against which all others are measured, ranked in descending order by their physiological proximity to the dominant caste" (Wilkerson 2020, 268). She is particularly concerned about an American racial caste system wherein "white" is considered normative, while non-white skin labels people as lesser and automatically subject to multiple disadvantages. The same might be said of a gay person in a homophobic community, a woman in a patriarchal culture, or an elder in an ageist society. So too are those with disabilities, who are so classified because they have a "non-normate" body, one that is not typical and standard (Reynolds 2022, 64).

This reductive objectification, whereby a person is viewed as being/having the wrong kind of body is, not surprisingly, experienced from within as deeply *demeaning and dehumanizing*. Fanon famously writes of his reaction to hearing a child say, "'Look, a Negro! Maman, a Negro!'. . . . my body was returned to me spread-eagled, disjointed, redone, draped in mourning on this white winter's day. The Negro is an animal, the Negro is bad, the Negro is wicked, the Negro is ugly" (Fanon 2008, 93). Yancy (2017, 17–49) writes of experiencing the "elevator effect": the white woman with whom he shares an elevator reflexively clutches her purse, viewing his black skin as indicative of someone threatening and criminal. Then too, he describes walking down the street and hearing the "ClickClickClick" of white drivers locking their car doors one after another (2017, xxiii–xxiv). These experiences are the very opposite of the embodied *communing* which we discussed earlier as a mode of healing.

The body that I am/have is thereby experienced as something *dispossessed, fragmented, estranged,* taken over in advance by the projections of others (Ngo 2017, 62–68). Many individuals subjected to this treatment feel the pressure to find remedial strategies. For example, this may involve a Black person deliberately whistling a nonthreatening song, wearing collegiate apparel, or making his body appear smaller (Ngo 2017, 56–67). In Yancy's case,

> I feel trapped. I no longer feel bodily expansiveness within the elevator, but corporeally constrained, limited. I now begin to calculate, paying almost neurotic attention to my body movements, making sure that this "Black object," which now feels like an appendage, a weight, is not too close, not too tall, not too threatening. (Yancy 2017, 32)

Along with this doubled awareness of the body, simultaneously experienced from within and as viewed by the hostile other, Frye describes oppression as involving *double binds* (1983, 1–16). For example, the sexually active woman risks being condemned as a "slut" whereas, if inactive, she may be mocked as a "prude" or "frigid." A disabled person might ask for help, but thereby draw attention to their dependency; or seek to do without it, but thus render themselves less mobile or vulnerable to injury. Again, it is a double bind. A member of a minority may speak out against discriminatory treatment but then be labeled as "angry," "not a team player"—or else remain docile, but thereby risk losing their dignity and shot at leadership positions.

Of course, despite the commonalities mentioned so far, different forms of embodied injustice play out differently. A young woman may find her appearance ogled in certain milieus, and even threatened by sexual predation. Conversely, but correlatively, an older woman may experience the indignity of becoming invisible now that she has lost her allure for the male gaze. Certain modes of disability may be immediately apparent and embarrassing—for example, being prone to epileptic seizures in public—while other modes, like chronic fatigue syndrome, may pass unnoticed and thus be unaddressed.

On this question of visibility and invisibility, Fanon draws on Sartre's analysis in *Anti-Semite and Jew* to distinguish between the situation of the Black and that of the Jew. Whereas the Black person is "overdetermined from the outside," unable to escape the white, objectifying gaze, a Jew "can go unnoticed" (Fanon 2008, 95). He is less detectable, more able to pass as a white person, but does not thereby escape an "overdetermination from within"—that is, the internalization of centuries of antisemitic caricatures that give rise to feelings of inferiority and self-hate. But as Weiss (2014) points out, these distinctions are by no means clear-cut. A Jewish person, by aspects of appearance, dress, or behavior, may be visibly different from others, and conversely, many Black people struggle with the internalized self-hatred that racism breeds.

In practice, there is often a synergy of external judgments/restrictions combined with internalized modes of oppression; and of doubled consciousness combined with double binds. Ultimately, all this serves to saturate one's corporeal schema (the umbrella term I will use here for the ways one experiences and employs one's own body). This is a last and crucial point to make about embodied injustice.

In her influential essay "Throwing Like a Girl," Young (2005, 27–45) describes a woman's constrained sense of her body in a sexist society. Instead of experiencing lived spatiality as the potential for action, she feels herself as positioned in space, and indeed as pressed to take up less space: for example, by walking in a compressed stride without the freedom to swing her arms. She loses access to the coordinated use of bodily powers which she was neither trained, nor given encouragement, to use in their totality. She ends up, for example, "throwing like a girl," that is, without drawing on the full power available in a unified employment of upper and lower body strength.

This problematic corporeal schema is also present for the Black person dealing with racism. Here Aho gives an overview of Fanon's account:

> Transformed into a brute object or thing by the judgmental gaze of the white European . . . the black person feels immobilized and incapacitated, finding it difficult to stretch into the world, to handle equipment, and to participate in public activities. The smooth, pre-conscious synergy that characterizes the European's existence is out of reach. He or she becomes imprisoned in a sphere of immanence, where one's physical motility and sense of self are constrained by skin color. (Aho 2020, 46)

As Ahmed (2007, 153) writes: "We could say that 'the corporeal schema' is already racialized; in other words, race does not just interrupt such a schema, but structures its mode of operation." These reverberating effects reach down to all layers of embodiment. To return to Yancy's examples, when surrounded by white people who are clutching their purses and locking car doors, one may become hyper-aware; tense one's muscles; experience gastric constriction, elevated pulse and blood pressure; and so on (Sekimoto and Brown 2020).

There is a danger that this schematic account of embodied injustice could fall prey to the kind of reductionism it is trying to critique. For example, though we have focused primarily on anti-Black racism, the issue of race in the United States is far more than a "black" and "white" matter. There are particular modes of discrimination that affect those who are Asian, Latino, Native American, and members of other groups (Alcoff 2006, 253–58). Moreover, no human being is simply and essentially defined by their race, gender, sexual preference, or disability. We dwell in the intersectionality of many different bodily and cultural attributes (Crenshaw 2023). Our multiplicitous selves may or may not blend into what feels like a unified identity. Ortega (2014) describes being a gay Latina, but one torn between her Hispanic heritage and that culture's homophobia.

And while acknowledging the painful constrictions brought about by embodied injustice in all its forms, we are far more than the sum of the *I can'ts* they impose on us. Ortega (2014) values and draws upon both her Latino and lesbian heritage. Weiss (2014) notes that to be a Jew is not just something defined simply by antisemitism, but also by rich traditional practices and celebrations. With various empowerment efforts ranging from the #MeToo and Black Lives Matter movements to the advances in gay, disability, and transgender visibility and rights (albeit ever imperiled), we gather individual and communal strength from, and on behalf of, all of our diverse identities.

That said, embodied injustice remains real and damaging in characteristic ways. Most relevant to this book, some of these patterns show considerable overlap with the experience of illness. When the body suffers injury, sickness, incapacity, or disfigurement, this can inaugurate changes in the corporeal schema analogous to those brought about by embodied injustice. The sick body surfaces as an object, not just a subject; one may feel constrained, fragmented, and marginalized. All these alterations in the corporeal schema may be intensified, not relieved, by contact with a depersonalized and disempowering medical system. This is not meant to equate the experience of illness with injustice; for example, the horrors of racism—social and economic exclusion, persecution, exploitation—do not descend on an individual simply because they develop rheumatoid arthritis. Nevertheless, I will investigage certain ways that embodied injustice is like a "socially caused illness."

The Example of Incarceration

In exploring the connections between illness and injustice, and what this means for our discussion of healing, I will turn to incarceration as a focal example. I do so for a number of reasons. For one, mass incarceration is one of the most potent and damaging manifestations of embodied injustice in my time and country. This has been widely recognized, including by those of different political persuasions. Books like *The New Jim Crow* (Alexander 2012) have drawn particular attention to the connection between mass incarceration and racism. It takes its place along with other historical manifestations—slavery, convict leasing, Jim Crow laws, redlining, and so on—as a way of constraining, punishing, and marginalizing the Black and brown body.

Our penitentiary system is the largest in the world, holding almost one-quarter of the world's prisoners, and leaving hundreds of thousands serving time for nonviolent, low-level offenses (Chettiar and Eisen 2016). Roughly two-thirds of the people so held are "minorities." According to the Department of Justice's Bureau of Prisons, over 38 percent of American prisoners are Black, and over 30 percent are Hispanic. At every level of the criminal justice system—what communities are surveilled by police; who is pulled over on the street or road; who is arrested, and then criminally prosecuted (e.g., for low-level drug offenses); and who is then actually sentenced to serve time—the racial disparities grow. One can attribute this to conscious and deliberate public policy, accompanied by implicit bias on the part of police, prosecutors, judges, and juries, but it begins with the embodied injustice we've been exploring. Black and brown bodies are perceived as intrinsically suspicious, dangerous, and potentially criminal, which then becomes a self-fulfilling prophecy. Ernest Drucker (2011), a public health expert, compares the contemporary spread of mass incarceration to a disease epidemic. Though not caused by a biological agent but laws, policies, and powerful political and economic interests, it has manifested explosive growth in particular populations and communities; has spread by proximity and exposure to previous cases; and is characterized by devastating outbreaks that cause untold human suffering and loss.

Imprisonment is not only a manifestation of embodied injustice, but serves as a powerful metaphor in itself. Fanon writes of the "imprisoning" gaze of the white man (2008, 92). In the words of Malcolm X: "You don't have to go behind bars to be in jail in this country. If you are born in this country with black skin you are already in jail, you are already confined, you are already watched over by a warden who poses as your mayor and poses as your governor and poses as your President" (Malcolm X 1971,

114). This metaphor of imprisonment is also applicable to other modes of embodied injustice besides racism. Frye (1983, 1–16) writes of how widespread sexism operates like a "birdcage": as long as one looks at individual wires in isolation (for example, a man opening a door for a woman), the problem remains invisible, but the total system of sexist attitudes, language, double binds, pressures, prohibitions, and punishments serves to effectively encage women.

In the *Republic*, Socrates suggests that to best understand justice in the soul, one can imagine it writ large in the form of a city: "If we watch a city coming into being in words, we may also see its justice and injustice come into being" (*Republic* 369a). Similarly, I would suggest, the penitentiary system shows embodied injustice "writ large." We see this in its purposes, architecture, rules and routines, and the way these exemplify segregation, surveillance, confinement, and deprivation. Unfortunately, this is no imaginary city but is all too real.

In my discussion I will draw on personal encounters and experiences, another reason I choose incarceration as a focal example. In addition to my ordinary university duties, I have served as a volunteer teacher at male maximum-security prisons on and off since the early 1990s, and most recently in a women's medium-security prison. In my classes over the years we have studied a variety of texts, including those of Plato, Lao Tzu, Buddhist teachers, pivotal African American thinkers and activists, Foucault on prisons, and the poetry of John Keats, as well as specific topics such as free will and determinism. Though prisons' educational resources are often focused on those approaching release, I feel particularly drawn to working with lifers and long-timers. These are students who are there for the long haul, so I could see them in repeat classes and build relationships with them over a long period. Moreover, long-timers, as they themselves told me, had needed years to settle in, mature, face their situation, think deeply about its causes and solutions, and become more philosophical in their quest to understand self and world. It is no cliché to say that I have learned as much from these students as they have from me. They use the philosophical toolkit in my classes in inspiring ways. Together we have published work about the dehumanizing experience of life on the streets and in prison, as well as the creative responses possible to such extreme conditions (Leder 2000; Leder and Greco 2014; Leder and Jessup Scholars 2014; Leder 2016a).

This, combined with my work on medicine, has given me opportunity to reflect on the topics now at hand. How do illness and incarceration alter the body–world relation in correlative ways, and how does this broaden the relevance of our discussions of healing? I will proceed systematically, as always building on the phenomenology of lived experience.

Constriction of Lived Space

Those suffering from chronic pain and illness, and those with long-term and life sentences, both inhabit a shrunken world (Aho and Aho 2009; Toombs 1992). In the former cases, this world-reduction emanates from the "inside out," triggered by bodily dysfunction. Pain exerts a kind of centripetal force, leading one's attention inward to the source of suffering. For example, in the case of my own neuropathy, my focus shrank to the size of a small oval-shaped patch of skin just above my left ankle. "It" kept sending me tingles, burns, and shocks. "It" was preventing me from my beloved stream-side strolls with my dog, and forced me to cancel an international trip to a conference. Pain and illness, as has been discussed, effect a narrowing of perceptual/cognitive focus and a limiting of possibilities. In severe cases this can take the form of a bedridden existence (van den Berg 1966). The world narrows down to the size of a room, a TV screen, the objects available on the end-table. Those who are less incapacitated nonetheless dwell in a reduced world, one which feels "unhomelike" (Svenaeus 2015).

While this displacement and constriction is largely initiated from within the sick person's body, in the case of the prisoner something similar is imposed from the outside. When incarcerated, a human being is deprived of most of their liberty of movement. Taken from home and community, they are confined, potentially for decades, in a small cell, perhaps the size of a bathroom in a large house. If they are not placed in administrative segregation (solitary confinement)—a long-term form of torture (widely overused in the United States) that often mandates twenty-three hours a day spent in the cell (Guenther 2013)—prisoners' movements are nonetheless restricted to certain prison buildings, perhaps including a walk to the cafeteria, limited time in a small exercise yard, or a stop in the prison library. Of course, Covid-19 introduced even more extreme confinements for prisoners without necessarily conferring protection from disease outbreaks.

This reduced world is in many ways reminiscent of that created by chronic pain/illness. For the prisoner's cell substitute a sickroom; for the severe restraint of agency imposed by the state, substitute that triggered by the recalcitrant body. Moreover, in the case of patient *hospitalization*, a clinical-architectural imperative institutes controls over movement similar to those used in prison, including monitored confinements to a room, locked areas, and permitted and prohibited pathways. Similarly, for the disabled, the blocks to free action can be exacerbated by social barriers that are functionally imprisoning (Wendell 1996). The lack of a ramp for an individual who is wheelchair-bound, or the lack of an elevator for someone unable to climb flights of stairs, may be restricting and exclusionary.

In comparing the experience of illness/disability and that of incarceration, it should be noted that many people suffer from both. Prisoners often develop physical problems which may be a consequence of the stressors, poor food, and inadequate health care often found in prisons. The restrictions imposed by illness and imprisonment then become synergistically confining.

Disruption of Lived Time

I turn now to shifts in temporal experience, drawing on my discussions from chapter 3 and elsewhere. Pain and illness can fracture lived time in paradoxical ways. On the one hand, they pull us relentlessly to the "now" of immediate bodily events: in my case, the nerve shock just above the ankle, or the aching lower back demanding a positional shift. The very insistence and aversiveness of pain is the body's way of requesting remedial action *now,* even if none may prove effective. Yet this *now* to which we are summoned is one from which we wish to flee. As Warraich notes: "Chronic pain mirrors incarceration; it essentially puts you in its cage, keeping you locked up in the penitentiary of the present. It becomes difficult to plan for the future and can very quickly shrink your life" (DuLong 2022). We may remember a pain- or illness-free time but are unable to reclaim it. Or our thoughts may drift to a future when our symptoms will be alleviated, and perhaps a cure is found—but again, we are unable to *realize* this future (make it real in the here and now), and we know the future might actually bring perpetual pain, a worsening of symptoms, or premature death (Toombs 1992). We are thus estranged from past, present, and future alike.

So, too, is incarceration something like a *chronic dis-ease* (that is, a loss of ease that lasts a long time, and which distorts our relation to time itself). The judge pronounces a temporal sentence—for example, *twenty years.* The prisoner will have to "serve time," it is said, or "do time." As with chronic pain and illness, long-term incarceration triggers a disruption of lived time's customary flow. The present closes in. No matter what escapes were accessible in sleep (and prisoners have told me they often dream they are free), each morning the prisoner awakens to the same present. The "now" begins to take on a repetitive quality, like a nightmare version of Nietzsche's eternal return as day succeeds day. This is not unlike the experience of those with chronic conditions, awakening each morning to the same prison of pain or limitation.

For incarcerated individuals, as for those entrapped by illness, there are efforts to escape this *now*. *Remembering* the past may summon happy recollections—but this healing strategy often has the downside of evoking feelings of regret and loss. Similarly, *anticipating* the future can restore hope and purposive action, yet, as earlier mentioned, it can also trigger frustration and a sense of endless anticipation that robs the present of meaning (Leder 2016a, 166–70). We will return to this topic when discussing the healing strategies available to the incarcerated individual.

Isolation

So far, I have talked as if patient and prisoner were individuals negotiating an uneasy relationship with restricted space, time, and action. But as discussed, we are profoundly social beings. States of existential disruption will manifest in, or even originate from, disturbances in our relations with others. Again, this is true for the ill and incarcerated alike.

Chronic pain and sickness, we have already seen, can isolate us from others, and in multiple ways. We are subject to bodily sensations and psychological struggles that no one else can fully share. Interior pains can indeed verge on the incommunicable—the crude language we use to characterize them (sharp, burning, aching, throbbing) is frustratingly imprecise and inexpressive (Scarry 1985, 162). Furthermore, pain and illness restrict our ability to participate in the shared social world of work and play. In Sophocles's play *Philoctetes*, the hero, a famed archer, has been abandoned for ten years on the desolate island of Lemnos after suffering a foul-smelling, oozing foot wound. This is a potent metaphor for many who dwell with chronic pain/illness as if on a remote island, separated off from friends and the daily flow of life (Leder 2016a, 13–23).

This isolation can be compounded by a kind of social exile. Philoctetes's comrades are repelled by his wound and his terrible cries, and finally want nothing to do with him. "Stigma is part of the complex of factors that transform impairment into disability," writes Love (2015, 173). Similarly, those with chronic pain or illness may find themselves stigmatized as different and disturbing.

This isolation is in many ways echoed by that of those imprisoned, for whom exile is socially constructed and intentional. The criminal, after all, has been judged a threat to society, mandating his removal. Thus, one is severed from one's community, family, and friends (though sometimes friends are waiting on the inside). Behind bars and barbed wire one's ability to communicate with the outer world is drastically reduced, as are civil liberties: materials in and out are censored; family visitations are intermittent, made unpleasant, and closely monitored; and solitary confinement is often applied in an arbitrary and prolonged way. Like Philoctetes, one has been exiled to a remote island.

And as with the Greek hero, few want to hear the cry of the wounded. My students have lamented how most of their friends and family members have dropped away over time, unable to bear the continued burden of the relationship or the humiliating security procedures that attend each visit. Meanwhile, prisoners know to keep a tough exterior, holding their emotion inside lest it be interpreted as weakness to be exploited within potentially violent institutions. (They provide "maximum security" for the outside world, but certainly not for those trapped within.) And this too can contribute to feelings of isolation even in the midst of overcrowding. Nor is the general society sympathetic to their plight. It assumes that criminals have brought their suffering on themselves as just recompense for the suffering they inflicted on others.

This does seem to be a key distinction between the isolation imposed on those judged guilty of a crime (though there are many in prison who are innocent and later exonerated), and therefore fit to be punished, and the isolation suffered by the innocent victim of illness or pain. However, as we have seen, the word "pain" derives from the Latin word for punishment, *poena.* The sufferer indeed often experiences pain-as-punishment (Buytendijk 1961, 50) and searches for what he or she might have done wrong, physically or morally, to bring on such suffering. The healthy may quietly concur with this harsh judgment, smugly complacent that their own virtue will keep them safe ("I never smoked or overate like her"). The sick person, like the criminal, not only suffers *deprivation* but also from the implicit charge of being *depraved.* Sometimes this can be reinforced by becoming a patient in the medical system. We have seen Oliver Sacks's and Arthur Frank's account of how, when brought low by serious illness, they felt judged as if they had existentially or morally failed.

Disempowerment and the Corporeal Schema

Patient and prisoner alike often undergo an experience of depersonalization and disempowerment. For the sick person, this is first initiated by pain and illness themselves. As discussed earlier, we may feel powerless to understand and control our bodily processes. These threaten to undermine our very life and personhood, as the daily routines and long-range projects that stabilize our identity begin to fall apart. Seeking help from the medical system can be a double-edged sword. It brings access to precious, sometimes even curative resources, but also the threat of being subject to medical language, practices, judgments, and institutions that can further the disempowerments triggered by illness (Frank 1991, 52–56). This includes the financial impact of expensive medical care itself, which can be devastating for patients and their families. Such may be compared to the reverberating financial impacts of incarceration, rendering one unable to make a living, thrusting families into poverty, and sometimes leaving one with debts and court costs after release.

In our discussion of *being-objectified* we have seen that the "patient"—a word sharing the same etymology as "passive"—must indeed be patient, and often kept waiting, half undressed, until the doctor strides in with an authoritative air. Physical examination then objectifies the body—the patient holds still and silent while being probed and poked (Baron 1985). This continues as the focus turns to the laboratory tests and imaging studies that are now accorded an epistemological place of honor. Their results are then presented to the patient in a way that may fail to attend to that person's own life-narrative (Charon 2008; Hawkins 1999). In *The Death of Ivan Ilych*, Tolstoy describes the suffering of his protagonist, a conventional man whose life has been uprooted by a painful and progressive illness:

> To Ivan Ilych only one question was important: was his case serious or not? But the doctor ignored that inappropriate question. From his point of view it was not the one under consideration, the real question was to decide between a floating kidney, chronic catarrh, or appendicitis. . . . "We sick people often put inappropriate questions. But tell me, in general, is this complaint dangerous or not?"
>
> The doctor looked at him sternly over his spectacles with one eye, as if to say, "Prisoner, if you will not keep to the questions put to you, I shall be obliged to have you removed from the court." (Tolstoy 1960, 122)

In *Discipline and Punish*, Foucault (1979) discusses the rise of a "microphysics of power" focused on meticulous control of the body, whether for penal, rehabilitative, educational, or therapeutic purposes. He analyzes how disciplinary structures employ technologies of surveillance and record-keeping, rendering bodies docile and utilizable. According to Foucault, such methods govern the modern prison, hospital, army, factory, and school alike. Thus it is no surprise, as in the story of Ivan Ilych, to see prisoners and patients treated alike despite the supposed differences in their situations. We hear this again in Sacks's account of his hospitalization:

> One's own clothes are replaced by an anonymous white nightgown, one's wrist is clasped by an identification bracelet with a number. One becomes subject to institutional rules and regulations. One is no longer a free agent; one no longer has rights; one is no longer in the world at large. It [is] strictly analogous to becoming a prisoner . . . One is no longer a person—one is now an inmate. (Sacks 1994, 27)

In Foucault's analysis, disciplinary institutions divide up space and time so that the location and behavior of individuals can be monitored and controlled. This is true for the hospital patient as well as the punch-clock worker, and the prisoner ordered for "count-out" many times a day. In a sense, the very "selfhood" of patient, worker, and prisoner is constituted by disciplinary modes (Foucault 1979, 170) such as the assignment of identification numbers, the logging of work performance, or the "tickets" issued for inmates' infractions. In speaking, for example, of someone with a "criminal *record*" we conflate their behavior, their very self, with the written record of their illegal acts. In the case of the hospital patient, the record can similarly become paramount, displacing the centrality of the lived body. The doctor may spend less time with ill persons than with written or computerized charts. Though these are labeled the "patient's chart," patients themselves are never permitted to write in them. The sick person remains an objectified body of record, not a subject *author-ized* to comment on his or her experience.

Moreover, this body is not only objectified but typified as deviant and devalued. In a hospital setting, the patient is often identified first and foremost by their disease; "the appendicitis in Room 27." Even worse, those in prison may find their identity reducible to the worst actions they ever committed—they are "criminals," "murderers," and therefore ever suspicious and potentially violent. When I and my Loyola students, including young women, received our mandatory orientation upon visiting the prison, we were warned over and over again to watch out for inappropriate touching, slipped notes, and the many other potential dangers the men posed. Nothing was said about their intrinsic humanity.

Not surprisingly all of this brings about the alteration and disruption of the *corporeal schema* that we discussed as typical of "embodied injustice." Iris Young (2005) spoke of the woman's body as objectified by the other's gaze, positioned in space, rather than experiencing lived spatiality as an arena for action—so too for the hospitalized and incarcerated person. In either case, one is placed in a bed or cell and is under near-constant surveillance. The penitentiary is filled with closed-circuit cameras, and "count-outs" are taken during the day to keep track of each inmate's position and actions. (We might add that the incarcerated person is also positioned in time, labeled as to exactly how many years, months, and days they have served and have left to go.)

We have seen how Fanon, Yancy, and Ahmed described the heightened self-awareness and restraint of those subject to racism. To some degree this applies to the hospitalized patient, and even more so to the prisoner. Catherine Cabeen, a dance professor teaching, as I did at the time, in a women's prison, pointed out to me the inability of her students to move freely, exercise, stretch, dance, sing, stand on a chair, have sex, or even give another person a hug. Guards were ever there to watch and intervene.

Finally, incarcerated persons face the kind of double bind described earlier as also characteristic of embodied injustice. In order not to receive a "ticket" that may prolong his sentence or lead to solitary confinement, the prisoner has to make sure that his body is docile, his actions nonthreatening. At the same time, to protect himself from victimization within the prison population, he has to project an air of strength, defend his bodily borders against invasion, and perhaps even commit an act of violence to establish his "credentials" so that others will let him be. Again, these double binds and stressors saturate all levels of the corporeal schema down to the visceral, and can lead to exaggerated muscle tension, high blood pressure, and other modes of (di)stress that compromise health and longevity. A disturbing number of my incarcerated students have died prematurely.

To some degree hospital patients, who are already stressed by an illness, may also suffer psychologically and physiologically from being subjected to an alien environment that is coupled with invasive procedures. This hardly seems conducive to healing. That said, there can also be genuine hospitality in hospitals, and genuine caring in health care. It is also true that institutional procedures often serve important diagnostic, therapeutic, and safety functions. Moreover, unlike the prisoner, those suffering from illness and disability often (though not always) retain the freedom to leave this clinical world at will.

The carceral environment is more totalizing and inescapable, and is usually crueler. There, the methods of depersonalization and disempowerment are used quite intentionally for punitive reasons, and to render prisoners more easily controllable. Whether this serves rehabilitative purposes—positively empowering an individual to reenter society as a contributing citizen—is dubious. It is also worth noting that for many in the U.S. prison system, disempowering experiences preexist imprisonment (Gramlich 2020). The men I worked with, predominately Black and often from inner-city Baltimore, had been subjected to poor and dangerous schools, broken neighborhoods, abandoned housing, severe family trauma, limited job opportunities, and all the other effects of poverty and racial discrimination. For a few, prison life might even seem preferable—at least three meals a day and housing were reliably provided. This is not an endorsement of incarceration but a powerful indictment of life on the streets.

The Chronically Ill and Incarcerated: A Healing Conversation?

What has been said suggests that there might be some healing in the very *communing*, the *giving* and *receiving* of help, that could result from dialogue between those who are ill and those who are incarcerated. Of course, there are significant obstacles to such a dialogue. Ill or disabled persons are often limited in terms of energy and mobility, and incarcerated individuals are segregated off, their communication with the outside world restricted. Nevertheless, if ways can be found to overcome these barriers, a conversation between the two groups might yield benefits to both.

For example, I have taught maximum-security prisoners an article by Havi Carel about her severe, progressive pulmonary disease. The reading was very well-received, leading to an e-mail contact with Dr. Carel. Her article triggered a sense of *communing* on the part of the men. They clearly identified with her predicament, in relation to both the confinements of prison itself, and the chronic illnesses and restricted breathing patterns it tends to breed.

But we make a mistake if we see incarcerated persons as always the ones in need. As mentioned, many of the men I have worked with have inspired me. Under conditions of severe long-term deprivation they maintain their dignity, empathy, sense of humor, intellectual aliveness, and joy in life. I have seriously thought of compiling a self-help book entitled *Life-Lessons from Lifers*, though I doubt it would sell well. Those who have survived, and even thrived, under long-term incarceration could be valuable teachers to us all, and perhaps especially to those grappling with disabling physical problems.

Communicative bridges between the two groups could also lead to other forms of reciprocal assistance. For example, at a prison where I taught for many years, certain inmates trained service dogs for incapacitated adults. Vince Greco, recently released after thirty-three years, comments,

> I guess waiting for a year while your canine partner is being trained in the prison is like being in prison and waiting for a year-long delayed

> release. Try placing yourself in the shoes of someone confined to a wheelchair or bed, who will be receiving a significant amount of freedom because prisoners are training their canine partners. (Leder and Greco 2014, 219–34)

Training service dogs is one way in which those who are incarcerated can *give* to those who are disabled. On the other side, prisoners, both while incarcerated and after release, need to *receive* the help of caring advocates on the outside. Those on the outside with chronic pain and illness, despite levels of incapacity, may be in a position not only to empathize but to act to help those inside. Whether this would take the form of prayer, pen-pal relationships, personal assistance, or political advocacy, we have seen that *giving* may also be a healing strategy for them, counteracting the involution of illness.

I will now turn from the (imagined) dialogue between the groups, to focus on how the healing strategies for illness previously discussed are applicable in prison. Rather than speaking for others, I will draw on the voices of incarcerated persons from our class discussions which, surprisingly enough, I was allowed at the time to audiotape (Leder 2000). I've been told there is no way that would be permitted anymore.

Note: I am happy to say that a few of these featured individuals, most recently John Woodland and Tray (Arlando Jones III), have been released after more than thirty years in prison and are doing great things. The latter immediately assumed a position in Georgetown's University Prisons and Justice Initiative, and recently addressed senators and other members of Congress, as well as four international delegations. The joy of witnessing such events, after many decades of incarceration, is hard to describe.

Escaping and Embracing the Body

Not surprisingly, those who are incarcerated often favor healing strategies that I've previously categorized as modes of "escaping the body" to reassert one's freedom. While the body is not the initiator of limitation, as it is for the sick, it is that whereby one can be handcuffed, locked up, and generally bound by the power of the state. In this regard, Mark Medley says:

> When you're really under twenty-four hour surveillance . . . there's also a way you can *resist* or *escape*. Autistic thinking. Total absorption in fantasy. "I'm building an island and this is what my water source will be, and the kinds of plants I'll have . . ." You can absorb yourself in this for

> hours and hours and resist being conditioned by the discipline. (Leder 2000, 44–45)

This should not be dismissed as "mere escapism." It is a valid strategy that I have called *transcending.* In this regard, fantasy literature can be popular in prison; Tray Jones, for example, passed much time pleasurably by reading every *Game of Thrones* novel. More broadly, Tony Chatman-Bey comments:

> You're stuck here physically and the only place you can grow and move is *mentally.* So we do. If a man goes to jail for five years, he'll read more books in that time than the average person will in twenty years. And reading itself can expand the mind. Books can take you anywhere, across the water, into space. (Leder 2000, 76)

Ironically, at my home university some students experience their philosophy courses, which are required by the Jesuit core curriculum, as a kind of coercion, time served before release to the outer world with a degree in hand. In prison, it was the reverse: the classroom was that rare zone of freedom behind all the bars and barbed wire.

Of course, there are many other venues which help those in prison to *transcend*, including religious and 12-step groups. As Charles Baxter, a Muslim imam, says:

> Man is created from one cell, right, and as man grows he adapts into another cell, and that cell's also a place for growth and development. When you read the Quran and the Bible you'll see that different prophets went to the *cave* for comfort and isolation. And the cell's like that cave. (Leder 2000, 56)

At Loyola University of Maryland we have distributed thousands of brochures on the use of meditation in prison, including a resource list of groups around the country that support it—this derived from a conference on contemplative practices in prisons, involving Christian-centered prayer, Buddhist mindfulness, Hindu *siddha yoga,* and so on. Having one's external life restricted can open the door to an inner journey.

In seeking to "escape the body," strategies of *ignoring* and *refusing* also have their place. In a discussion about whether a prison could truly be a "home," John Woodland had this to say:

> We always had a concept around here about keeping yourself distant from prison activities and the prison mentality. . . . don't think about

> fixing no cell up to make it comfortable. Let it stay raggedy. You want to keep a mindset that this is not some place for me to get comfortable. (Leder 2000, 57)

John would rather *ignore* and *refuse* his entrapment than slip into the mindset of a perpetually institutionalized person. In general, *refusing* is a frequently chosen strategy to preserve one's dignity and independence in prison, whether declining to rat out another inmate, comply with regulations, or bow to the power of correctional officers. Not surprisingly, *refusing* has its shadow-side: it can lead to "tickets" that may lead to solitary confinement and lengthened prison time. Then too, one must endure the psychological distress of always feeling in conflict with one's environment.

In reply to Woodland, Charles Baxter took a different tack:

> (laughing) I call my cell my *palace*. As a matter of fact I just got it painted last week and paid the dude four packs to do it. He painted the floors, my ceiling, the whole thing. I got my oriental rugs laid down. I don't care where I'm at, I'm going to make it heaven while I'm there. Even in this hellhole, I'm going to find some heaven. (Leder 2000, 57)

This is akin to healing strategies that involve "embracing the body" rather than seeking to escape it. Baxter *accepts* and *cares* for his embodied situation. An article by Bollnow (1961) that we discussed in class clarifies the close relation between one's cell and one's body, insofar as any room we inhabit serves as an extension of our physical capacities—for example, the bedroom, bathroom, kitchen, and dining room of a normal house.

Yet Arlando (Tray) Jones III—who himself has published two memoirs with my university's press (2010, 2019)—brings up a problem with viewing the cell as an extension of one's body:

> But you can never really have a home in here. Because the officers could come with the key anytime they want and uproot you. Like right now, everything I own I brought out with me (my toothbrush and all) because *I'm the cell,* my own body, rather than some hole cut out of space. (Leder 2000, 56)

Despite the disrupted corporeal schema described earlier, the challenge, then, is to live out the body authentically. For example, while sinister associations persist about prisoners getting "ripped" (muscle-toned) from lifting weights, or having multiple tattoos, these can be forms of positively embracing the body, and *transforming* it (another healing strategy) into a vehicle for personal expression rather than something state-controlled.

Temporal Strategies

For inmates serving long sentences, it is no surprise that temporal healing strategies also come to the fore. Here, Woodland makes a pithy but telling comment:

> Quite a few guys try to live in the past. I like living in the future, thinking about what my life is going to be. But I think one thing most of us try to avoid is the *present*. Because the present here is the most painful. (Leder 2000, 86)

Those who "live in the past" employ the healing strategy of *remembering*. One may recall the family and friends, money, sex, drugs, and freedom that used to brighten life—but as Woodland implies, this strategy has its shadow-side. Ruminating on times past may lead to bitter regrets about lost opportunities and mistaken decisions. And even if that remembered pre-prison world seems positive, it may be colored by fantasy, no longer be recoverable, or be bound together with the criminal activities that led to imprisonment. Too often, returning to the old neighborhood, friends, and activities is one element that feeds the high rate of recidivism in the United States, with most ex-convicts back in prison within five years of release. (It should be noted, though, that the carceral system markedly worsens this problem by releasing people without adequate reentry support, and then re-jailing people for minor parole violations.)

Focusing not so much on *remembering* but on the future, Woodland's preference (as quoted above) would correspond to the earlier-discussed healing strategy of *anticipation*. This can be necessary to survival. Many "lifers" have suggested that the belief that they will not die in prison serves as a crucial lifeline. Otherwise, they may grow depressed, "zap out," and perhaps even commit suicide. Hope also motivates their activities for personal and professional growth. Then too, toward the end of sentence, the prisoner needs to formulate a pre-release plan for where he will live, and so on, even to be considered for release. Yet there is a dark side to all this focus on the future, one discussed earlier through Minkowski's term "expectation." Over-focus on a release date—which might be decades off—can lead to lived time becoming stagnant and the present deprived of richness, as one waits interminably for that future day to arrive.

That said, and despite Woodland's comment about the painfulness of the present, I have also met incarcerated individuals who practice appreciative *presencing*. Just as Carel found that her life sentence, and possible death sentence, from severe pulmonary illness surprisingly led her to "amplified enthusiasm and joy" wherein "all my energy and happiness are funneled into the *now*" (Carel 2014, 146), so do some incarcerated individuals learn to value precious moments of life, even those of a lifer.

While studying a Buddhist-inflected book called *Awakening Joy* (Baraz and Alexander 2012), one man spoke in class about how affected he was by a simple teaching: instead of saying "I have to" about daily activities, the author recommended saying "*I get to.*" Starting with breakfast, my student experienced a newly grateful mode of *presencing*. "I said to myself 'I don't *have to* go to breakfast, I *get to* go. A lot of people don't have enough food . . . but I do!'" I have been inspired by maximum-security tales of joy from those who awaken to their senses; laugh with a friend; read literature and take classes; pray and meditate; and appreciate being alive when so many friends are in the ground. It reminds me that if they can do this while in prison, surely I can better appreciate my own well-off life.

Presencing can also fruitfully blend with other temporal strategies. One class member, "Q," put it this way:

> To me, time is like a dragon I have to slay. If I can master the present, I will have used my time to *redeem* time. Then I can go back and offer something to people who never had to be in that situation . . . I get up in the morning at 8:30 and I don't get back to my cell until about 10 p.m. Between those times I'm constantly involved in activities that are beneficial and what I want to do. . . . The time flies for me, you know? Sometimes I can't even find enough hours to complete what I wanted. (Leder 2000, 73)

Wayne Brown, another class member, replied: "I call this *'doing time'*—when you use every available moment for your benefit. When you have time to sit back and mope and worry, is when *time begins to do you*" (Leder 2000, 86).

These accounts show how different strategies synergize. *Presencing* in an enriched "now" goes hand in hand with *anticipating* a better future, one which involves *giving* to others. This sense of purpose also constitutes a *re-envisioning* of one's life, a crucial modality of healing accessed by many incarcerated individuals. Though there may be regrets about previous choices, or simply the blunders that led one to be caught, prison time can also be "redeemed" by pivoting to a new narrative of one's life and identity. This can involve a self-examination which, as Woodland notes, "can be a real gut-wrenching experience" (Leder 2000, 167), but also a gateway to something new.

Studying materials ranging from Martin Buber's *The Way of Life according to the Teachings of Hasidism* to *The Autobiography of Malcolm X* led to fruitful discussions of this "turning" that many of my students were seeking or had accomplished. Just as someone with cancer might end up saying, "This was the best thing that ever happened to me," so I have occasionally heard that about being in prison. "It slowed me down compared to life on the streets"; "if it wasn't for prison, I'd be dead"; "it made me take a new look at my life and where I wanted to go"; "I finally understood what my grandmother was trying to tell me all those years."

This notion of penitential reflection and self-transformation is of course built into the very history and etymology of the "penitentiary" itself (Guenther 2013). Unfortunately, the penitentiary system has done precious little to support, and much to obstruct, this process. Nonetheless, some incarcerated men and women accomplish it themselves. It is a shame that the extreme long-term sentences handed out in the United States leave so many languishing in prison for decades after a youthful crime—as if this were still the same individual, one whose *re-envisioning* of self is dubious or impossible, just a tale constructed to fool the parole board.

Communing, Receiving, and Giving

Though it is possible, for example, to accomplish spiritual *transcendence* or *re-envisioning* on one's own, most of the healing strategies mentioned earlier are best maintained when those in prison can access supportive others. These can be friends and family who write and visit; teachers and other volunteers from outside; a kind librarian, social worker, or even a respectful correctional officer. Often those in prison turn to one another through mentoring, friendships, or spiritually based groups. In discussing illness, I spoke of how *communing* can often be best accomplished with others who share the same condition, including its restrictions and frustrations, as in the Parkinson's disease support group. To fully feel and understand what a prisoner goes through, it helps to be one yourself.

Prison relationships don't, of course, always go in this supportive direction. As it is used as a one-size-fits-all "solution" to a range of social and psychological problems, prison can press together men and women with psychiatric difficulties, anger management problems, sociopathic tendencies, traumatic histories, neurological deficits, and so on. Battles for power, space, and scarce resources not surprisingly ensue. However, Tray Jones comments on the *communing* that can develop even in such an environment, and its radiating effects on one's lifeworld:

> But when I was in the cell with T—the only cell buddy that I really got along with—a bond developed, and in our closeness we were so brotherly. . . . It seemed like I had *more* room in the cell with him than I do now when I'm alone. We'd play cards and talk, and it felt like there was a lot of room! (Leder 2000, 58)

Surely, the healing strategies of *receiving* from, and *giving* to others, are as crucial in surviving chronic incarceration as they are with chronic illness. Jones, for example, told me of a single encounter that happened years ago but affected him profoundly. A "little old white-haired lady that used to teach English here" noticed he had a cold and made him a cup of tea. "But the thing was how gentle she was and the smile she always had. It's just the whole relationship was so unconditional." In a dark environment, a small ray of light means much to the one ready to *receive.* In our classroom I was touched by the appreciation the students expressed for my presence, our classroom discussions, and for others in the course with whom they'd shared hard times and joys over the course of decades.

However, the carceral system can be disruptive to human relationships in so many ways. One day I found out that the class represented in this chapter had disappeared; with no notice, many of the men at the Maryland Penitentiary had been transferred to a new maximum-security facility. I have not seen most of these people since. Sometimes, I have been told, prisoners are even transferred simply because they developed too many close relations with others. These examples of "fraternizing" are viewed as a security threat insofar as power centers and plotting may develop outside the purview of the guards. In this sense, *communing, giving,* and *receiving* are read as something to be surveilled and interrupted.

It should also be noted that incarcerated people can also develop deeply meaningful relationships with animals such as service dogs, stray cats, and even rodents. The Jessup Correctional Institution at which I taught for many years was, surprisingly enough, a designated wildlife sanctuary for migrating geese who often chose to reside there all year round—it was indeed a place of "maximum security" for them to raise their goslings. Vincent Greco spoke of how he loved to feed the birds though this was frowned on by prison staff, and the things he learned from them. "I never saw a parent goose physically abusing or plain ignoring one of their goslings" (Leder 2016a, 208). Zaeed Zakaria comments: "When I first seen a goose my eyes widened and my heart began to feel joy because I was looking at a creature Allah created. I felt sincere peace, but more so I was inclined to feel humble and to feel compassion" (Leder 2016a, 208). Those in prison *give* to these animals who themselves are often refugees, *receiving* back inspiration and affection. Paradoxically, *communing* with animals can help restore one's humanity: the animal's gaze is one of the few in such an institution that does not label you as a "criminal."

But often, those I have met in prison most want to *give* back to their family, who they feel they have hurt or abandoned, and to the wider community of young men and women like themselves who may need positive redirection. Yes, this can be a ploy to tell the parole board, "I should be released because I have so much to contribute," and these declarations are often viewed suspiciously. But my experience is that this desire to *give* seems quite sincere, and is almost a primal need welling up within the spirit. The imprisoned men and women I've known have found multiple ways to do this while still incarcerated, through supporting friends, participating in the Quaker-initiated Alternatives to Violence program present in many prisons, sponsoring or participating in conferences, helping run religious groups, and mentoring young people influenced by gang culture.

* * *

In closing, it is also important to shift the focus from individual healing to things which can only be brought about by sociopolitical change. After all, we have seen that imprisonment functions as something like a *socially caused chronic illness*. Despite the rhetoric of "rehabilitation," it is hard to see how we make people better by deliberately sickening them. Our culture of mass incarceration is bloated, racist, and deeply inhumane, an example of embodied injustice writ large. It treats human beings, often those arriving from disadvantaged settings and limited options, as if they were objects to be warehoused, predatory animals to be caged, or savages who deserve to be punished over decades for a single criminal act. We have seen that who is actually surveilled, prosecuted, and imprisoned is vectored by racism and classism. Many are imprisoned who are later exonerated, perhaps victims of prejudice or prosecutorial misconduct. And instead of being geared toward redemptive therapeutic, educational, and job training programs, incarceration often leaves people far worse off than when they went in—having made criminal contacts, become more out of touch with the modern world (since internet access in prison is prohibited in most states), and being burdened now with the label of "convicted felon" that can close off jobs, housing, and social services. The not surprising result is a very high recidivism rate—prison is very good at creating future prisoners. And for every person incarcerated there is so much collateral damage—children who grow up without a parent, emotional and financial disturbance for entire families, communities torn asunder by all the persons gone missing.

In this context, our focus on personal healing strategies should not displace the need for a kind of "preventive medicine," that is, the reduction, reformation, or abolition of our current prison system. We need modes of "criminal justice" that are less criminal and more just.

7

Elder Wisdom: Re-possibilizing Later Life

In this chapter I focus special attention on the "aged"—those who experience themselves, or find themselves defined by others, as "old." Like the incarcerated, older persons may feel the pressure of both life-constriction and social marginalization. Again, we are dealing with a mode of "embodied injustice," this time in the form of ageism rather than sexism or racism. In *The Coming of Age* Simone de Beauvoir, most famous for her feminist work, writes that the old man "becomes, and to a far more radical extent than a woman, a mere object. She is necessary to society whereas he is of no worth at all. He cannot be used in barter, nor for reproductive purposes, nor as a producer: he is no longer anything but a burden" (Beauvoir 1996, 89). Of course, there are traditional societies that particularly value the aged and see the richness of our later life both for self and community. However, many modern Western societies, focused as they are on technological innovation, economic productivity, and youthful vitality and sexuality, devalue the aged body to the point of mockery and revulsion. Unlike other modes of discrimination, ageism potentially awaits us all. Still, we would probably rather deal with ageism than suffer a premature death.

But what is it to age well? In this chapter I will focus primarily not on the pathologies of embodied injustice, as in our previous chapter on prisons, but on our various life-affirming responses to the biological and sociological assaults of age. I will try not to simply recapitulate the earlier discussion of twenty healing strategies used in the face of illness and impairment, though much of it is directly applicable to the trials that come with the aging body. I will start by a brief and suggestive sketch of the phenomenology of "growing old" which, more than illness and incarceration, is fundamentally ambiguous, associated as it is with both potential losses and gains. I will quickly survey these in relation to (1) the body itself, (2) its temporal horizons, and (3) its worldly involvements. Later I will critique our society's customary models of "aging well," and turn to more inspired healing strategies drawn from a variety of cultures and spiritual traditions.

Bodily Losses and Gains Associated with Aging

Bodily Losses

1. *Loss of vitality and strength.* As we get older we may find ourselves simply unable to do things we once could. We may experience diminished muscular strength, energy, and endurance. In general, we may feel more fragile and do more guarding and restriction of activity, or suffer when we neglect such precautions. In the dialectic of the body's *I can/I can't,* the balance seems to tip ever more toward the latter.

2. *Accumulation of aches, illnesses, and impairments.* There are many possible "fixes" when a technological device gets old and malfunctions. There may be replacement hardware, software updates, a reset procedure, or we simply buy a new one. But this cannot be done for the aging body. Over the course of time, like an old and "buggy" computer, we tend to accumulate aches and injuries that never quite heal; chronic illnesses that develop or spread as we age; decreased immune function that leaves us more susceptible to acute illnesses; and so on. We may also develop various forms of cognitive deterioration that can threaten our core identity. To a degree, diet, exercise, medications, surgery, and even organ transplantation can extend our quality and length of life. But science fiction scenarios aside, the only "cure" for these accumulating ailments is death.

3. *Loss of physical attractiveness.* Many older people, at least in our culture, look in the mirror and are disturbed—or even horrified—at what they see. There are unwanted sags, wrinkles, and flab. The sense of this as "ugly" is based on a youth-centered cultural norm. There is much beauty to be seen in an aged face whose every wrinkle may record a life well-lived. However, it is undeniable that the body ages past its prime reproductive years, and so it makes biological sense that, if nothing else, it would become less sexually alluring in our later years. The billions of dollars spent on anti-aging creams, hair dyes, Botox injections, and cosmetic surgeries are demonstrations of the way we view our aged body not only as an *object-for-others,* but as one increasingly past its prime.

In a sexist society, this takes on a gendered vector. In Beauvoir's words, "As men see it, a woman's purpose in life is to be an erotic object; when she grows old and ugly she loses the place allotted her in society: she becomes a monstrum that excites revulsion and even dread" (Beauvoir 2011, 123).

4. *Loss of productive value.* When we grow old, we may be viewed not only as less attractive, but as less productive of economic and social value. In a world oriented toward profit-making and technological innovation, the aged body can seem slow, unable to work long hours, hidebound in its long-held habits, and possessing a knowledge base that is increasingly out of date. After all, "you can't teach an old dog new tricks."

While there is a lot of ageism in the dismissal—metaphorical and often literal—of older employees, again there are kernels of undeniable truth. The old body often simply cannot keep up with the young, at least in tasks that demand strength, endurance, or simply comfort with the latest zeitgeist and software. Again, the needle here tilts toward the *I can't* when compared to the abilities of younger competitors. This may also affect one's finances; many older individuals who have been downsized or retired may find themselves suffering monetary losses.

Bodily Gains

1. *Accumulation of skills and experience.* The losses mentioned above are, however, balanced out by a series of gains. Even if the older body has less energy, and perhaps some outdated knowledge and habits, it has also likely accumulated valuable skills and experience. An older carpenter, compared to a newly minted associate, might eye a structural challenge and know the proper solution; he or she has seen enough houses, and been through enough failed and successful rebuilds, to know how to best approach the issue. As a teacher I might not be as energetic as some younger colleagues or as conversant with new teaching software. However, I have learned more than a few pedagogical tricks in my decades, and compared to my young self, I know better how to guide an upper-level seminar discussion, or be compassionate with first-year students while also holding them accountable. The worth of long experience should not be discounted.

2. *Liberation from restraints.* The social marginalization mentioned earlier can also open up zones of individual freedom. An aging woman, no longer the focus of a sexualized male gaze, may feel freer to stop conforming to the "feminine ideal," for example by letting go of chronic dieting. This can go hand in hand with experiencing menopause as liberating, despite any social messages that one's prime has passed. The needle tilts a bit more toward experiencing the *body-as-subject* than as *object-for-others*, enhancing a sense of power and autonomy.

There are many other examples of liberation from restraint. An older parent may find pleasures in the empty nest after the fatigue of full-time child-minding and housekeeping. Someone retiring from a job, while perhaps suffering economic and social costs, may also gain freedom of time and action. Again, the needle tilts back toward the *I can*. The famed neurologist and author Oliver Sacks wrote as he approached age eighty:

> I do not think of old age as an ever grimmer time that one must somehow endure and make the best of, but as a time of leisure and freedom, freed from the factitious urgencies of earlier days, free to explore whatever I wish, and to bind the thoughts and feelings of a lifetime together. (Sacks 2013)

3. *Positive transformations in the face of limitation.* The real physical losses—of energy, endurance, and sometimes health—that come with age are undeniable. We have, however, explored in this book how bodily limitations can themselves trigger personal gains. Perhaps someone hyperactive in young adulthood learns to slow down in later years because she has to; she can finally appreciate the shifting cloud patterns in the sky, or play patiently with a grandchild. Perhaps she has developed an aching arthritic knee, but this has deepened her resilience, and her ability to experience *communion* with others. These are new modes of the *I can* which help balance out all the *can'ts* of the aging body. Then too, the very frailties of aging may guide us to be more attentive to our bodily needs. As mentioned earlier, the healing strategies involving in *listening* to and *caring* for the body with proper diet, exercise, breathing, and sleep patterns may be a gift of age. When young we can get away with various forms of self-abuse which aging makes all but impossible. Our body then becomes the great teacher to which we must finally listen.

Temporal Losses and Gains

As we focused on in chapter 3, the embodied self is profoundly temporal. In my phraseology, "I'm time" means always being open to *restoring* or *transforming*, and *re-envisioning* one's past, present, and future and their interrelation. What, briefly, are some of the temporal losses and gains that occur as we reach our later years?

Temporal Losses

1. *Accumulation of losses and regrets.* Just as we spoke of the gradual accumulation of aches, injuries, and illnesses, so too can a long life involve

a buildup of other losses. Robert Butler introduced the notion of "life review" as developmentally appropriate to the later years, often to positive effect (R. Butler 2002). But we can also survey our life and see youthful dreams unfulfilled; relationships that ended, and perhaps badly; disappointments in our work-life and career; family dynamics that did not live up to our hopes; or opportunities that never materialized or were mishandled. We cannot wipe our memory clean as we might do with a computer, or install new software to eradicate these flaws.

2. *The loss of open-ended futurity.* Our past may be growing, but commensurately our future shrinks. As we reach our later years we realize limitations in the amount of time and opportunity that remains. How long will I stay healthy? Active? Able to work? Travel? Take my dog on long walks? So open-ended in youth, the temporal horizon becomes more limited. Death, which may have felt distant and abstract when we were young, may now become much more real, and for some imminent. We may sense our demise approaching with the passage of each birthday. We earlier termed this somewhat dysfunctional relation to time that of "expectation," wherein we do not purposefully move forward into the future but feel it coming toward us. Even if we long to stop time, or attempt various physical and psychological modes of evasion and postponement, death still resolutely approaches.

Temporal Gains

1. *Accumulation of past and present satisfactions.* Balancing the above, our review of an ever-lengthening past need not bring only regrets, but also reconciliations. For example, we may find meaning even in the "failures" and disappointments we experienced along the way. Perhaps we now sense a reason behind events which at the time were simply painful. Being fired from a job, or losing a relationship, may have opened the door to better ones, or at least taught us valuable lessons. This relates to what I mentioned earlier: our accumulation of experience yields holistic perspectives that we didn't have access to in our youth.

We may also accumulate many happy memories that glow from a distance—of travel, special occasions, the birth of a child, or even of our own childhood. If my experience is any guide, we may actually feel closer to our early memories than we did in mid-adulthood. It is if they resonate in a timeless realm, but we needed a long life to be able to see through and past time, and rejoin these originating moments. The most famous literary representation of this timeless experience is evoked for the older Proust when a madeleine dipped in tea suddenly triggers vivid memories of his childhood in Combray. His age has not taken him farther from, but actually closer to his beginnings, which leap to life as he continues to meditate on them as a semi-invalid in a solitary room. This involves what we earlier termed *chronic healing*; Proust has gone "in search of lost time" and found much to heal *khronos* (time) itself.

2. *Death-enhanced life.* The loss of open-ended futurity can also bring gains that resonate throughout our temporal fields. A sense of limited time can pull us into *presencing*, with deepened mindfulness and gratitude. Who knows how many changes of season I will witness? I now pay closer attention to the advent of spring with its new-budding leaves, or to the wild change of colors that announce the fall. There is not a lot of time to waste, and so we may laser in on the precious *now.*

As we become more present, we may also seek reconciliation with the past—to get back in touch with a long-lost friend, or apologize to our children for deficits in our parenting (Shachter-Shalomi and Miller 1997). We know we have only a limited time left to straighten accounts.

In relation to the future, the growing proximity to death may deepen our spirituality, that we may better accept mortality, or turn our attention toward an afterlife. As W. B. Yeats famously writes, in "Sailing to Byzantium":

> An aged man is but a paltry thing,
> A tattered coat upon a stick, unless
> Soul clap its hands and sing, and louder sing
> For every tatter in its mortal dress (Yeats 2000, 80)

One way for the soul to "clap its hands," philosophers and spiritual traditions agree, is to take "death as our companion." Awareness of our own and others' impermanence can point us toward existential authenticity, wiser decisions, and greater appreciation and compassion.

Worldly Losses and Gains

I now turn from losses and gains focused on the body per se, and on the temporality of growing old, to focus on changes in the world around us as we age.

Worldly Losses

1. *The loss of companions.* Understood in a broad way, this includes the fact that children grow up and move away, and we may lose touch with friends

and other family members who live at a distance. These days of remote video interfacing can definitely lessen the loss, but never fully eradicate the "remoteness" of the electronic interface.

Then too, as we grow old we lose an increasing number of life companions to death. First to go may be the generation of musicians, politicians, spiritual leaders, and so on that we grew up with and who helped define our life and world. We may also lose our grandparents, and then our parents, the latter so central to our youthful world and identity. Even though the loss of one or both parents is "natural" and "expected," this may not soften the blow. If we live long enough, we then see friends and associates die one by one. Old age can be a time of loneliness and melancholia.

2. *The loss of one's place in the world.* As we age, we may feel increasingly peripheral to, disengaged from, or even incompetent with regard to the new forms the world is taking. We may not understand all the technical innovations and applications that drive our society and prove necessary to accessing health care and other services. We may not relate to newer music, movies, or cultural trends.

Geographically, we may also have had to move away from the home of our youth or adulthood for any number of reasons, including downsizing, relocating to "be near the kids," or entering a retirement community or facility. Even if we age in place, we may witness the green spaces that defined our town eradicated for new real estate developments until "this is no longer the place I knew." More broadly, we may feel that the world in general seems to have gotten markedly worse in many ways, such as global climate change, increasing economic inequality, and massive political dysfunction.

Worldly Gains

1. *Deepening of companionship.* There are gains that balance the losses I've just described, and in many ways are their flip side. Though we lose people over the years, long life can also support a deepening of companionship. We may "re-meet" our children as mature adults, maybe now parents themselves, and have a mutual understanding that wasn't possible before. We may still have friendships that have now lasted decades. Each Thanksgiving I gather with college buddies and their families, some of whom I have now known for over fifty years. This shared history adds layers of richness and meaning to our relationships.

This book also has addressed how, as energy and health diminish, this need not diminish our relationships; physical and social losses can actually open up deepened experiences of *communing*, *giving*, and *receiving* compared to what we had in our youthful days of carefree independence.

2. *Enhanced appreciation of the world.* The changes in the world around us are not always a cause for grieving. We may appreciate that we have lived long enough to witness and benefit from new developments. Perhaps the progress of medical science has given us access to much improved medications or surgeries. We may be delighted to be able to speak with friends and family members across the country via video calls and "virtual reunions." It may be a boon to be able to watch from home our choice of streaming movies rather than be subject to the limited choice and long journeys associated with local theaters. I, as mentioned earlier, also love the new availability of audiobooks.

On the social level, we may see areas of meaningful advance, for example in the alleviation of homophobia and certain forms of sexism. Even though it has become harder to believe in the modernist dream of continued world progress, certain changes are clearly improvements, or at least hopeful and revitalizing.

The Problems with "Successful Aging"

I have tried to impartially sketch some of the many losses and gains that come with aging, including those related to the body itself, its temporal horizons, and worldly relations. We should not seek to sugarcoat the losses. The Buddhist meditation teacher and psychotherapist David Chernikoff starts his "Aging and Awakening" workshops with a session in which all the participants are encouraged to complain in an exaggerated fashion about their problems, voicing their sufferings honestly (Chernikoff 2021, 103–5). Only then are they freed up to turn toward creative *re-envisioning*. However, for many individuals that positive turn may never happen. As said, our ageist culture tends to emphasize the losses of later life far more than the gains. As Aho notes,

> This is strange because unlike other "isms"—such as sexism or racism—ageism isn't directed at an amorphous "other" with a different gender or skin tone, but toward our own future self. Understood this way, ageism looks like a kind of self-hatred of who we will one day become. (Aho 2022)

Ironically, this pervasive ageism goes hand in hand with an unprecedented surge in the numbers of people living to an older age. Since

1900 average life expectancy has increased from 47 years to 77 in the United States, with those age 65 and above forming the fastest-growing age group. A good half of those who, in the history of humankind, have ever reached this senior age are alive today. In Japan the mean life span is 85. All these added decades suggest an important shift in the trajectory of a human life (Roszak 2009). In many societies, or at least those with the necessary protections and social safety net, elderhood is no longer the accomplishment of a privileged few, but an expected part of the human life span.

However, our vision of how to age well has failed to keep pace with our abilities to extend life. I will briefly turn a critical eye on four models of "successful aging" embedded in our social practices and discourse.

First is what I term the *preventive* model of a good old age: this concentrates on the prevention of disease, disability, and death. One has aged well when one has successfully defeated, or at least delayed, many of the earlier mentioned bodily and mental modes of deterioration associated with later life. Maybe enough lifestyle changes, physical therapy, medications, plastic surgeries, and even organ transplants can keep us youthful and healthy into our later years.

A second model of successful aging focuses more on *prosperity*. No one wants to outlive their financial resources, and age into destitution and neglect. In the United States we keep careful watch over our personal retirement funds, worrying whether they will hold out, and we hope that Social Security will remain solvent and sufficient. A good old age is thus seen as one that is financially secure, with some people aspiring to wealth accumulation for self or heirs.

Then too, there is the model of *productive* aging. I earlier discussed the perceived diminishment of productive value in elders. In later life we still want to feel useful, vigorous, contributory, and respected. Within our society this is often demonstrated by our continued capacity for work, whether this takes the form of corporate employment, "blue-collar" labor, giving our family financial and emotional support, house maintenance, or active volunteerism. When we're focused on successful aging as involving "productivity," we may delay retirement as long as possible, or be urged to fill our retired years with contributory labors. (I have talked with people who say they never have been so busy since they retired—now everyone thinks them free to join committees, take on service positions, or care for the grandchildren.) Even in the area of intimacy we are encouraged to keep sexually active, for example, through direct-to-consumer TV advertisements for the treatment of "male erectile dysfunction." The natural lessening of libido is medicalized as a preventable disease: this shows how the *preventive* and *productive* models of successful aging synergize, along with the *pleasure* model I now turn to.

We are familiar with the vision of the "golden years" as a time for *pleasure*, perhaps to finally rest and play, and enjoy the fruits of our lifelong labors. I mentioned that later life may liberate us from prior constraints. Ads may monetize the new possibility of late-life enjoyments in the form of cruise-ship travel, high-end retirement communities, or other seductions for those with the requisite funds. Rather than remaining productive members of a capitalist economy, here seniors are switched to the role of pleasure-seeking consumers.

However, I will suggest that all these images of "successful aging," respectively involving the four "P's" of prevention, prosperity, productivity, and pleasure, are deficient. Moreover, *they are deficient in similar ways* though their foci seem to differ, and sometimes stand in opposition.

First, they *fail to define what is unique and meaningful about later life.* Many cultures and religions, as we shall soon see, revere elderhood as a special time of life that offers distinctive opportunities and benefits to both the individual and their community (Schachter-Shalomi and Miller 1995). By contrast, the visions of "successful aging" that I've just discussed focus mainly on prolonging the goods associated with midlife, as if this period could and should be extended indefinitely. While the prevention of later-life illness and poverty, the maintenance of productivity, and the pursuit of pleasures are all worthy goals, they tell us little about what is uniquely valuable about later life.

Furthermore, though positive on the surface, these models implicitly continue to associate later life with its potential *losses*—sickness, poverty, disability, depression—albeit as enemies that can be overcome. As such, these ideals of successful aging still embody the cultural fear of, and resistance to, the diminishments associated with old age. "Successful aging" becomes a kind of negative of a negative, rather than envisioned as a positive life stage in itself.

Finally, these models of successful aging necessarily create classes of individuals who, by definition, have "failed." One well-regarded book by Rowe and Kahn (1998) summarizes more than a decade of research supported by the MacArthur Foundation. In the book, successful aging is characterized as (1) involving a low risk of disease and related disabilities; (2) a high level of functioning, both physical and mental; and (3) a continued active engagement with life. "In sum, we were trying to pinpoint the many factors that put one octogenarian on cross-country skis and another in a wheelchair" (Rowe and Kahn 1998, xii). But necessarily, many of us will end up like that wheelchair-bound person. We have seen that in old age we may unavoidably struggle with illness and disability. Many of us will also live with financial stress through no fault of our own; perhaps be unwilling or unable to maintain our midlife productivity; or be without the funds or inclination to pay for consumerist pleasures. Does this mean that all such people have aged *unsuccessfully*? For example, we need to know far more about that person in the wheelchair, his or her dreams, prayers, friendships, and character (Hillman 1999), before using that person as a cautionary tale.

Ultimately, these models of "successful aging" do not explore in a holistic and deep way the existential meaning of a human life (Leder 1998; Crowther et al. 2002). Physical health, financial prosperity, productivity, and pleasure capture surface modes of well-being which, admittedly, are of great importance. Who would not want these, when they're attainable? But a person may be lacking in one or more of these, and despite such deficits, or even *because of* such deficits, can still build a rich and meaningful life, and be "healed" in the sense we have used throughout this book.

In re-envisioning what it is to age well, we don't need to reinvent the wheel—in this case the *weal*, or well-being, possible in old age. When surveying cultural, historical, and religious traditions, we find many positive images associated with the elder to inspire us. In my book *Spiritual Passages* (1997) I take up twelve such images; here I will briefly develop four as a path into this larger terrain. In keeping with this chapter's alliterative flourish (for good or ill) I will call these, respectively, the elder as "Contemplative," "Contributor," "Compassionate Companion," and "Creative."

The Contemplative

> When a householder sees his skin wrinkled, and his hair white, and the sons of his sons, then he may resort to the forest. . . . Let him always be industrious in privately reciting the Veda; let him be patient of hardships . . . and compassionate toward all living creatures. . . . In summer, let him expose himself to the heat of five fires, during the rainy season live under the open sky, and in winter be dressed in wet clothes, thus gradually increasing the rigour of his austerities. . . .
>
> Let him always wander alone, without any companion, in order to attain final liberation. . . . All that has been declared above depends on meditation. (Doniger and Smith, 1991)

To a twenty-first-century Western reader, this ancient Hindu text presents a forbidding vision of aging well. It is starkly opposed to all models of "successful aging" hitherto discussed. This forest elder is not manifesting financial prosperity or customary forms of social productivity. He or she is not in pursuit of pleasure or illness prevention—quite the contrary, as indicated by the challenging austerities that are voluntarily undertaken.

To make sense of this, we need to place it back in its original context. In the Hindu tradition, spiritual realization is commonly viewed as the ultimate goal of life. Elderhood provides unique opportunities to move toward, or even attain, enlightenment. In busy midlife, social dharmic duties weigh heavily; one is busy raising a family, making a living, caring for elders, contributing to the community. Later life is seen as a time when one can finally turn these responsibilities over to the next generation. This represents the gain earlier discussed as "liberation from restraints." One is now freer to focus with a single-minded energy on the life-aim of spiritual awakening.

Furthermore, the aging process presents a challenging, but ultimately helpful curriculum in this regard (Ram Dass 2001). It presses one to move beyond identification with the body, now deteriorating; to transcend all the social roles (parent, worker, community member) that had previously defined one but which are now being altered or left behind; and to face the fact of death, and therefore the question of eternal life. We are thus pushed beyond the shell of the ego-self. Here is what we termed "positive transformations in the face of limitation" and the "death-enhanced life"—potential gains associated with elderhood.

Especially given our society's emphasis on productivity, the elder-as-contemplative is a somewhat countercultural ideal, yet it has much to teach us. Instead of resisting the losses associated with aging, the Indian model suggests how we might, by leaning into them, uncover some rich gains. Few of us can or would literally go live in a forest, yet some contemporary applications can easily be imagined. (Even in India, this solitary retreat is rare; it is more likely that elders may join an ashram, a spiritual community.) For example, clearing out the clutter in our attic, or downsizing to a smaller living quarters, has an element of the forest retreat: this can be a time to simplify and refocus our life. So too, can the transition to becoming an empty-nester or retiring from one's job. As Thoreau wrote, "I love a broad margin to my life. . . . I realized what the Orientals mean by contemplation and the forsaking of works" (1983, 156–57). Countering the losses associated with social marginalization is this "broad margin" that later life may bring.

The Hindu model focuses on transcendence found through retreat, scriptural study, and meditation. Yet contemplation can take many forms: the enjoyment and creation of art; wanderings in nature (there are reasons why the renunciate pursues his or her quest, like Thoreau, *in the forest*); taking periodic retreats for self-exploration; ritualizing important transitions like retirement; keeping a Sabbath rhythm to one's daily and weekly life; and so on.

In our rush-rush multitasking culture, elders are often mocked for talking, walking, or driving slowly, or sitting around without meaningful doings. It is true that diminished activity can be a sign of deterioration and disability. Yet, paradoxically, this is sometimes a sign of *existential health*: the contemplative elder reminds us all to slow down and be more present. In terms of our earlier discussed strategies of healing, we thus see *presencing*, the *re-envisioning* of our life-narrative, and *transcending* all at play. We may rise out of our customary sense of the limited body-egoic self to an experience of unity with Spirit and universe, the ultimate goal of the Hindu retreatant. I will turn more toward this theme in the book's final chapter.

The Contributor

> I am an Eagle Clan Mother of the Onondaga nation. . . . People choose a clan mother by watching how she has lived her life and cared for her family . . . because that's evidence that she will take care of all the people as if they were her children. . . . Clan mothers also have the duty of selecting a candidate for leadership chief in the clan. . . . If we see him going in a way that is not acceptable, we must approach him and remind him of his responsibilities. . . . One of my deepest concerns right now is about our youth. . . . I tell them, if you find yourself in a position where you have to make a major decision, think about the things that are taught in the [Onondaga] Longhouse, and ask yourself, "Is this going to bring harm to myself, or to any other living thing?" Basically, that's what we call respect—respect for yourself, respect for people around you, and respect for the earth. (S. Johnson 1994, 194)

At first glance, this archetype of "aging well" looks quite opposed to the first one we examined. Rather than departing on a contemplative retreat the elder, in this case represented by an Eagle Clan Mother of the Onondagas (one of the six Iroquois nations), remains in active service within the tribe. This example of the "Contributor" archetype is obviously not the same as our "productive" model of successful aging, either. The Eagle Clan Mother is not focused on producing anything in the usual economic or technological sense. Rather, she serves as a mentor, caregiver, and wisdom-keeper.

From whence comes the wisdom often associated with elderhood, at least in traditional cultures? One source is the earlier discussed "accumulation of skills and experience" with age. The elder is not only a living record of tribal history, but has hopefully learned from a personal history filled with mistakes as well as achievements. He or she is able to share these lessons, and gracefully mentor those youth who are willing to receive them.

If "she has lived her life well," the elder has experienced and demonstrated responsibility. For example, she may have had children (though this is hardly a prerequisite for maturity and compassion) and been deepened by the journey of parenting. Yet the fact that her kids are now grown up and independent allows an expansion of the sphere of concern such "that she will take care of all the people as if they were her children." In youth and midlife, the focus is often on establishing our identity and safeguarding our personal interests and family; elderhood can free us up to participate even more widely in the open-hearted *giving* discussed in chapter 5.

Our concern can even expand to future generations and the earth. Having lived a long time, we can see how far-reaching consequences must be considered before rushing into action. In the words of Oren Lyons, Faith Keeper of the Turtle Clan of the Onondaga Nation: "We are looking ahead, as is one of the first mandates given to us as chiefs . . . to make every decision that we make relate to the welfare and well-being of the seventh generation to come . . . We consider: will this be to the benefit of the seventh generation?" (Lyons 1980, 203–4).

This far-sighted elder wisdom is not an automatic result of having lived a long time. We may find it exemplified in certain public figures—Nelson Mandela, the Dalai Lama, Mother Theresa, and Thich Nhat Hanh come to my mind—but it is sadly lacking in other older political or religious leaders who shall remain nameless. This pattern may be reduplicated within our family. One grandfather may be wise and loving, while another is a bull-headed curmudgeon. Why the difference?

Part of the answer might lie in the individual's realization, or lack thereof, of the previous archetype of the Contemplative. While at first glance this seemed the opposite of the Contributor, these two archetypes can play a synergistic role. Those who have contemplated the nature of self and spirit, the wishes and feelings of others, the consequences of one's actions and the state of one's character, are far more likely to manifest contributory wisdom in later years.

As we look at the world around us, filled as it is with superficiality and short-sightedness, threatened by racism, tribalism, and warfare, along with terribly destructive global dangers like climate change and species eradication, we have never been more in need of elder wisdom. Schachter-Shalomi and Miller have proposed establishing a council of elders who, like the Eagle Clan Mother, could remind our world leaders of their responsibilities (1995, 67). Some more modest programs exemplify the archetype of the Contributor in action. For example, the AARP's

Experience Corps matches thousands of older adults with young children at risk, in a mentoring/tutoring process that enriches all participants. The AARP also offers annual prizes honoring individuals over fifty who have tackled major social problems in a creative way. In the words of CEO Jo Ann Jenkins, "The AARP Purpose Prize is all about a new story of aging—focusing on experience and innovation and the idea that our aging population is an untapped resource full of possibilities" (AARP 2017). As our population ages, the historically unprecedented number of elders is usually cast as a social burden. But what if it were also seen as a social asset, a reservoir of contributory wisdom, a source of *giving* from which we all can *receive*? This could serve not only personal but cultural and global healing.

The Compassionate Companion

What follows is written by a Maryknoll Sister, the principal of a Peruvian school until crippling progressive rheumatoid arthritis forced her back to the United States for surgery:

> I remember thinking that even though my hands were going to be broken and crooked, they would still be sacred to me. I'd use them to bring something to somebody, I didn't know what. My hands could be the compassionate hands of Christ as much as the hands of the doctors and nurses.
>
> So I sought to be able to enter into the world of the sick, and to live with the mystery of suffering. I saw that I had to enter into my own experience of pain, and to face up to it, and to allow myself to be changed by it. Without that nothing could be done. I saw that healing comes from owning our own wounds in the first step to moving beyond them.
>
> I returned to Peru at a lower altitude. Almost everything had changed, especially my attitude toward the people I was working with. I could feel their terrible poverty and pain in a whole new way. In fact it seemed as if I was seeing it for the first time. How often I'd rushed around trying to solve people's problems without really seeing them. . . . And so my ministry changed. It became the ministry of walking together. . . . Our pain and weakness and deformity proved to be teachers of a great mystery, a small introduction into the kind of dying from which new spirit is born. (Ram Dass and Gorman 2003, 90–91)

We have outlined some of the losses experienced by the aging body, including the aches, illnesses, and afflictions that accumulate over time. But the above story illustrates a skillful response, embracing what I will term the role of the "Compassionate Companion." Faced with such suffering, any of us could become resentful and self-pitying, yet the Maryknoll Sister journeys in the opposite direction. Inspired by Christ, she transmutes her pain into insight and compassion for the plight of those she serves. She is actualizing the gain of "deepening companionship" we discussed earlier.

While introduced through a Christian-inflected tale, this archetype hardly belongs to any single tradition. Buddhism, for example, is equally attuned to the centrality of suffering in human existence—that was Buddha's First Noble Truth. Having seen the old man, sick man, and corpse, Siddhartha Gautama not only foresaw his own suffering, but better understood that of others. Along with wisdom (*prajna*), compassion (*karuna*) becomes one of the two great Buddhist virtues, enjoining us to relieve the suffering of all sentient creatures.

Before developing rheumatoid arthritis, the Sister had tried to do this but had "rushed around trying to solve people's problems without really seeing them." There is an overtone of unconscious superiority, of doing good on behalf of those in need. Then an encounter with age and illness exposes her own vulnerability. She is no longer above, yet neither is she below, others. In "the ministry of walking together" she is a compassionate companion on the journey; the necessity of pain also opens the opportunity to love. This archetype is inherently non-hierarchical, replacing the ideal of an independent old age with an embrace of our interdependence. This epitomizes the healing strategy of *communing*, in which the very boundary between *giving* and *receiving* has dissolved.

The Creative

> And God said to Abraham, "As for your wife Sarai, you shall not call her Sarai, but her name shall be Sarah. I will bless her; indeed I will give you a son by her. . . . Now Abraham and Sarah were old, advanced in years; Sarah had stopped having the periods of women. And Sarah laughed to herself, saying, "Now that I am withered, am I to have enjoyment—with my husband so old?". . . .
>
> Now Abraham was a hundred years old when his son Isaac was born to him. Sarah said, "God has brought me laughter; everyone who hears will laugh with me." (Gen. 17:15, 18:11–12, 21:5–6)

As discussed in this book's first chapter when focused on Itzhak Perlman, this biblical passage involves a linguistic joke: the name "Isaac" comes from the Hebrew word meaning "to laugh." Isaac's very existence involves a kind of cosmic joke—God bringing forth a child from such elderly parents! Moreover, Sarah and Abraham undergo their own (re)birth, symbolized by a name-change and a journey to a new land.

This story serves to introduce the archetype of the elder as Creative. New lands, new identities, new births, can happen even late in life. Through teaching this material in lectures and workshops, I have met inspiring elders who have become later-life environmental activists; taken up new careers; explored spiritual practices far afield from their earlier religious training; become a teacher after years of learning, or a learner after years of teaching; separated after decades of marriage to explore an independent selfhood; pulled up stakes to move to a new city, or an intentional community; and learned to face death head-on without fear. This goes against the stereotype of the elderly as static and stodgy. It turns out that you can teach an old dog new tricks; the *I can* remains vigorously operative, not just the *I can't.* But much depends on whether the individual is still exploratory, creative, and receptive to the call of spirit, as were Sarah and Abraham.

Again, this archetype is not confined to the Judeo-Christian tradition. Chuang Tzu, the Chinese Daoist author, tells the tale of four old friends who are also masters in the way of the Dao. One falls ill with a disease that distorts his body: "My head sticks up like a hunchback and my vital organs are on top of me. My chin is hidden in my navel, and my shoulders are above my head." Yet he seems "calm at heart and unconcerned," free of resistance and resentment. "Perhaps in time he'll transform my left arm into a rooster. In that case, I'll keep watch on the night. Or perhaps in time he'll transform my right arm into a crossbow pellet and I'll shoot down an owl for roasting" (Chuang Tzu 1964, 81). This is a humorous example of embodied *transformation,* accompanying the *re-envisioning* that is available if one flows creatively with change. Resistance to change, in Daoism as in Buddhism, is a central source of suffering. As Carl Jung writes:

> A human being would certainly not grow to be seventy or eighty if this longevity had no meaning for the species. The afternoon of human life must certainly have a significance of its own and cannot be merely a pitiful appendage to life's morning. . . . Whoever carries over to this afternoon the law of the morning, or the natural aim, must pay for it with damage to his soul. (Jung 1933, 109)

* * *

This chapter has asked, "what is it to age well?" After introducing the losses and gains that are characteristic of later life, and criticizing some of the models of successful aging prevalent in our society, I have turned instead to traditional, often transcultural, archetypes that are still applicable in the twenty-first century. Though there are many others, I have focused on that of the elder as Contemplative, Contributor, Compassionate Companion, and Creative.

One might ask how these relate to one another, and to one's own life journey. There is no univocal answer. I have chosen these four images for their complementarity. An element of introspective withdrawal, as found in the Contemplative, is balanced by the social involvements that mark the Contributor. The Compassionate Companion lives with and learns from suffering and mortality. The Creative, on the other hand, is associated with rebirth, humor, and vitality. A full experience of later life might incorporate elements of all four archetypes, perhaps held in a yin-yang balance. In the process, we minimize losses and actualize many of the gains of age mentioned in this chapter, along with the modes of healing treated in the book's initial sections. As discussed earlier, these modes of healing unfold on a "chessboard," or "keyboard" that we seek to play upon with skill, as appropriate to our shifting needs.

At times, one or another archetype might appropriately predominate for a given character type or situation. For example, someone might take a contemplative bent in later life either because this was a lifelong disposition, or for the opposite reason—that earlier decades were so busy that now having a "broad margin on life" is a welcome switch. Another person may find it more natural and satisfying to fill their time with contributory activities as long as they are able, whether this takes the form of caring for grandchildren, mentoring younger colleagues, or political activism. Such predilections can change from year to year as we age, depending on alterations in our social, financial, and physical condition, or simply in response to new inward promptings.

There is then no one way to actualize healing in later life. Withdrawal and contribution; sadness and humor; confronting death and experiencing rebirth; there are many forms that "aging well" can take, whether—to return to Rowe and Kahn's example—we do so by whipping along on cross-country skis . . . or sitting quietly in a wheelchair.

Part 3

The Inside-Out Body

8

Inside Insights and the "Inferior Interior"

In this book I have examined not just the effects of illness and incapacity, but the healing strategies available to cope with these forms of embodied limitation. In the book's first part we moved from the personal to interpersonal dimensions of healing. In the second part we turned toward broader social issues, with a special focus on incarceration and aging.

In contrast to this movement outward, I now pivot inward. We will explore those visceral recesses of the body that are nearly inaccessible to experience, but crucial in illness prevention and healing. The goal is to go deeper (pun intended), by reexamining lived embodiment using a different experiential taxonomy than previously. I earlier discussed fundamental structures like the *I am/I have* dichotomy, or that of the *I can('t)*. But I now reapproach the body with a focus on the relevance to healing of what constitutes its "inside" or "outside." Spoiler alert: We will find that this very division is suspect, that the body is always and intrinsically "inside-out." In this chapter I start with "interoception" of the body interior; in chapter 9 I turn to breathing, that life-sustaining movement of air inside and out; and in the book's last chapter I discuss the radically non-dual experience of body–universe connectivity, that which reveals possibly the fullest sense of healing and wholeness available to us as humans.

But to begin, exactly what is "interoception"? The term has been used in a variety of ways. Sherrington (1906) introduced the notion of "interoceptors" to refer specifically to receptors on, and perceptions of, the *visceral* region (as opposed to proprioception and exteroception). Over time, the word "interoception" has also been given an expanded meaning and used to refer to *all* perceptions of our own body, including those with a musculoskeletal or skin origin (Ceunen et al. 2016, 743). Proceeding phenomenologically, we do find that the lived body operates as an integrated whole in ways that can weave together visceral interoception, proprioception, body-surface sensation, and even our outward-focused perception and motility. Still, I will focus on *visceral* interoception—placed in dialogue with biomedical perspectives—and briefly trace its significance vis-à-vis the body and its lifeworld, Western philosophical history, modern disciplinary practices, and the implications of all this for our healing strategies.

The Personal and Pre-personal

Initially, "interoceptive" is distinguished from "exteroceptive" experience by its personal and private nature. It is true that if I gaze at a tree, I have my own perception of it that no one else exactly shares. I regard it from a certain angle, and it may summon up meanings and associations that are particular to me. Yet the tree always remains publicly available. Others view it, and we can compare, and for the most part agree on, many of our perceptions; for example, that it is a twenty-foot-tall maple tree sporting the brilliant orange leaves of fall. The interoceptive world is not sharable in this same way. *You* cannot experience the queasiness *I* feel in my stomach. Only I directly apprehend it. What Scarry writes about pain could be generalized to the interoceptive field:

> Pain enters into our midst as at once something that cannot be denied and something that cannot be confirmed (thus it comes to be cited in philosophic discourse as an example of conviction, or alternatively as an example of skepticism). To have pain is to have *certainty*; to hear about pain is to have *doubt*. (Scarry 1985, 13)

That interoception constitutes a private, personal field of experience has a number of ramifications. Research has shown that there is a good deal of variability in the levels of sensitivity and vigilance individuals have relative to their inner body (Herbert and Pollatos 2012). We cannot assume that the same processes will elicit the same experiences for different individuals, or even for the same individual at different times. In a medical context, this contributes to the difficulty of deducing the nature and severity of disease simply from a patient's report of internal symptoms. Hence the heavy reliance on laboratory reports and imaging devices which yield intersubjective data.

Moreover, the personal nature of interoception can make it hard for a patient to even communicate these experiences. When seeing a clinician I might point to the relevant bodily region, and describe what I feel—"there's a kind of dull aching around here now and then, and sometimes a sharp pain"—but there is still a struggle with imprecise language (Scarry 1985, 162). The other person cannot directly share the object of reference. He or she must "take my word for it," but the words I have at my disposal are disappointingly crude. "Aching," "sharp," "bloated," "crampy": this sort of language is less than exact. Contrast this, for example, with the ability of a paint store to present hundreds of slightly different color shades, each with its own designator, such as "teal," "turquoise," "aqua," "jade," "sage," "edgewater," "valley mist," and so on. This kind of subtlety of discrimination and labeling is possible because these colors manifest in a shared world which we see and name together.

While *personal* to each individual, interoception also gives us glimpses of a *pre-personal* level of embodiment. Organismic functions involving circulation, respiration, digestion, the production of blood cells, the filtering of toxins, and so on largely proceed without the need, and often the possibility, of conscious awareness and control (Leder 1990, 36–68; Ricoeur 1966). Our life arose from a pre-personal process of embryological organ growth, and each night we lapse back into a blind reliance upon these organs to sustain us when we fall asleep. During the day, these pre-personal calls may overturn our personal agenda: for example, in the middle of an engrossing movie I discover I simply must run out to the bathroom.

Paradoxically, interoceptive experience can both subvert and reinforce a sense of self–body dualism. When I gaze in a mirror, the hazel-colored eyes I see looking back at me don't experientially coincide with my eyes-as-lived, the power of sight that organizes the visible world; there is a gap between the eyes as seen and seer that makes me feel separable from the physical body. Yet this is not the same for the interoceptive field. When I have a cramp in my midsection I feel it *from within*. Initially, there seems to be no divergence between the perceived and perceiving. There is simply cramping. Students of traditions like Hinduism and Buddhism often work with attention to body sensations to foster "non-dual" experience (Loy 1988), as the subject–object split dissolves. Yet the kind of non-duality triggered by insistent interoceptions may also take on a threatening quality. Inner experience, such as a severe stomachache, can feel trapping, overwhelming, inescapable. Earlier we compared pain and illness to incarceration. It is hard to establish any distance from that which seizes you from within.

Thus, while interoception could be said to subvert self–body dualism, in other ways it reinforces it. In the West we tend to identify our core self as somewhere up in our head, where our brain and most of our exteroceptive senses reside. From this vantage point what unfolds in the stomach can seem distant, something *non-I* which I look down upon, literally and metaphorically. Moreover, insofar as we are receiving from a pre-personal, organismic level, the bodily *I can* is here replaced by a kind of *it can* (for example, my stomach can digest food), or in some cases, *it can't* (I feel like I have to throw up). As I explore elsewhere, philosophical dualisms, such as Descartes's famous mind–body split, may have their origins, or at least part of their appeal, in such experiences of divergence between the volitional self and our necessary, but often burdensome, viscerality (Leder 1990, 126–48).

This dualistic split is not present in all cultures. Nor must the managerial and pre-personal levels of the embodied self always clash. In the next chapter, we will focus on the act of breathing, which intertwines those two levels and potentially in salutary ways: the meditator practicing abdominal breathing can increase oxygenation, slow the heart, lower blood pressure, improve digestion, and provoke other positive effects mediated through the parasympathetic nervous system. And as we have seen in our discussion of *listening* to and *caring* for the body, one can be responsive to inner signals taken as helpful information. To head for bed when fatigued; to lay off a food that causes stomach upset; to notice the signs of mounting anxiety and take remedial measures; these are all ways of positively attending to and learning from interoceptive cues—about which I will say more at the end of this chapter.

The Inaccessible, Indistinct, and Intermittent

The previous section focused on the ambiguous relation between our visceral body and our "self." Now I turn more specifically to the sort of access we have to this inner body. First, it seems that there are regions that are simply *inaccessible,* a kind of organismic absence at the heart of our biological life. Hidden as they are in the depths of pre-personal anonymity, certain organs, tissues, and functions may disappear entirely from our conscious perception, their functions manifest only through indirect sources. This can include important regions of the visceral body, such as the alveoli of the lungs or the parenchyma of the liver, and even the brain itself taken as an organ. (Headaches arise from the tissues, blood vessels, and nerves surrounding the brain, not from the brain itself.)

In some ways, this recessive absence is beneficial. It frees us up to focus on our conscious projects as vital processes are silently managed by our body. In other ways, such interoceptive gaps can prove problematic. For example, certain cancers are more deadly because they progress asymptomatically. By the time a patient experiences problems, the growth of a large mass and metastases to distant regions have already occurred.

While the inner body is not entirely inaccessible, what interoceptive awareness we have, when compared to exteroception, is often marked by various modes of *indistinctness.* We scan the outer world with our classical five senses, which synesthetically intertwine with one or another (Merleau-Ponty 2012; Jonas 1966; E. Straus 1963). Through vision we survey a world of objects seamlessly arrayed in depth, gazing at galaxies billions of light years away or homing in on the minute patterns of a small flower. Hearing alerts us in all directions to passing events, including the whispering of leaves in the wind, or the subtle complexities of spoken language in a face-to-face encounter. With touch I experience the proximate with precision; our fingertips can distinguish stimuli to the accuracy of a millimeter. Yet by contrast, the inner body yields a far more *indistinct* landscape. Physiologically, our bodily interior is replete with a host of specialized sensors that minutely monitor the slightest variations of the inner milieu—but on the subjective level we have only a dim sense of what is going on in there, manifesting for example as queasy feelings or a slight heaviness.

This indistinctness can take the form of spatial ambiguity. When asked about a "stomachache" we may point at our midsection, but this hardly coincides with the outlines of a particular organ. Nor does the "ache" have anything like the qualitative precision that our exteroceptive senses, used singly and in combination, often yield (Leder 1990, 39–42). Moreover, due to the complexity of our organs' spatial and physiological relationships, and neural distortions like "referred pain," we may not even be sure if what we experience reliably correlates with the "what" and "where" of the originating organic processes. As discussed earlier, in clinical situations the patient and doctor alike are involved in trying to decode, with the help of the patient's history and diagnostic tests, these indistinct interoceptive messages (Svenaeus 2001; Gogel and Terry 1987; Leder 2016a, 87–105).

Then too, interoceptive experience often exhibits what Ricoeur calls the "strange mixture of the local and the non-local" (1966, 412) that attends vital functions. A chest pain may be "right here" in a certain sense, but may also be experienced as reverberating throughout the discomforted body, and can even, as I will later discuss, color our experience of the outer world. Proust, that consummate literary phenomenologist, poses an interesting question in *The Guermantes Way*: "Is there not such a thing as diffused bodily pain, radiating out into parts outside the affected area, but leaving them and disappearing completely the moment the practitioner lays his finger on the precise spot from which it springs?" (2002, 114). The interoceptive field may combine specific pains, tickles, and spasms with diffused and confusing regional effects.

This sensory field is often not only qualitatively and spatially indistinct in such ways, but temporally *intermittent.* By contrast, the world of vision exhibits a sense of constancy. As long as our eyes are open the world fills in around us, continuous in time. Within that world we can see our external body, which is always present. Yet interoception yields a more intermittent register, surfacing to and disappearing from awareness at different times. For example, though I take more than 20,000 breaths a day, I do not consciously attend to the vast majority of them, nor to my shifting oxygen/carbon dioxide balance. For most of us, most of the time, visceral interoception remains intermittent, often reaching awareness only at times of demand: "I'm really hungry," or "I may be getting my period."

From an evolutionary viewpoint, it seems logical that conscious awareness would often be most needed when intervention is called for to assist bodily homeostasis, for example, when we are ill and need to take to bed. Times of unproblematic health free us up to focus on outer-world activities (Leder and Jacobson 2014). Yet interoception can also be intermittent insofar as it comes to the fore at special times in the life-course—for example, puberty, pregnancy, menopause, and as we have seen, old age, as well as the dying process itself.

The Inside-Out Body: Interpretive, Emotive, Purposive, Projective

My treatment of visceral interoception so far has been somewhat provisional and oversimplified, focusing on it as a pre-personal sensory field. This analysis needs to be expanded to address the complexity of the relationship between our sensations and our cognitive interpretations, emotive responses, and goal-oriented actions—in general, all the ways in which visceral processes arise from and return to the body-lifeworld relation. I will treat these as aspects of what I will call the "inside-out body." Together they challenge the very notion of a pure "interoceptive" field.

One popular mode of research on interoception explores the degree to which individuals become aware of their own heartbeat or can be trained to do so (Herbert and Pollatos 2012, 693). While interesting results have been obtained, this is an example of a case of interoception treated as composed of isolated sensations, separated off from the interpretive and practical contexts of everyday life.

Let's instead consider a context in which heartbeat sensitivity might naturally rise. A woman has a light breakfast with coffee and goes to the gym for an early morning swim. By the end she notices that her heart is racing. What's going on? Perhaps it was too much coffee—if so, better cut back on the caffeine buzz. Or she might interpret this as the sign of a good aerobic workout—after all, you're supposed to get your heart rate up. But perhaps she is worried—is this pounding in her chest a sign of how out of shape she is? She might even fear that this is truly a cause for alarm—could it be an arrhythmia, or even the start of a heart attack?

In all these cases she is not simply experiencing a pure sensation, but a sensation-as-interpreted, and thereby one resonant with a certain quality and meaning. An elevated heart rate, if taken to signify a healthy aerobic workout, feels very different from one associated with danger, even if the interoceptive stimulus is the same. In the latter case, the heart pounds with an ominous, distressing quality like a stranger knocking on the door in the middle of the night. This is *heartbeat-as-threat*, each pulsation feeling like a potential assault.

A number of points might be made here. First, and most obviously, interoceptive experience is never "pure sensation" but is always shaped by interpretation. In this it is no different from exteroception; as touched on earlier, Heidegger (1962) and Gadamer (1984) suggest that *all* experience is necessarily "hermeneutical," that is, interpretive (Palmer 1969). The swimmer's various interpretations of her rapid heartbeat are not just idiosyncratic but draw upon Western understandings of anatomy and physiology. She may have seen pictures of the heart, studied it in classes, and understands that life depends on its mechanical pump-function. Our cultural training feeds into and forms our interoceptive experience.

Our body is, so to speak, turned inside-out. Interoception is shaped by information we receive from outside sources. Moreover, in the West, the body (and even the bodily interior) is largely thematized as if an external object, that thing which can be opened on the pathologist's table, or imaged through an MRI (Foucault 1975, 124–72; Leder 1990, 146–48). Hence the swimmer does not feel a series of sensory impressions; rather, she feels *her heart*, that quasi-external object residing within her chest.

Sensations not only provoke such interpretations, but interpretations can provoke sensation. An example is provided by Groopman, himself an oncologist who, in being treated for a hand problem, received a bone scan which seemed to show metastatic rib cancer. "I generally think of myself as reasonably well put together psychologically, but within moments my chest began to ache. When I touched my ribs, they hurt" (2007, 265–66). Even when further tests showed he was cancer-free, the pain continued for several hours afterwards. Fortunately, he recovered from this distressing experience which mimicked that of the disease he feared. Certain individuals, often labeled hypochondriacs, suffer from an over-vigilant and catastrophizing turn of mind which can make the interoceptive field a place of nightmares.

For sensation is not only *interpretive* but also *emotive.* We have seen that for the swimmer her pounding heart may be suffused with an aura of elation, worry, or terror. At times, this emotional tone is even the predominant quality and significance of inner-body experience. We speak of having a "heavy heart," "heartache," or even a "broken heart." These expressions relate to real sensations in the chest area that can accompany grief. The heart is often experienced, or at least understood, as the emotional center of love; we say "you're in my heart," or send a heart-shaped Valentine's Day card. The heart is also viewed as a place of intuitive knowledge, as in "I know in my heart . . ." Others might refer to having a "gut feeling," or more negatively, a "gut-wrenching" experience. Of course, just where in the body we experience our cognitive and emotional responses can differ among individuals and cultures. The Chinese refer to *xin,* the "heart-mind," and to the lower *dantian,* below the navel, as a crucial energy center. Hindus describe a series of "chakras" (energy-wheels) running up and down the spine, mediating, for example, sexual urges, interpersonal love, or transpersonal insights.

These examples suggest that interoceptive experience is not only *interpretive* and *emotive,* but also *purposive* (Herbert and Pollatos 2012), that is, generative of urges and actions. Returning to the example of the swimmer, depending on how she interprets her quickened heartbeat, she may feel the need to catch her breath; moderate her caffeine intake; swim a few more laps to get in better shape; or immediately exit the pool and phone her doctor. She may later talk with friends or conduct internet searches, before deciding what if anything to do. But the sense of a prereflective *call to action,* a push or pull in certain directions, wells up within interoceptive experience itself. Fatigue beckons us to sit down. Heartburn calls out for a glass of milk. Here too, we see the principle of the inside-out body at play, for the inner body is both affected by, and motivates our actions toward, the external world.

Taken collectively, this suggests that interoception is what I will term *projective.* This word derives from the Latin *jacere,* "to throw," and *pro,* "forth." Interoception is more than simply internal sensation; it is also "thrown forth" into the lifeworld and its endeavors. As Sartre writes, "'coenesthesia' rarely appears without being surpassed toward the world by a transcendent project" (1956, 436). Earlier, in the section on "the inaccessible, indistinct, and intermittent," I contrasted those recessive features of visceral experience with the richness of exteroception. This contrast was also developed in my earlier book *The Absent Body* (1990). Yet we should be careful not to overemphasize such splits. The lived body is not simply a collection of discrete organs and regions, but operates in a unified fashion as embedded in a lifeworld.

Let me take a personal example. When working too long on this chapter, I begin to feel fatigued. My head swims; the words I am writing no longer come easily. I begin to feel a bit distracted and irritable. I have some stomach queasiness from the tea I've been drinking. Am I hungry? Not sure. What time is it? Past twelve. Though confused, tired, and a bit depressed, I don't want to knock off before finishing this section—but I'm having trouble even parsing the words on the computer screen. It's time to take a break and have some lunch.

In this example I note certain interoceptive cues (queasy stomach, fatigue, irritability, depressive feelings). Yet these are blended seamlessly with alterations in my experienced lifeworld, for example how the computer words appear, and even my dimmed sense of what I am trying to say. To use Heidegger's term, the world is always experienced through a certain *mood* (1962, 172–79)—in this instance, irritation and confusion. Using a more embodied perspective than Heidegger does, this means we encounter the world as somewhat filtered through inner-body states which help determine our emotions, perceptions, and desires. In fact, often we come to know our internal states only indirectly through noting changes in the outside world. That the words on the computer screen no longer make sense helps clarify to me that I am growing hypoglycemic. Again, this is a manifestation of how the internal body *pro-jects*, is thrown-forth into its surrounding world.

This involves a temporal, not merely a spatial, self-transcendence, casting us into past and future. When regarded as a collection of isolable sensations, interoception seems to manifest as pure *presence*. I feel a tickle *now*. A pain *now*. Everything is simply *now*. But interoceptive experience also has a thicker temporality. My hypoglycemic state developed gradually, imperceptibly unfolding until it pushed through into self-awareness. Moreover it refers to the past—when did I last eat?—and the future—what should I have for lunch? If my issues were more serious than transitory low blood sugar, the horizon of futurity might take on even greater meaning. For example, the return of pain for someone with a chronic condition can raise the specter of continued disability, deterioration, or even death. Again, these resonances are not simply subsequent to the sensation, but are felt within it, adding ominous weight to what otherwise might be a minor tug.

A projective temporality manifests even on the pre-personal interoceptive level, composed of habits and anticipations. As mentioned earlier, I have noticed that simply *thinking* of drinking a glass of orange juice will provoke acid release and a burning sensation in my throat. On a visceral level, my body, which has been shaped by past experience, anticipates the citric acid it is about to receive and responds accordingly. The visceral body thus has its own sensorimotor *pro-jects*, cast forth across space and time.

Inside Insights: Revaluing the "Inferior Interior"

The previous analyses have hovered ambiguously between the universal and the culturally specific. Certain features, such as the inaccessibility of certain bodily regions, all but devoid of consciously available sensory receptors, would presumably be true for humans in general. Other aspects of the interoceptive landscape—for example, our degree of awareness, the places in the body we most sense and emote, and the interpretive models we use—not only differ among individuals, but among different cultures and historical periods. This is a job for medical anthropologists, sociologists, historians, and others to investigate. I have mainly focused on contemporary Western experience. Yet it is valuable to reflect on how this itself was historically shaped, and how this heritage may be problematic.

Beginning in the seventeenth century a new conception of the material world, and the human body, was proposed and gained a certain ascendancy. This has been referred to as "the death of nature" (Merchant 1980)—that is, nature, and most particularly the human body, came to be understood according to the metaphor of an inanimate machine. For Descartes, the mind or soul (*res cogitans*) is the repository of conscious thought, including perceptual experience, imagination, rationality, memory, and the like. The body (*res extensa*), like the rest of the natural world, simply operates as a machine, according to material properties and forces (Burtt 1952; Descartes 1911). For example, the heart in time came to be understood as a mechanical pump, using muscular force triggered by electrical impulses. This soul–body dualism also gave rise to a monistic variant, ascendant in contemporary science, in which the mind or soul disappears entirely, or is considered simply as an epiphenomenon of mechanistic processes. The book *L'Homme Machine* (*Machine Man*) by Julian de La Mettrie, an eighteenth-century French physician and philosopher, is one famous and early example of this position (1996). Foucault examines the reverberating power of this model:

> The great book of *Man-the-Machine* was written simultaneously in two registers: the anatomico-metaphysical register, of which Descartes wrote the first pages and which the physicians and philosophers continued, and the

> technico-political register, which was constituted by a whole set of regulations and by empirical and calculated methods relating to the army, the school and the hospital, for controlling or correcting the operations of the body. (Foucault 1979, 136)

When the body is reconceived as a machine, its placement and action can be minutely controlled and made to serve the ends of military, educational, medical, or industrial institutions.

To some extent we still live in such an era, and this shapes our interoceptive experience in crucial ways. First, it fosters a tendency to *overlook* (literally and metaphorically) the inner body's sensory field. Insofar as we inhabit something like a body-machine, we need not attend to its messages. Again, experience and wisdom are viewed as the possession of the mind, while the body is something we use, devoid of higher consciousness. Thus we are acculturated to dismiss interoceptive experience; we look elsewhere, higher in our hierarchy of value, to messages from the external world or from within our own intellect.

Hence the interoceptive field comes to be regarded as what I term the *inferior interior.* Descartes and other philosophers valorized the rational powers of the intellect. Theologians looked to the soul that human beings uniquely possess, with its capacity to worship the divine, read scripture, and exercise moral judgment. This, then, is the *superior interior,* that belonging to the "mind" or "soul." For this is where rational reflection, meditative prayer, and the deliberative processes necessary to function in our complex, bureaucratized, and technologized world take place. In school, we are mostly trained to think much, and think better. All the input we receive from the external world—a ceaseless flow of language, data, and images needing absorption and processing—leads us back into that cogitating mind, rehearsing its sub-vocalized language, memories, and symbolic representations. By contrast with this *superior interior,* messages arising from our bodily interior take on secondary status. Schools do not teach us, for the most part, to pay attention to our interoceptive sensations. These sensations are not publicly available, nor do they contribute to our required studies and activity patterns. Similarly, employers are not interested in hearing about our aches and twinges. They want us to be present for and focused on outward tasks. Hence, interoception implicitly becomes the "inferior interior."

Without coaching and validation, it is difficult to pick up on and understand interoceptive messages. As we have seen, they are nonverbal, private, often subtle, intermittent, indistinct and ambiguous. It is not necessarily that we lack knowledge per se about our inner physiology—for example, we may have learned a lot about diet, digestion, and gut bacteria from school or internet searches. Yet at the same time we may lack the training to help us notice and utilize the signals arising from within our lived body.

In addition to *overlooking* inner-body messages, we often energetically *override* them. Foucault, in the quote just mentioned, writes of the "technico-political register" according to which man-the-machine is disciplined. School attendance is mandatory, as are the rooms you occupy at which times, the chairs you sit in (often ill-fitted to the body), and how you face and address your teachers. Prisons, as we have seen, engage in their own modes of intensive surveillance and restriction of the body. So too, companies are busy with time-clocks to be punched, workspaces that are divided, phone conversations to be recorded, or remote computer usage to be measured. The body, as Foucault writes, is micromanaged, rendered docile in the face of power, even while its utility is maximized (1979, 135–69).

Discipline, according to Foucault, is most effective when it is internalized so that individuals manage their own bodies in accordance with the larger systems in which they are embedded. Again, this leads many of us not only to overlook but to actively override interoceptive messages. True, we may have thoughts like, "I'm exhausted, I don't want to work today"; "I'm tired of sitting in this office and staring at a computer—I need to go for a run"; "This air I'm breathing makes me feel sick"; or "This project is giving me a headache." But such interoceptive messages are overridden in the name of being a good worker. Even our consumerist modes of entertainment—also mandatory for the capitalist engine to hum at full throttle—involve overriding internal messages. We drink too much, exhaust ourselves in expensive travel to distant destinations in search of relaxation; get too little sleep and are too sedentary as we interface with our electronic screens; and then we over-exercise, trying to "get back in shape." This of course refers to the shape of our *outer* body, whose appearance is viewed as of paramount importance, with special pressures placed on women in our sexist culture. All the while we lose touch with our inner body, and whatever guidance we could derive from its messages.

In this light, we can revisit some of the healing strategies treated in chapter 2 under the rubric of "escaping the body." These include modes of *ignoring* bodily messages, for example, ones of pain or impairment; *refusing* to be limited by them; and *objectifying* and *transcending* them in a kind of lived dualism whereby the essential self separates from the troublesome body. We suggested how these can serve as adaptive strategies whereby we protect ourselves from being restricted or overwhelmed by physical challenges. However, as mentioned, these strategies all have their shadow-sides. In general, they play into the cultural gestalt of disconnecting from and disciplining the inner body rather than attending to its messages. We can see now that these are not simply strategies willingly adopted by individuals, but are often forced upon them by disciplinary institutions. At such times they are not so much healing as alienating.

Instead, I turn to the value of recovering what I will call *inside insight.* There are interoceptive cues that suggest what will support or deplete our energy; what assists or impairs our digestion; the effects of different patterns of respiration, with their potential to relieve or increase stress; and so on. In clinical research, a pattern of "body awareness" or "somatic awareness" has often been associated with anxiety, bodily hypervigilance, and catastrophizing in a way that can intensify pain and distress. (Here a healing strategy such as *ignoring* may in fact be helpful.) But there are positive modes of body awareness that should also be recognized (Mehling et al. 2012). If we develop *in-sight*—that is, learning to look within—the inner body offers up a wealth of information and requests that can be of value for our health and welfare. Yes, this body often "knows" more than our preoccupied, driven mind or the pressurized society in which we dwell. Nietzsche, as quoted earlier, aptly said, "There is more reason in your body than in your best wisdom" (1954, 146–47).

But to do us any good we have to recover the capacity to attend to these bodily messages, even if they are intermittent and indistinct. There are many cultures and traditions more focused on this than ours, and their methods have now become available in the West. To name but a few, there is Buddhist *vipassana* meditation, which teaches careful, sustained attention to the breath and other bodily sensations, or what we earlier called the strategy of *witnessing*; this has given rise to mindfulness protocols that are now popular in integrative medicine (Kabat-Zinn 2013). There are Chinese medical practices such as acupuncture, and meditative/martial art/exercise/dance forms like qigong and tai chi (Jahnke 2002) that work with our bodily qi (vital energy). Hinduism has given rise to hatha yoga postures and to *pranayama*—breath-control techniques (Rosen 2002)—to render the body strong and flexible, tone inner organs, and move *prana* (vital energy) through the different chakras (energy centers). I will say more on these practices in the next two chapters.

Admittedly, these systems may map the inner body in ways that differ from Western anatomy and physiology. Some of them may or may not be proven to have direct medical benefits; studies are beginning to explore the mechanisms and efficacy of "alternative" treatments such as acupuncture and yoga used in a variety of clinical contexts. It is unclear whether qi or the chakras will ever register as anatomico/physiological realities in the Western sense. But they certainly do speak to the phenomenological experience of the inner body as interpreted by different cultures and employed in their health practices. These Eastern systems have been accompanied by a proliferation of Western holistic, body-centered therapies such as Alexander Technique, the Feldenkrais Method, Healing Touch, massage therapy, and reflexology. Again, regardless of proof of their efficacy, these treatment systems are indications of a growing desire to get back in touch with the body rather than ignoring and overriding its messages (Mehling et al. 2011).

This resonates with our treatment in chapter 2 of a number of healing strategies grouped under the rubric of "embracing the body." Instead of trying to free ourselves from embodiment at times of discomfort or dysfunction, we could read such messages as invitations to move closer. We can seek to *witness* and *accept* whatever signals our body is sending us; and *listen* to them closely so as to be better able to *care* for our body, perhaps assisted by practitioners who share this orientation. For example, over the years I have worked with a massage therapist who is an expert in craniosacral and energy healing, as well as with an acupuncturist and, finally, a practitioner of Alexander Technique. While all of these therapists conceptualize the body in different ways, each one taught me how to better attend to my bodily experience and adjust it both within and outside our treatment sessions.

This focus on *inside insights* should not lead us to ignore the fact that many illnesses are not caused solely by our individual practices, nor can they be fixed by them. We have carcinogens in our food and water. Agricultural subsidies help assure a never-ending, inexpensive stream of unhealthy foods filled with corn syrup and fat. As examined in the discussion of "embodied injustice," racism, sexism, and homophobia, as well as unemployment, poverty, unsafe streets, productivity pressure, or simply reading the daily news, can send our blood pressure soaring. A shadow-side of any over-exclusive focus on inside insights is that these can be used to distract us from the political reform needed to create a health-supportive world. However, they can also awaken the need for change as we grow more sensitive, through inside insights, to what environmental factors sicken us or are healing.

That said, each person can still do what is possible to maintain inner awareness and health even within aversive environments. Also, as mentioned, groups disadvantaged within the culture—for example, women, persons of color, transgender individuals—are often neglected, mistrusted, and misdiagnosed within the medical system. This can make the need to listen to one's body (rather than turning to the "experts") even more important for those with socially devalued bodies.

Paradoxically, it was a concern with health maintenance that motivated Descartes to develop the mechanical view of the body that is here critiqued. As he writes in his *Discourse on Method*:

> It is possible to attain knowledge which is very useful in life . . . principally because it brings about the preservation of health, which is without doubt the chief blessing and the foundation of all other blessings in this life. . . . We could be free of an infinitude of maladies both of body and mind, and even also possibly of the infirmities of age, if we had sufficient knowledge of their causes, and of all the remedies with which nature has provided us. (Descartes 1911, 119–20)

It is true that Cartesian medicine, with its diagnostic technologies, chemical pills, and surgical repairs or transplants, has for many offered great relief of suffering and helped prolong the human life span. (In my case, I mentioned the value of a nerve surgery after I had seemingly exhausted attempts at self-healing.) Yet this model also has its shadow-side, as explored in the section on the healing strategy of *being-objectified* in chapter 4. The Cartesian notion of the body-machine, and the repairs to it, can distract our focus from developing an inner-body awareness that could prevent certain disease processes for which modern medicine offers only end-stage treatment (Leder 2016a, 56–83). There is a temptation, when downing another cheeseburger and fries, to believe that we can always take a cholesterol-lowering statin, or later have a cardiac procedure to open up or replace clogged arteries. This is symptomatic of an exaggerated cultural fantasy of a "fix-all" medicine. Greater awareness and valuing of our inner-body signals (I feel a bit sick after eating that burger and fries) might forestall the need for many of those pills and procedures.

To pay greater attention to interoceptive messages—what kinds of foods sit well, how much sleep and movement we need, what subtle symptoms of imbalance are manifesting that might lead to chronic problems—constitutes an ever-available resource for preventive medicine. And these inside insights are free; they involve no costly insurance premiums and co-pays. They might forestall expensive and burdensome doctor visits, invasive laboratory studies, prescription drugs laden with side effects, and emergency organ repairs and transplants which don't always work. Those who are healthy may remain so longer and improve the texture of their day-to-day life. Even those already struggling with chronic diseases or age-related debilities may find ways to monitor and moderate these, improving their quality of life and reducing the need for medical services.

Of course, inside insights will not prevent or cure all our problems. As previously mentioned, many ailments have an environmental etiology, and some have a genetic component. In addition, some diseases, or disease-predisposing factors, may develop in relative "silence" within the body. We may not become aware of high blood pressure or elevated cholesterol simply by introspection. Certain cancers, like pancreatic ones, may grow in organs that don't give the conscious mind any sensory feedback; and these can be the most deadly ones, lying hidden until they have grown and spread. There thus remains the great value of Cartesian-style methods such as measuring blood pressure, laboratory analysis of blood samples, tests for cancer markers, and diagnostic imaging techniques like CT scans and MRIs. Ideally, we should be able to hold in proper balance the information gained from without and from within, the use of Cartesian-style treatment methods along with forms of self-care and alternative healing. Thus, we can harmoniously play the "keyboard" of different healing strategies.

However, it is difficult to find this harmony and balance in a culture that leans excessively toward what could be called *interoceptive bypassing*. When we choose to refuse, ignore, or transcend the troublesome body, this can involve a kind of personal interoceptive bypassing, that is, avoiding or suppressing signals from within. When a practitioner relies too exclusively on diagnostics labs and images, and treatments such as pills and surgeries, without attending to the patient's inner experience, this is a form of medical interoceptive bypassing. While such bypassing is sometimes legitimate, it often stands in the way of illness prevention and healing. There may be supplements to, but no substitute for, the power of inside insights.

9

Breath as the Hinge of Dis-ease and Healing

Having begun with the body's interior depths, I turn now to the act and experience of *breathing*, that interface between our inner body and the outer world. This will extend our examination of the "inside-out body." Here we will also see that breathing is involved in many healing strategies, supplementing our earlier discussions. Finally, an examination of the breath will form a bridge to the last chapter of the book, in which we focus on expanding and transcending the body as customarily experienced. Breathing has long been used for practices of mindfulness and meditation that can dissolve identification with the separate self, facilitating what I will term the "transparent body."

As with other "inside insights," Western medical science has been guilty of under-thematizing the importance of the breath in disease and healing. One reason is economic: most clinical trials are funded in search of highly profitable treatments such as pharmaceuticals and surgeries. Much less research is done on low-cost or no-cost approaches, such as the use of breathing techniques in disease prevention and symptom reduction. In fact, the more effective breath techniques prove to be, the less profit is to be made from drug sales. Moreover, what research there is on breath control often employs it as but one component of a larger program—for example, involving hatha yoga or mindfulness protocols—making it difficult to tease out the efficacy of breath per se, especially since no one type of breathing is consistently examined across different studies.

As in the previous chapter, I will supplement a phenomenological approach with references to Western biomedical perspectives on the body. In this and the next chapter, I will also make use of Asian traditions that have attended to the breath over thousands of years of study and practice.

I will organize this discussion through an overarching metaphor: that our breathing functions as a multidimensional *hinge* within the lived body. A "hinge" is defined as something like a joint or flexible surface that holds together two parts, allowing them to swing relative to one another. For example, a door hinge both connects the door to a wall and also allows separation between them, permitting the door to open and shut. Our breathing, as I will trace out, serves as a living hinge between the conscious and unconscious body; the voluntary and the involuntary; physical dualities such as left and right nostril, nose and mouth, chest and abdomen; the inside and outside world, and the flow of receiving/returning that links them; and periods of movement and rest. And finally, the breath seems to form a hinge between the material and immaterial realms, the physical and the transcendent.

In all these ways, our breathing can also act as a hinge between illness and healing in the lived body. Swinging freely, the breath can be the source of psychophysical flexibility, openness, and wholeness, whereas illness can result from a frozen or defective hinge, or states in which we become patently unhinged. Deficient breathing can manifest in forms of physiological dysfunction, both acute and chronic, sometimes mediated through experiences of elevated stress, anxiety, or depression. While this does not necessarily lead to sickness, it is a source of *dis-ease*: that is, a loss (*dis*) of *ease*—a loss of comfort, flow, and well-being.

The Conscious and Unconscious

A first thing to notice about our breathing is the way we usually *don't* notice it—it hovers on the edge, a kind of hinge between the conscious and unconscious realms. We take some fifteen thousand breaths a day but most of these spring to life and die away without penetrating our awareness. As explored in the last chapter, they exist in that indistinct and intermittent space characteristic of viscerality. Even as I write, my breathing proceeds silently, autonomously, at most a kind of subliminal background to my focused work. Scientists tell us the respiratory act is triggered by physiological events—for example, the buildup of carbon dioxide and acidosis—and is controlled by brain centers such as the brainstem's medulla oblongata and pons that operate without the need for reflexive awareness. Instead of saying *I breathe*, we might say *it breathes*, freeing the "I," the ego-self, to focus on outward tasks.

But one can of course pause at any moment and become aware of one's breath. *Try it.* Sense the air entering through the nose and throat with accompanying tickling or sucking sensations. Also easily apprehensible is the lift and fall of the chest, and the swelling of the belly. (Science tells us that this is the result of contractions of intercostal, diaphragmatic, and abdominal muscles, along with secondary respiratory muscles, creating volume-pressure changes; Farhi 1996, 47–68). With some work, this awareness can be rendered more subtle, just as a chef is trained to notice flavors that a novice would miss. For example, practitioners of Buddhist *vipassana* (awareness) meditation grow adept at experiencing the slight coolness in the nostrils upon inhalation, whereas exhaled air feels warmer as a result of its travels through the body interior. This cultivated awareness would be an example of the healing strategy I earlier characterized as *witnessing*. *Witnessing* in some ways draws us closer to our body—we have access to what I termed "inside insights"—but at the same time it creates some distance between the self and the body whose sensations it objectively observes. We earlier examined how this witnessing stance can help free us from being overwhelmed by pain and distress. It can also be associated with the healing strategies of *listening* to and *caring* for one's body: even when we're not trying to "fix" our breathing, simply attending to it may cause it to shift in a beneficial direction. For example, becoming aware that our breathing is rapid and shallow may gradually permit it to slow and deepen, even if, or because, we are not forcing that change. We are simply, so to speak, taking time to watch and "catch our breath."

Cultivating breath awareness is a key spiritual practice used in the Buddhist Eightfold Path, Hindu *raja yoga,* Daoist energy-based methods (more on this in the next chapter), and many other spiritual traditions. Our breathing is ideal as a meditative focus: it is ever available, repetitive, and intimately connected with our energy, mood, and thoughts, as well as the universe around us. The breath can thus be used to gain one-pointed focus; calm the restless mind and body; promote energy flow; and investigate and experience the deep sources of vitality.

Yet, as said, breathing also belongs to the visceral dimension, and as such not only does it often proceed subconsciously, but some aspects of it remain largely inaccessible. We are not immediately aware of our seventy million microscopic alveoli, which together have the surface area of a football field, though this is the place where the "business" of respiration is accomplished—oxygen and carbon dioxide diffuse to and from blood-carrying capillaries. Furthermore, during sleep, breath in its totality slips beneath our awareness. As a hinge, breath can form our passage from wakeful consciousness into a dormant, unconscious state. Many an insomnia specialist counsels breath awareness or deep breathing as the way to tune out our busy mind and world and lull ourselves to sleep.

Of course, just as other visceral regions speak up particularly at times of dysfunction, problematic breathing can seize our attention, and even that of others. Perhaps our partner complains about middle-of-the-night snoring. We may feel unjustly accused—why blame me for my unconscious acts? Or we might suffer from sleep apnea, which can create thirty or more arousals (micro-awakenings) an hour, causing blood pressure to soar during the night and setting the stage for potential long-term health problems. Through the night, the sufferer—and I have been one—hovers on the restless borderline of conscious/unconscious states. The hinge of breath has become unhinged, provoking experiential as well as functional dis-ease. After years of using a helpful dental device as a corrective, I have recently transitioned to the gold standard of treatment for serious sleep apnea, the CPAP (continuous positive airway pressure) machine. Though long delaying the move, I have found this device surprisingly easy to adjust to and even enjoy: through the healing strategy of *incorporation*, a physically external object has become a part of my nighttime corporeal schema, assisting the depth and consistency of my breathing.

The diagnosis of sleep apnea involves undergoing a sleep study either at home or in a lab setting. In my first experience, my body was wired up to electrodes while the lab assistant counseled me to "just go to sleep" so data collection could begin. Good luck! That sleep lab was the site of perhaps my most sleepless night ever. My very consciousness of *trying* to fall asleep unhinged my ability to sink into unconsciousness. Such is the sad and paradoxical fate of many who suffer from insomnia.

The Voluntary and the Involuntary

This brings us to the next topic: breathing is a hinge not only between the conscious and unconscious levels, but the volitional and involuntary. Scientists tell us that as an action triggered by neural, chemical, and hormonal signals to subcortical brain centers, respiration is largely driven by the autonomic nervous system, from the Greek *auto-nomos*, meaning "self-ruled," or "run by its own laws." As part of the *it can*, breathing does not need *my* intervention, and in fact the latter can be counterproductive.

Here is an example: *Pause right now. Try to breathe "correctly." Make sure to get enough air, and then expel all carbon dioxide with a strong outbreath. Remember, your life depends on it!* You may find that this willed act disrupts your breath's natural flow, introducing some measure of bodily confusion and discomfort. For Daoists, the breath is a prime example of the principle that *wu-wei*, a kind of "action/non-action" characterized by effortless flow, is the best way to navigate life (Smith 1991, 207–11).

Yet simply leaving our breathing patterns just as they are may allow problems to continue unaddressed. In our modern high-pressure, multitasking world, bodies often manifest unhealthy patterns of constricted, shallow respiration. This is particularly associated with certain postures (slumped over, or wearing tight clothes over clenched tummies) and with "chest breathing," which develops as we age and is associated with sympathetic nervous system (fight-or-flight) activation. Chest breathing, which does not make use of the large diaphragm muscle, tends to be rapid, shallow, characterized by insufficient oxygenation and unnecessary adrenaline and cortisol release. This has been correlated with a number of stress-related disease patterns, both acute and chronic. Such breathing is contrasted with "diaphragmatic" or "abdominal" breathing, which leads to a much fuller lung expansion and oxygenation. Sometimes disordered breathing also constitutes a disease state in itself, as with chronic obstructive pulmonary disease (COPD)—often involving bronchitis or emphysema—making it difficult to get enough air.

Learning to deepen and direct our breathing can thus be essential to disease control and prevention. For example, sufferers of COPD can train in techniques to improve respiratory efficiency, such as pursed lips and diaphragmatic breathing. More broadly, Dr. Herbert Benson advocated the use of the "relaxation response," which employs the breath along with the use of calming words and images as a no-cost, noninvasive treatment for a wide range of diseases, including cardiovascular chest pain, anxiety and depression, hypertension, infertility, hot flashes, migraines, and chronic pain (Benson and Proctor 2010; Brown and Gerbarg 2009, 54–62). In the words of James Gordon, a professor of psychiatry at George Washington University, "Slow, deep breathing is probably the single best anti-stress medicine we have. . . . Heart rate slows, blood pressure decreases, muscles relax, anxiety eases and the mind calms" (Krucoff 2000, 14). Similarly, Andrew Weil, a professor of medicine at the University of Arizona, and a leader in the field of integrative medicine, calls breathing

> the simplest and most powerful technique you can use for protecting your health. I have seen breath control alone achieve remarkable results: lowering blood pressure, ending heart arrhythmias, improving long-standing patterns of poor digestion, increasing blood circulation throughout the body, decreasing anxiety . . . and improving sleep and energy cycles. (Krucoff 2000, 15)

If such statements are to be believed, we have free and immediate access to a powerful health restorative, though many of us fail to use it. Again, our breathing patterns tend toward the unconscious and involuntary—unless we use breath-as-hinge to intentionally open the door to healing.

Directions on how to work with the breath vary according to teacher and practice. Benson counsels simply breathing "slowly and naturally" to evoke the relaxation response (Benson and Proctor 2010, 9). This may be easier said than done. For Western adults, habitual breathing patterns may be far from "natural," if that word refers to the far healthier abdominal breathing often seen in babies and young children, when the belly swells on each in-breath.

As mentioned, "mindfulness" approaches favor cultivating an awareness of the breath without trying to judge or transform it in any way (Kornfield 1993, 60–63). There are other spiritual practices—for example, those from the Hindu pranayama tradition—that emphasize a variety of voluntary interventions, including ones that render the inhalation and exhalation even in length; prolong one or the other, or the pause between them; emphasize nasal breathing, either deliberately balanced or unbalanced between the nostrils; develop diaphragmatic "full-body" breath; direct the breath-energy up and down the spinal chakras or follow it entirely out of the body on exhalation; or associate the breath with a mantra, chanting, or imagery. Sometimes these are designed as time-limited meditation practices, but they can also serve to re-pattern our habitual form of breathing. These approaches would be examples of healing strategies described earlier that involve *caring* for the body by *transforming* its patterns of usage.

Yet, we have seen that healing strategies have limits and shadow-sides. Practicing a breath-control technique for twenty minutes a day may be ineffective in changing long-term unconscious habits. In fact, such techniques can even do harm, instituting artificial patterns (holding your breath, forcing your breath) that take us farther away from any "natural" rhythm. To find the latter, the yoga teacher Donna Farhi advocates a kind of Aristotelian mean:

> At one end of the spectrum is the unconscious, involuntary breath; at the other end is breathing that is controlled and regulated by the will, such as the classic breathing exercises done by yogis. Between these two extremes lies the "essential" breath, a conscious flow that arises out of the depth of our being and dissolves effortlessly back into our core. . . . To access this essential breath, we must first be able to focus on and perceive our own breathing process; that is, we must make the unconscious conscious. (Farhi 1996, 9)

As the quote suggests, the two hinges we have been exploring—that between the breath as conscious/unconscious, and as voluntary/involuntary—are closely related. Problems, Farhi suggests, can arise when the hinge swings too far in either direction. She suggests using what we have termed "inside insights" to arrive at balanced essential breath.

Physical Dialectics: The "Where" of Breath

Due to its centrality in sustaining life, our breathing operates through a number of paired systems, which are in some ways both redundant and complementary. Here too we see the hinge structure at play. For example, as we have mentioned, we can inhale primarily through the nose or the mouth, and with an emphasis on the chest muscles or the large diaphragmatic muscle that separates chest and abdomen. (The mechanics of breathing are of course far more complex, but we will work here with a simplified treatment.) In a certain sense, either member of these pairs "can get the job done," but not all usage patterns are created equal. The nose has certain particle filters for dust and allergens that the mouth lacks. The large diaphragm can open up greater lower lung capacity, and more efficient oxygenation than a breath that is mostly reliant on chest muscle contractions. And a combination of nasal inhalation with abdominal deep breathing tends to trigger the vagus nerve and parasympathetic nervous system, slowing the heart rate, relaxing sphincters, increasing intestinal and glandular activity, and often calming the mind. As mentioned, the yogic tradition also invokes another dialectic—that between the two nostrils. These are believed to be the terminus point for paired energy channels (*iḍa* on the left, *pingala* on the right), each with its different properties that together need rebalancing. Hence the practice of *Naḍi Shodhana* (Feuerstein 1997, 127, 194–95, 219–20), that is, alternate nostril breathing.

Thus, the development and healing of dis-ease is related to the physical dialectics of respiration, though these are recruited differently by various medical and spiritual systems. The emphasis might be on swinging breath more toward one pole than another (e.g., diaphragmatic rather than chest breathing); incorporating the fullness of the spectrum (as in the yogic "three-part" breath, with a progressive abdominal, chest, and clavicular component); or in establishing balance, as in alternate nostril practices (Krucoff 2013, 42–43; Lewis 1997, 33).

While speaking of the physical dialectics of respiration, it is helpful to reclarify that it is the *lived body* that breathes, not simply an objectified correlate. There is thus first-person experience of where breath takes place, which may differ from a third-person scientific analysis of respiration. In some cultures, this borderline is porous. We see this, for example, in the Indian accounts of *praṇa*, and the Chinese focus on qi: these life energies associated with the breath follow pathways through a "subtle body" that can be mapped from outside (though not in ways that correspond to a Western paradigm), but also felt and guided from within.

More generally, breathing techniques can be performed, and experienced, virtually anywhere. We can experience breathing from, or to, any part of our body. A meditation practice that I employ involves following the breath upward on inhalation, and on exhalation down into the sacrum, or lower body—though this seems to reverse the Western account of respiratory physiology. In the next chapter, I will discuss a Chinese qigong practice which uses the breath and visualization to direct universal vital energies toward any body part in need, which proved extremely helpful with my own neuropathy. I have also learned to expand awareness by breathing "outside my body"—for example, three feet to the left or right of where I stand. This may not seem to be physiologically possible, but phenomenologically it is and can prove quite expansive.

The In and Out

This brings us to breath as a hinge between the inner and outer. Of course, respiration functions by always swinging between these two poles. This constant communication of the within and without, of receiving and returning, is at the heart of our organic survival. If we're deprived of this exchange even for a brief while, we die. Again, this point can be brought home by a brief experiment: *Stop breathing right now, say for 60–90 seconds. How does it feel?* You may find yourself gasping for air, but with a renewed appreciation of the larger forces that sustain us.

Much else that is characteristic of human life rides along with this movement of air through our body (E. Straus 1952b, 674–95). Like our animal cousins, we can sniff the air, noting the scents of potential predators and prey, terrain, and weather—or in the modern world, of alluring foods, as well as toxic gas fumes. On the out-breath we use our mouth to shape air into meaningful sounds—words that label the things around us, communicate with others, voice our prayers, and sing forth our songs. Then too, our words, subvocalized, become one of the primary bases for our sense of an "inner mind" engaged in private monologue. Earlier, we called this the *superior interior*, an experiential source of Cartesian mind–body dualism, even though our thoughts have an embodied source (Leder 1990, 121–25). And the sounds we make, when transcribed into written signs, become reproducible and transmittable across space and time, allowing for the development of complex human science and cultures. Yet this all began with the simple act of breathing in and out.

This balance of in and out is central to some of the healing practices we have already been discussing. As modern Westerners we are often reminded to breathe more deeply, yet *trying to* do this through intensifying inhalation can have a paradoxically opposite effect as we constrict muscles in our effort to suck in more air (Lewis 1997, 41). Some teachers emphasize instead lengthening exhalation. By emptying the lungs more fully the next inhalation naturally deepens. But this hardly touches on the variety of techniques taught by ancient and contemporary traditions that play with the in-out hinge. For example, in yogic practices, *kapalabhati,* or "skull-shining breath," employs fast, vigorous exhalations to cleanse the sinuses and respiratory passages, improve circulation, tone muscles and visceral organs, and calm the mind. In "against-the-grain breath" (*viloma pranayama*), both inhalations and exhalations are broken into a series of brief steps and pauses, thereby intensifying our breath awareness and control. Various kinds of "ratio breathing" teach one to maintain inhalations and exhalations for specific counts, either to deliberately equalize their length (*sama-vritti*) or to establish unequal ratios (*visama-vritti*), each with its own benefits (Rosen 2002, 227–53).

In any case, the cycle of inhalation and exhalation reminds us that our breathing and our lived body are self-transcending and thoroughly interdependent with the universe as a whole. Western science shows that we are sustained by breathing in the oxygen released by plant life, and then exhaling carbon dioxide, an essential nutrient for plants. And as Lewis writes (1997, 9): "For the *Daoist,* breathing, when it is natural, helps open us to the vast scales of heaven and earth—to the cosmic alchemy that takes place when the radiations of the sun interact with the substances of the earth to produce the energies of life." Breathing well is not just a personal but a communal and planetary affair, expanding our notion of the "healing body" beyond conventional limits.

In Tibetan Buddhism, *tonglen* meditations use the in/out hinge of the breath as an instrument for the development and expression of expansive compassion. One imagines oneself as breathing in the suffering of specific others (sometimes visualized as a dark or hot smoke), and then breathing out to them a sense of spaciousness, positive energy, or specific gifts that would bring relief (Chödrön 1994, 38–39). This well-wishing breath can gradually be extended to all suffering sentient creatures. This also helps relieve our own suffering: as we have seen, in *giving,* we ourselves *receive* healing, an experiential hinge whereby self and other are interconnected.

For Zen Buddhists, the simple awareness of breath flow can help us awaken from the delusion of the isolated self, that fundamental source of our sufferings. In attending to the hinge of the in-breath and out-breath, we see that all is in flux and interconnected at every moment. There simply is no solid, stable, and separate "I." In the words of Shunryu Suzuki:

> When we practice zazen [seated meditation] our mind always follows our breathing. When we inhale, the air comes into the inner world. When we exhale, the air goes out to the outer world. The inner world is limitless, and the outer world is also limitless. We say "inner world" or "outer world," but actually there is just one whole world. In this limitless world, our throat is like a swinging door. The air comes in and goes out like someone passing through a swinging door. If you think, "I breathe," the "I" is extra. There is no you to say "I." What we call "I" is just a swinging door which moves when we inhale and when we exhale. (S. Suzuki 1970, 29)

The Zen teacher Thich Nhat Hanh recognizes the ecological implications of this body–world reciprocity. He writes of the sun as "the great heart outside of our body," pumping energy to all life, and the forests as "our lungs outside of our bodies" (Hanh 1991, 103–6). When we cut the forests down, or poison them with acid rain, we are damaging our very own body. The deeper we penetrate within ourselves, the more we discover the totality of the external universe, including the exploding supernovae, so distant in space and time, from which our carbon atoms were created. This, then, is a profound corollary of the "inside-out" nature of the body we have been investigating in this book's part 3.

That the body is "inside-out" is one reason why the personal is political and vice versa. For example, during the Covid-19 epidemic, many individuals and government officials exhibited a fierce resistance to wearing masks. Though irrational in ignoring the science of disease transmission, this can be understood as a "visceral" response; after all, masks may seem to *restrict one's very breathing* (even if this is not physiologically the case). To some it can feel as if the government is wrapping itself around their very mouth and nose, choking off their ability to breathe freely.

Perhaps on the other end of the political spectrum, we see the Black Lives Matter movement adopting as its slogan, "I can't breathe." Eric Garner was under suspicion of selling loose cigarettes on a street in Staten Island. When not immediately compliant with a police order to stop, he was put in a chokehold and thrown to the ground, his face pressed into the pavement. Restrained by four officers, eleven times he gasped out those words, "*I can't breathe*" before losing consciousness, never to regain it. The medical examiner ruled his death a homicide caused by compression of the neck and chest while under police restraint.

"I can't breathe" not only recalled Eric Garner's fate but serves as a metaphor for the experience of Black people in the United States in ways we explored in chapter 6. George Yancy recalls the case of Eric Harris, a Black male shot in the back supposedly by accident. With a police officer's knee on his head, Harris was heard to scream, "Oh my God, I'm losing my breath." As Yancy writes, "That plea was met with a ruthless response: 'Fuck your breath'. . . . the callous and haunting articulation of a form of contempt, in this case, for Black male life" (Yancy 2017, 3–4).

Even outside of overtly violent interactions, racism, as embodied injustice, can make it hard to breathe. When living under the threat of hostile gazes and discriminatory treatment, one can constantly feel as if in a chokehold, as if pressed to the pavement. The fight-or-flight shallow breathing and hormone-release characteristic of anger or anxiety can then become a low-level chronic reality, leading to physiological stressors like high blood pressure, with the risk of consequent disease or premature death.

Then too, there is the issue of inferior air quality distributed according to race and social class. A Johns Hopkins study found that 17 percent of black children and 20 percent of Puerto Rican children exhibited asthma, compared with just 10 percent of white children (Keet et al. 2015). This could not simply be attributed to living in urban environments. Rather, race, ethnicity, and income seemed to be key factors in determining who suffered from asthmatic coughing, wheezing, and breathlessness. Roach and other pest allergens, indoor smoke, and air pollution may have played a part, and of course, these are not equitably distributed in our society. For example, environmentally "dirty" incinerators and factories are far more likely to be located in poor and minority areas. Real estate is cheaper there. Moreover, the residents may not have the political clout—the ability to make campaign contributions or call up friends in the mayor's office—to have such projects stopped or relocated. The effects of global climate change and pollution are also often worse in more vulnerable or impoverished countries, and many of the most "unbreathable" cities are in India, China, Saudi Arabia, and Bangladesh.

Smoking—one of the worst causes of breathing difficulties and diseases, including bronchitis, emphysema, and lung cancer—also has a sociopolitical dimension. In the United States there is a growing gap between the affluent, who have seen a sharp drop in smoking rates, and poor and working-class communities where there has been far less of a decline. Ali H. Mokdad, author of a key study on the issue, says, "Smoking is leaving these fancy places, these big urban areas . . . but it has remained in these poor and rural areas. They are getting left behind" (Tavernise and Gebeloff 2014).

Not only racism and poverty, but sexism can lead to breathing disorders. For many centuries Western women were pressured (literally as well as metaphorically) into corsets and girdles that flattened the tummy while severely restricting breathing. An ideal of the "beautiful body" took precedence over its proper functioning, privileging the "object body" subordinated to the male gaze over the "subject body" of the woman herself. Even today, there is pressure to choose beauty over comfort. A flat stomach and tight jeans are fashionable for women, and demands are growing for men to have "six-pack abs"—though guys still are given far more leeway for paunch.

Sometimes we think of political issues like "freedom" and "equality" in abstract terms which apply to us as "citizens." But these also apply to us as *bodies*, as beings who breathe. Are we physically and psychologically able to breathe freely? Do we have equal access to clean and healthy air? We are reminded of the embodied nature of our democratic ideals by Emma Lazarus's poem engraved on the plaque at the Statue of Liberty:

> "Keep, ancient lands, your storied pomp!" cries she
> With silent lips. "Give me your tired, your poor,
> Your huddled masses yearning to breathe free . . ."

Movement and Stillness

We have been examining the hinge of the in-out exchange involved in breathing, including its cosmological and political dimensions. But we should pause to note that breathing also embodies—a pause. There is the flow of air on inhalation and exhalation, yes, but between them there is a rest, a moment that can be infinitesimal . . . or deliberately extended to great length . . . . wherein the breath becomes *still.* There are two moments, actually: the pause after inhalation has peaked, but before exhalation—the midpoint of a breath—and the pause at the end of exhalation before the next breath is taken. Certain traditions work deeply not only with the movement of breath, but with these moments of stillness.

This can be used for health purposes—lengthening the breath pauses can facilitate relaxation, and a deeper in-breath as the need for oxygen builds. But certain meditation practices also use these pauses as portals to awakening. In Buddhist terms, the "form" of breath movement is seen to arise from and disappear into the "formless." In the Hindu tradition this gap, suspending movement and thought, provides a gateway to a deep *samadhi* state. Swami Muktananda teaches the ancient Upanishadic use of the mantra *hamsa,* which, while having certain Sanskrit meanings associated with liberation, is also said to be the sound the breath itself makes, and therefore a natural mantra repeated within us thousands of times every day since birth.

> When the breath comes in with the sound *haṃ* and merges inside, there is a fraction of a moment that is completely still and free of thought. This is the *madhyadeśa*, the space between the breaths. This is where you have to focus in meditation. To focus on that space is the highest meditation and the highest knowledge. That still space between the breaths, that space where no thoughts exist, is the true goal of the mantra. It is a miraculous space. . . . the space of God, of Supreme Consciousness, of the Self. (Muktananda 1992, 38)

With a Western focus on productive activity, we may view our breathing as simply the constant movement of goods coming in and waste products eliminated. Efficiency is key for the Cartesian body-as-machine. But we then risk overlooking the physical/spiritual significance of those moments of stillness which the breath arises from and to which it ever returns.

The Visible and Invisible

This opens up consideration of a final hinge intrinsic to breathing, and one key to spiritual traditions: that between the visible and invisible. Our breath seems to hover in a liminal space. We can feel our breath, and even see it if, for example, we blow on a piece of paper. Yet the breath, of itself, remains invisible (unless it's particularly cold out). It has no weight, color, or measurable size, unlike the rest of our fleshy body. It can thus seem *almost disembodied* in its thin materiality, though it is the very principle keeping the body alive. When breath departs, vitality goes with it, and we are left with an inert corpse.

This is one reason why the Greek word *psyche,* and the Latin *anima* and *spiritus,* which could be translated as "soul" or "spirit," all derive from the word for "breath." These concepts have been interpreted in diverse ways, by Aristotle in *De Anima* and Plato in the *Phaedo* and the *Republic.* Any detailed analysis of this is beyond the bounds of this work. Suffice it to say that the soul can be conceptualized either as the living principle that animates a body, or as what we might call "mind" or "spirit," which is potentially separable from the body, and eternal. From whence comes this sense of a soul–body split? It is reasonable to infer that *respiration*—so integral to life, and yet invisible, almost immaterial—was one phenomenological *inspiration* leading to Greco-Christian, and then Cartesian, modes of dualism with the notion of a spirit that animates, but which is also separable from, the body. The invisible breath thus can be associated not only with corporeal life but also, paradoxically, with a disincarnate realm. The breath appears/disappears, seems material/immaterial, is of this world but otherworldly, in its invisible comings and goings.

This chapter, indeed this book as a whole, has had a focus on preventing or recovering from bodily illness. But a certain kind of otherworldly dualism implies that embodied life is intrinsically a kind of illness, that which plunges the soul into painful limitation. With Socrates's last words he is said to have asked that a cock be sacrificed to Asclepius, the Greek god of healing (Plato 1993, 185). Nietzsche (1954, 272) writes, "This ridiculous and terrible 'last word' means for those who have ears: 'O, Crito, *life is a disease*'. . . . Socrates, Socrates *suffered life*." From this point of view, it is not breath which relieves disease, but the *cessation* of breath which does so.

This is indeed a dualistic position articulated at times by Plato's Socrates—that the philosopher's soul frees itself from the prison of the body first by intellectual contemplation of the Forms and then, ultimately, by physical death. In this book's last chapter I reject this point of view, while retaining sympathy for a kind of transcendent impulse that carries us beyond the body, at least as usually conceived and experienced. However, I will suggest that this spiritual urge is best approached not through the lens of dualism but through a rigorous *non-dual* pathway. This path is already suggested by the breath itself, which forms a hinge between inside and outside, self and other, and the realms of the visible and invisible.

10

The Transparent Body

An exploration of the potential non-duality of inside and outside, self and other, even life and death, brings us to the final chapter of this book. In the first chapter I wrote not only of the sense of "impossibility" that can attend bodily incapacities, and the spirit of "I'm possibility" that can allow for healing transformations, but also how bodily breakdown can open onto the "'I am' possibility"—that is, the idea of an "I am" (as the biblical God, Ex. 3:14, said his name was "*I am that I am*") that outruns the egoic body–mind complex. What is this "I am" experience?

This question was echoed in the healing strategy of *transcendence* discussed in chapter 2. Among the modes of transcendence—intellectual, escapist, artistic—that sick people use to escape bodily confines, is a spiritual sense of connection to a transpersonal reality. This also relates to other elements on the "chessboard" of healing strategies discussed earlier; for example, the sense of *witnessing* without involvement; *transforming* our habitual ways; a sense of (timeless) *presence*; and of *communing* with others, *giving* and *receiving* beyond our sense of separated identity.

However, at a certain point this sense of a transpersonal reality threatens to upend the metaphorical chessboard previously outlined. That is, it resists confinement to our customary mode of embodiment and the moves it makes possible. A chessboard is essentially a two-dimensional square surface. But in reality this board exists in a larger three-dimensional world that overleaps its limits. What if we could move entirely off the board, for example by escaping vertically?

The book will conclude with a discussion of a "transparent body"—one no longer considered as the bedrock of separate identity so much as a conduit to a transpersonal Whole, drawing fully on the body's "inside-out" nature. This could be considered as a last, or *twenty-first* healing strategy. Alternatively, as said, one could consider this as more than just another strategy within the game. After all, vertical movement doesn't exist as a sanctioned play in the rules of chess—we have left the match behind. That is the sense of those who have "awakened," having discovered that the whole game was illusory, including the entrapment of illness, impairment, and mortality (Yogananda 1986, 169). In many spiritual and philosophic traditions, this awareness is considered the ultimate healing, not only *of* the body but *from* the body.

Before proceeding with an analysis of this "twenty-first strategy which is beyond all strategies," it may be helpful to introduce an autobiographical note. I have long been attracted to various Asian traditions and have read, taught, and used practices drawn from Daoism, Buddhism, and Hinduism. These, along with my work in the 12-step program, have opened up a number of spiritual experiences that challenged my customary assumptions about reality. In my own explorations I have been most drawn to Advaita (non-dual) Vedanta as first articulated in the Upanishads of ancient India. ("Vedanta" means the "end of the Vedas," and the Upanishads are the "last" or most recent texts in the Vedas.) This will be the initial focus here, though toward the end I will increasingly turn to Buddhist and Daoist material, as well as briefly refering to key figures in the Western tradition such as Descartes and Kant.

As such, this chapter will be both more philosophically technical and spiritually expansive than previous ones. I want to proceed with great care, step by step, especially because we are venturing into seemingly "mystical" territory. If this is not of interest to the reader, one may omit this chapter entirely, or at least skip to the closing sections where I speak of cultivating the "transparent body" and its direct help with "non-dual bodily healing."

While, as mentioned, I found myself most drawn to Advaitic teachings, I also found them most problematic. My philosophical work has largely focused on the import of the lived body. Advaitic teachings, however, emphasize *disassociation from the body.* This is not because the body can interfere with, or distract us, from the workings of the rational mind—that Platonic critique so influential in the West. From the Vedantic point of view, the ordinary rational mind is just as problematic as the body, nor are mind and body genuinely separated. Our mind–body-generated thoughts, perceptions, and desires all lead us to see ourselves as finite beings separated from an external world. But in truth, according to Vedanta, our deepest consciousness and identity participate in a unitary, world-inclusive, unlimited Being. When probed from within, we discover that the true Self or Atman is none other than Brahman (divine energy). This realization is recorded in the *Chandogya Upanishad* (Easwaran 1987, 119–52) and elsewhere through the repeated invocation: *tat tvam asi,* "you are That!"

"Advaita" means non-dual: there is no true separation between self and other, or between self, world, and God. Of course, in its own way, a phenomenology of the lived body also embraces non-dualism. Recent chapters, exploring the inside-out nature of interoception and breathing, have pointed toward profound mind-body and self-world interconnections. Perhaps "healing," most broadly conceived, is about healing those rifts between "mind" and "body," "self" and "world," and even "self" and "God" which are so characteristic of our modern world, and which manifest as physical, psychological, and spiritual dis-ease. In this chapter, we are thus not abandoning the theme of this book, embodied healing, but seeking to open it to its farthest horizons.

We will do so by examining, paradoxical as it may sound, *the duality of two forms of non-dualism.* One form, derived from phenomenology, emphasizes the centrality of embodiment, whereas Advaitic non-dualism resolutely decenters our embodiment. We had a foreshadowing of this in chapter 2 when we investigated experiences that *I am* my body, but also ones that *I have* a body separable from the true self. The former intuition led toward strategies of "embracing the body," while the latter led toward those that focus on "escaping the body." We now reencounter this question not simply on the therapeutic, but on the ontological plane. Who or what am I really: a limited body, or transcendent being shining in and through my flesh?

At this point it may legitimately be said that we have gone beyond the bounds of phenomenology, since that approach "brackets" off any metaphysical presumptions or conclusions. It is true that this chapter is written more in the mode of speculative inquiry, taking off from but not adhering exclusively to phenomenological description. However, it is worth noting that the later Merleau-Ponty (1968) in his unfinished writings on "the flesh," and Heidegger throughout his works, were not afraid to connect lived experience with ontological reflection. Perhaps there is no experience that doesn't arise from, or lead toward, some intuition of the nature of reality itself.

I have noted that the phenomenology of a Merleau-Ponty tends to emphasize the ways I am my body, while Vedanta teaches that I am not; it might seem that if one view is correct, the other is simply wrong. But perhaps this itself is a dualistic way of thinking—that there is a simple yes/no, right/wrong dichotomy at play. When probing more deeply, we can find sympathies of spirit and method between the two approaches. Both paths seek to surpass conventional dualisms by a return to "the things themselves," to employ Husserl's phrase, that is, the evidence provided by immediate experience. Without trying to deny their conflict, I will also suggest ways in which these systems complement and supplement each other.

In this discussion I am especially indebted to a set of "direct path" teachings, particularly those of Rupert Spira (2016). For those interested, he is in a lineage going back to Ramana Maharshi (1988), Nisargadatta Maharaj (1973), and Krishna Menon Atmananda (1978) in India, and routed in the West through Jean Klein (2006) and Francis Lucille (2006).

In the tradition of the ancient *jnana yoga* (yoga of wisdom) dating back to the Upanishads, "direct path" teachings tend to (a) strip away the cultural baggage of ancient India or other spiritual systems; (b) focus on direct experiences which are immediately accessible to all, rather than esoteric spiritual states; and (c) render central an inquiry into the true nature of the self, with "Who am I?" considered the crucial question. Particularly in the cases of Klein, Lucille, and Spira, Vedantic elements are also supplemented by practices influenced by hatha yoga and Kashmir Shaivism which focus on the body as central to liberatory experience. These teachings help to move past the facile dichotomy between identifying as a body or rejecting the body, and frame the journey to physical and spiritual healing as dialectical in nature.

But how to begin this dialectical examination? In my first book, *The Absent Body*, I found it fruitful to investigate the various ways in which the body absents itself from experience despite, or actually because of, its centrality in human life. I will similarly enter here through an exploration of radical absence—in this case, a *zero point* or *null-point*. This will take us through a series of onto-experiential reflections, after which we will reflect on its direct relevance to healing.

The Cartesian and Phenomenological Null-point

Edmund Husserl, the founder of phenomenology, did much groundbreaking work on the lived body that is sometimes overlooked by scholarship, focused as it has been on his other contributions. In *Ideas II*, Husserl writes that

> all spatial being necessarily appears in such a way that it appears either nearer or farther, above or below, right or left. . . . Body then has, for its particular Ego, the unique distinction of bearing in itself the zero point [*nullpunkt*] of all these orientations. One of its spatial points, even if not an actually seen one, is also always characterized in the mode of ultimate central here. (Husserl 1989, 166)

That is, wherever we go, here we are. As we change positions, the lifeworld rotates around us: what was left is now right, what was near is now far, but our body always remains as the orientational zero point of the sensorimotor field. Edward Casey comments:

> Husserl adverts to the geometric idea of the null or zero point in a deliberate if ironic borrowing from Descartes. Just as the zero point in analytic geometry (i.e., the point where the X, Y, and Z axes coincide) is posited as stationary and invariant, so my body as *Nullpunkt* has the peculiar property of seeming always unmoving in relation to the surrounding world. (Casey 1997, 218)

We thus have two related but contrasting conceptions of the null-point. The concept employed in Cartesian geometry relates to an idealized physical world in which everything has a measurable extension. Any point in the mathematical world, or the material world it refers to, can be chosen as the zero point of orientation. For example, in hanging a painting I can measure my zero point, perhaps one equidistant between two side walls, make a pencil dot there, and use this to position the artwork. I thus use geometry to align the material world.

But in hanging that painting I probably chose to place it at or near eye-level. I am thus reminded of my lived body, that subjective null-point which orients my experienced world. Of course, the eyes with which I see the painting and its surroundings never themselves appear in the visual field they survey. This is another meaning present in the metaphor of the null-point. Putting aside for a moment any mirror phenomena, our eyes are what we see *from*; they are the origin of our visual field, and thus we do not see them as objects within that field (Polanyi 1969, 138–58).

Descartes's null-point of analytic geometry is embedded in his dualist metaphysics. Excluding all attributes of consciousness which belong to *res cogitans*, the physical world remains as sheer *res extensa* to be characterized mathematically (Descartes 1911). In this world, which lays the groundwork for the Newtonian conception of absolute space, there is no natural null-point insofar as any point can serve equally in that role. Of course, the notion of a "point" is itself a mathematical abstraction; it has nullity at its heart, for it is without physical dimension.

The phenomenological notion of the embodied null-point is appreciably different. It undoes the dualism of *res extensa* and *res cogitans* insofar as it is a zero point associated with our bodily position in space, and thus orients an experiential, not a strictly material world. Our subjectivity is corporeal and vice versa. Our body is not simply a physical thing in the world, or a mathematical abstraction, but that which perceives, and that perception is vectored by desire, motility, active goals. In Casey's words again, this phenomenological null-point represents a "deliberate if ironic borrowing from Descartes," but now used in a way that is *non-mathematical, non-dualist, and therefore anti-Cartesian.*

The Null-point in Advaita Vedanta

Advaita Vedantic teachings provide yet a third reading of the null-point. They suggest that our primordial Awareness can neither be captured by a physicalist description of the world nor identified with the lived body. The body, after all, is a limited object that is changing over time like other worldly things. Interoceptions, kinesthesias, and visual images of the body appear in our consciousness, and are identified as part of our "self." Other experienced things—that book over there, the sky glimpsed through a window—we label as the "outside world," and therefore as "non-self." But from the Vedantic perspective this sense of a multiplicity of separate objects and subjects is deceptive, a kind of *maya*, or "illusion," that obscures the fundamental unity of the field of Awareness within which the world manifests. *However, that Awareness represents a null-point at the heart of experience*; it can nowhere be located as a limited thing since it underlies and outruns all particular experiences. (I will only sparingly employ religious language like Atman, Brahman, or God, and will prefer instead the term "Awareness," with its links to personal experience, though the capitalization suggests that it grounds but also transcends that of the individual mind.)

One analogy for the field of Awareness is that of a TV, computer, or movie screen (Spira 2008). These screens allow for an indefinite range of images to flash across their surface. The screen disappears insofar as it itself is not visible in the movie. It cannot be identified with any object, or even subject, therein. It is not the hero of the movie, even if the hero is often on-screen and the film is also filled with POV (point-of-view) shots from that hero's perspective. Something similar might apply to our embodied self. It appears as the hero of our life story. Moreover, the lived body can be compared to the camera which yields the POV shots by which the surrounding world is seen from a particular perspective. Nonetheless, the body is still not the "screen" of Awareness in which all worldly images are projected. Of course, when absorbed in a movie we suspend disbelief, that we may better immerse ourselves in its plot (Yogananda 1986, 114–15); similarly in life we are caught in *maya*, an illusion comparable to being lost in a movie. (To complete this metaphor, we have to somehow imagine an *aware* screen, not simply an insensate stretch of vinyl observed by others.)

Just as the notion of the lived body as null-point drew on, but ironically reversed, its Cartesian meaning, this Vedantic null-point can be said to draw on, but ironically reverse, the lived body as null-point. Phenomenologically, we said that the perceiving eye orients us but absents itself from the visual field, rooted as it is in the limitations of being embodied. There is no "view from nowhere" (Nagel 1989): we always see from a particular perspective, glimpsing what lies in front of us but not what is behind us, nor our eyes themselves. But what of the Vedantic "I," the Awareness which underlies all that we witness? It too is an experiential null-point—not because it is rooted in a limited body, but because it is *unlimited*, beyond all bodily form. It might be called the Formless, Emptiness (*sūnyatā* in Buddhism), Consciousness, Brahman. That which is formless allows all form to manifest, just as the blank screen allows an indefinite number of movies to be shown. Awareness is thus a kind of *null-point* (absence) that is also *all-points* (presence), since it is both everywhere and nowhere in particular to be found.

The Nowhere as Now-Here

By a pleasing coincidence, the English word *nowhere* can be broken down alphabetically into *now* and *here*; this provides an avenue for further probing the structure of Awareness. First, we can notice that all of our personal awareness unfolds in the *now.* No one has ever lived a single moment in the past or future, though memory and anticipation may form part of our present experience. Even people in the seventeenth century didn't live in the "past" despite what we learned in history class. They inhabited their present, that is, with the same experience of the living *now* that illuminates every moment of our own existence.

Moreover, we always find ourselves not only *now* but *here.* I became particularly aware of this when traveling through China with my daughter on a whirlwind trip. Whatever room, city, or region I awoke in, which was hard to keep track of, I was nonetheless always right *here* to myself and the surroundings, even before I had a clear idea of where we were geographically.

We saw that for Husserl our perception is oriented by the lived body as null-point, which he calls "the ultimate central here" (1989, 166) from which objects appear as near or far. But, taking an Advaitic turn, we could call everything we experience *equally here, equally near.* In a film, an actor we see in the foreground, or a mountain pictured in the deep background, are actually on the same plane of the screen, and are in truth equidistant from the observer. The magic of the movies has simply created a spatial illusion. Similarly, all of our experiences at any given moment could be said to be equally present *right here,* even if we tend to read them through the lens of dispersion. That is, my sense of bodily fatigue, the thoughts in my mind, the computer I stare at, the trees and birdsong outside, are all equally right *here* within my awareness. When discarding conditioned dualities, investigation also reveals all of this as a *unified field.* I can shift my attention from my bodily sensation of fatigue to my thoughts without ever encountering a border that separates "body" from "mind." I can then allow my attention to drift to the birdsong outside my window without encountering a hard border that separates "self" and "other." Consciousness thus moves freely among its sectors.

It is true that in ordinary perception, which is also shaped by our scientific understanding, we apprehend the world as composed of material forms distributed across space and time. Yet to invoke a Western referent, Kant's *Critique of Pure Reason* (1929, 65–82) suggests that "space" and "time" are actually a priori forms of intuition whereby consciousness apprehends the world. Thus, we do not dwell in space and time so much as *space and time dwell within us,* structuring our experience of a determinate world.

Realizing this not just conceptually but experientially—as I will later explore—involves a gestalt flip akin to that found with perceptual illusions whereby you suddenly switch your sense of what is figure and ground (for example, seeing the profile of two faces versus the outline of a single vase). We can experience ourselves as one small thing within the spatiotemporal world, or flip our perception so that we sense the world as manifesting within the Self, that ever-present field of Awareness.

Kant (1929, 257–75) restricted metaphysical speculation, asserting that we could not know the thing-in-itself (noumenon) but only the thing as it appears to an experiencer (phenomenon). Vedanta would beg to differ by suggesting that there are yogic modes of knowledge whereby we can come to know the true nature of reality. Often, these yogas are thought of as involving long-term strenuous practices that finally make available special mystical revelations. But "direct path" teachings suggest that these truths are always already there, if overlooked, in the midst of ordinary experience.

After all, we have suggested that experientially the *now* is a realm we always abide in, not just an infinitesimal moment on a timeline. While the clock hands continue to rotate or the digital numbers flip, we always remain rooted in the *now* whose stillness and constancy allow us to apprehend temporal flow, like someone sitting on the bank apprehends a river rushing by. That is, the ever-present *now* is what allows us to experience the *new*—the constant change and impermanence of all worldly things (a central focus of Buddhist teachings).

In this view, the *now* we always inhabit—as opposed to the "time-right-now," a moment registered by a clock—could thus be called "eternal." This term does not imply something everlasting in time but something atemporal, outside of time, since Awareness is the place within which time makes its appearance. Similarly, the experiential *here* is not a Cartesian point in space or a limited place. Instead, the lived *here* of experience could be said to be "in-finite"—that is, it doesn't have measurable dimensions like a bounded, finite thing within the sensory field. Rather, the entirety of our sensory field always unfolds within the *here*.

Of course, "eternal" and "infinite" are often qualities attributed to the Divine. This "direct path" phenomenology suggests a way to make sense of the Upanishadic teaching that the true self, or Atman, is a manifestation of Brahman. The skeptical reader need not agree with this conclusion; I have no desire to persuade, just explore. Nonetheless, this exploration suggests that a "mystical" viewpoint can emerge directly from the phenomenology of everyday experience, not its negation.

Descartes's First and Second Meditations, which inaugurated the subjective turn in modern Western philosophy, led him to similarly unconventional territory. He too reflected on the centrality of awareness itself—*cogito ergo sum* (Descartes 1911, 144–57). Only this was indubitable, not the existence of an independent material world. Later he attempted to regain the world by demonstrating the existence of a non-deceptive God. Descartes argued that the very idea of God must prove God's actuality, since Descartes could not have derived the thought of an omnipotent, omniscient Being from within his own limited self (Descartes 1911, 157–71). (Most commentators have found this proof thoroughly unconvincing.) The Vedantic "proof" of God takes an opposite approach. It is based not on our sense of limitation, but on the discovery within the self of limitless depths, the eternal and the infinite in the sense described above.

The true Self as God? This can sound grandiose and solipsistic if we were to identify limitless Awareness with the individual self—in my case, "Drew Leder." This egoic self is clearly located in time and space, and is defined and constrained by my history, social relations, and bodily characteristics. As we have seen, experiences of illness, impairment, and aging make us particularly conscious of such limits.

Yet, according to Vedanta, the Awareness, that zero point at the heart of my experience, is not the sole possession of an individual bodymind but arises from an experiential matrix common to all. Metaphorically this situation might be compared to a set of property owners, each of whom has sunk a private water well on their land, and is thereby convinced that it is "their water" alone—though actually they are all tapping into one and the same groundwater source hidden beneath the surface. Awareness is similarly viewed as that common source we all draw upon, though it is filtered through our individual lived body. A more contemporary analogy might be the way in which, to gain access to a transpersonal internet, we nonetheless need to use our personal computer and browser.

Why would the infinite choose to manifest through these diverse, seemingly separate forms and thereby fall prey to illusion? One answer Hinduism gives is that this allows for the *lila* (play) of determinate and novel experience. Brahman needs to limit, divide, and even forget itself so that a world may manifest. To use an example from Spira, imagine we are trying to photograph a butterfly, but simultaneously from an infinite number of different perspectives as an omniscient being might—the result would simply be a blur. To photograph the butterfly effectively, a shot must be taken at a particular time and from a definite distance and angle. Similarly, infinite Awareness has to limit and localize itself in order to have the play (*lila*) of defined experience. Lived bodies enable it to view the world, which is also none other than Itself, from an indefinite variety of perspectives.

So then, yes, in a sense, there is no "view from nowhere" within embodied experience. We are always located *somewhere in particular,* using our rich but limited range of sensorimotor powers. Yet, paradoxically, Vedanta would assert that in another sense *every view is ultimately a view from nowhere*—that is, each a manifestation of the *now-here* of Aware Presence.

The Dream Body

So how to summarize the relation between a conventional phenomenology of the body, as used throughout this book, and this Vedantic orientation toward infinite Awareness? First, some commonalities between them should be noted: (1) both engage in a careful examination of experience, and are phenomenological in spirit; (2) both reject our current ruling paradigm of scientific, even eliminative, materialism; and (3) both to a degree are non-dualist analyses of experience. That is, they do away with the notion of consciousness and materiality as substances independent of each other. Though phenomenology accepts a distinction between noetic and noematic poles, both it and Vedanta challenge any firm dualisms of subject and object, self and other, perceiver and perceived, and recognize the interpenetration of these polarities.

That said, there remain clear points of opposition between these two non-dualisms. Merleau-Ponty's phenomenology centers on the corporeality of the lived body and flesh. To imagine some transcendent, immaterial consciousness is to fall into delusion. Vedanta would say the opposite—identification with the limited body-mind is itself the core delusion that keeps us trapped in suffering.

Yet I would suggest that a certain reconciliation is offered by reference to the *dream body*. Descartes famously reflects: "How often has it happened to me that in the night I dreamt that I found myself in this particular place, that I was dressed and seated near the fire, whilst in reality I was lying undressed in bed?" (Descartes 1911, 145–46). In the Sixth Meditation he finally dismisses the possibility that he might simply have been dreaming the entirety of the physical world (1911, 199)—though not for particularly persuasive reasons.

Vedantic and "direct path" teachings take more seriously the dream analogy (Spira 2008, 173–84). In Spira's words: "Awareness assumes the form of the finite mind by identifying itself with the body, through the agency of which it knows the world, in the same way that at night our own mind collapses into the mind of the dreamed character from whose point of view the dreamed world is known" (Spira 2007, 21).

To speak personally, I once had a "lucid dream"—one in which you know you are dreaming—because I was flying through the air, which I knew to be unnatural. Being a philosopher (apparently even in my sleep), I decided to test Descartes's original postulate by checking to see if this dream-world was every bit as vivid and detailed as real life. Yes, I discovered, it was!—and have ever since recalled that dream. But I'll choose another example to focus on: I recently dreamt I was on a boat traveling through India (though I've never been there in real life). When the boat docked, other people boarded or left while I stepped onto solid land. I remember getting on a train which I then discovered was going in the wrong direction, much to my distress . . . and so the dream proceeded with all the anxious vibrancy of real life.

Upon awakening I realized that the entirety of that Indian world, and the people and events that took place within it, were the product of my own sleeping consciousness. Myself as dreamer had produced the dream-Drew, a kind of avatar stand-in for self, but I had equally created all the others sitting beside "me," as well as the boat, train, and the Indian setting. All this multiplicity was but the product of a singular mind. And yet within this world I had identified, or really misidentified, with only one small part, witnessing everything from that point of view. This *dream-body* served as the null-point around which the dream-world was oriented, and through which this world was experienced. In a dream, as in a film, the "camera" has to be placed somewhere. There is almost always a virtual lived body from whose perspective a dream is witnessed.

Only upon awakening did I become aware of another experiential null-point, the most crucial of all—that is, myself, fast asleep in bed. This was my true self and had been so all along. Yet that dreamer was nowhere to be found in the dream-world he had created. I was thus in a state of delusion or ignorance until I awakened. From the Vedantic point of view, the phenomenology of the dream state should be taken seriously as a powerful clue to the way we are deluded within our usual waking reality (Yogananda 1986, 22–24).

In an ordinary dream there is but one figure who crystallizes the dreamer's viewpoint. But, as discussed in chapters 4 and 5, we deeply experience ourselves as accompanied by co-subjectivities. To adjust our metaphor, we thus need to imagine that Awareness's dream simultaneously localizes itself through a multiplicity of lived bodies. Here the movie metaphor usefully supplements, and even merges with, that of the dream. The people sitting in a theater enter a kind of shared "dream state" when the lights go out (Eberwein 2014). While watching the film together they share its simulated world, even though each member of the audience also interprets it in an individual way. In such a fashion, when awake we experience a common world even if it is always viewed from our unique embodied perspective.

The Limits of the Ultimate Medicine?

What does all this have to do with *healing*, the central theme of this book? From an Advaitic viewpoint, awakening from the delusion that our self is but a limited, decaying body is in fact the deepest source of healing possible. In Sri Nisargadatta Maharaj's words:

> So long as you identify yourself as the body, your experience of pain and sorrow will increase day by day. That is why you must give up this identification, and you should take yourself as the consciousness. If you take yourself as the body, it means you have forgotten your true Self, which is the *atman*. And sorrow results for the one who forgets himself. . . . If you identify yourself with the body, you will feel that you are dying, but in reality there is no death because you are not the body. Let the body be there or not be there, your existence is always there; it is eternal. (Nisargadatta 2001, 65)

This ultimate medicine is thus not about the healing *of* the body per se (though the relaxation that accompanies awakenings may support good health)—it is primarily focused on healing *from* the body. We come to identify not with our skin-bound form but with the Unlimited.

Yet there may be limitations involved with this move toward the Unlimited, as often conceptualized and practiced in this Advaitic tradition. I will mention three of them:

1. At times this negation of the body is accompanied by an overly negative view of its role in human affairs. We see much the same in the West, as in Socrates calling for the sacrifice of a cock to Asclepius, implying that embodied life is a kind of disease. It is also echoed in Descartes's fear of perceptual error, as well as bodily disease and death, which helps motivate his resolute dualism. Christian theology has famously often warned against the sins of the flesh. We find this too in many Eastern sources: in the words of the Theravadan Buddhist "Rhinoceros Discourse," "the body is a calamity, an excrescence, a danger, a disease, a dart of sorrow, a fear to me" (Stryk 1968, 221). Elsewhere I provide a phenomenological reading of this aversion: the body particularly calls for our attention when, like Heidegger's "broken tool," it stands forth as problematic in experiences of uncontrolled lust, perceptual error, pain, illness, or impending death. These times which force us to thematize the body may also tilt our view of it unduly toward the negative (Leder 1990, 126–48). This can surface in adverse Advaitic descriptions of the body.

2. Advaitic writings, both ancient and contemporary, can also fall prey to an overly reified view of the body. It is seen as a material object like others in the world. Even our sense of "inner experience" is said to be reducible to interoceptive and kinesthetic signals which themselves are simply objects that appear within the field of Awareness.

But this characterization of "body" may be unduly limited. Phenomenology has illuminated the profound ways that the lived body underlies our subjectivity through its perceptual-motor skills, desires, habits, tacit knowledge, and expressive and goal-oriented activities. We also explored in chapter 4 how embodied subjectivity is the root of experiences of empathy and communion. When we see pain on the face of another, we feel it within ourselves. This sense of embodied connection is enshrined in the Christian doctrine that God chose to incarnate, and the Mahayana Buddhist belief in bodhisattvas deliberately reborn into samsara so that they may relieve the suffering of all sentient creatures. Embodied existence is a much richer, multidimensional thing than is sometimes acknowledged in Advaitic teachings.

3. And finally, if, as suggested above, Advaita adopts an overly limited view of the body, focusing on the object-body rather than on the body-as-subject, this may limit the effectiveness of Advaitic liberatory methods. One such practice, both traditional and contemporary, is the *neti neti* (not this, not that) approach. One continually remembers that one is not identical to any of the limited transitory objects that surface to Awareness, including those associated with the body. Yet this *neti neti* disassociation

from the body may seem less convincing if it does not account for the full range of experiences that make one feel *I am my body*. This also suggests the dialectical possibility that after work spent on *escaping the body* (I am *not* this, *not* that) there can, and perhaps must, be a return to *embracing the body* (I *am* this, *am* that), albeit in a new, expanded way. Let us now turn in this direction as a pathway toward healing.

The Return to the Body and World

Initially, in seeking to relate a phenomenology of the body and the Advaitic perspective, we might adopt a "two truths" account that is often favored in Hinduism and Buddhism. That is, there is both a relative and an absolute description of experience, with each having its own domain of validity. Within the "relative" world of multiplicity, the phenomenological account of lived embodiment would hold. It clarifies the many ways in which the body plays a key role in constituting our subjectivity and lifeworld. But in shifting to the "absolute" perspective, we become aware of a divine Awareness analogous to the dreamer, for whom the lived body is a kind of avatar channeling consciousness. We reread the body not as the place wherein consciousness originates, but as its conduit.

However, we can also take this *structural* (relative/absolute) analysis and *temporalize* it, to illustrate dialectical progression on the path. Here I will utilize examples from Buddhist literature, seeking not to muddle diverse religions, but to clarify stages of non-dual experience and their relation to the body. A famous saying from the Zen master Ch'ing-yuan reads:

> Before I had studied Zen for thirty years, I saw mountains as mountains, and waters as waters. When I arrived at a more intimate knowledge, I came to the point where I saw that mountains are not mountains, and waters are not waters. But now that I have got its very substance I am at rest. For it's just that I see mountains once again as mountains, and waters once again as waters. (Watts 1957, 126)

One interpretation of this passage is that the non-dual path commences with a move toward the absolute that takes one away from everyday experience. The mountains are no longer seen as mountains, the waters are not waters, and we might add, my body is not "my body" anymore. This turn away from the world is also enshrined in the Vedantic *sanyassin* (renunciate) tradition. One seeks to free oneself from absorption in worldly attachments and aversions, and from a materialistic interpretation of reality. In Buddhism, a similar break with the world is particularly emphasized in the Theravadan monastic tradition.

However, Mahayana traditions (Zen is a form of Mahayana Buddhism) also encourage a movement back into the world, allowing one's insights to be integrated into everyday life. Once again, mountains are mountains, and waters are waters. A famous Zen poem reads:

> My daily activities are not different,
> Only I am naturally in harmony with them . . .
> Drawing water, carrying firewood,
> This is supernatural power, this the marvelous activity. (Smith 1991, 138)

These Buddhist references suggest the importance of re-embracing the world as part of the spiritual journey. Here, I would contend that a phenomenology of the body can be a natural ally, sharing as it does certain commonalities of insight. As Aho writes in a phenomenological vein:

> Our embodied, sensory-motor capacities constitute space, they create and open up an experiential field through which we can handle and engage with things. Understood this way, my body does not end at the skin as if I were a bounded corporeal object. It stretches beyond itself and is everywhere in my experience of the world. It extends seamlessly into the keyboard on which I type these words; it stretches to the trees and the lawn outside my office window; it reaches toward the sun and clouds in the distance. (Aho 2022, 51)

In an earlier work I called this the "ecstatic" dimension of lived embodiment (Leder 1990, 11–35). The body is self-transcendent, ever leaping beyond itself. Those who are spiritually inclined may seek extraordinary "out of body" experiences (Rogo 1983), as also reported by those who have undergone near-death experiences (Moody 1975). But it could be said that *ordinary life always already involves "out of body" experiences*: this enables Aho to sees the distant sun and create words on the keyboard. Again, we may discover that "drawing water, carrying firewood, this is supernatural power, this the marvelous activity" as our body wonderfully constitutes and gears into its world.

This self-transcendent capacity of the body is explored in phenomenology, but not really accounted for. That discipline resolutely eschews metaphysical explanations, whether materialist or idealist. But embodied self-transcendence, I would suggest, is not consistent with reductive, eliminative materialism. While hardly proving the converse, phenomenological perspectives are consonant with the possibility we have been exploring—that of a transcendent Awareness channeled through the lived body. As Spira says:

> Although you have understood that consciousness is not limited *to* your body, it does perceive *through* your body, and therefore you feel (quite rightly so) that your body is full of consciousness. But just because this room is full of space doesn't mean that the space is limited to or generated by the room. . . . [Similarly it] doesn't mean that the consciousness that your body is full of is limited to your body or generated by it. (Spira 2018, audio)

If the body is like a "room," this implies that it is located, perspectival, limited—sitting here in my office, I cannot see into other rooms. Similarly, the sensations, perceptions, thoughts, and emotions of one individual will be separated off from that of another. But the metaphor of "space" suggests that an unlimited field of Awareness might underlie all limited consciousnesses despite their manifest divisions.

What is existentially at stake here cannot be overstated. Again we return to Nisargadatta Maharaj's words: "If you identify yourself with the body, you will feel that you are dying, but in reality there is no death because you are not the body. Let the body be there or not be there, your existence is always there; it is eternal" (Nisargadatta 2006, 61). In this book on illness, aging, and inevitable death, an identification with transcendent Awareness would be, as Nisargadatta says, "the ultimate medicine" (in our words, the ultimate "healing"). This sense of wholeness is not based on the promise of eternal survival as a separate individual, or through its successive reincarnations. Rather, it suggests that identification with "the separate self" is the problem, building an imaginary prison which results in deep suffering, including the kinds explored in this book. See through its walls, experience one's Source as unlimited space, and then we realize that we have always ever been free. In Zen parlance, the self does not age and die because it was never born to begin with (Bankei 2000).

But how can we dissolve these walls without losing our appreciation of embodied life? Phenomenology itself does not usually offer specific techniques for self-development and self-awakening. However, "direct path" teachers do suggest ways to blend what we have called *escaping* and *embracing* the body, expanding our sense of the "marvelous activity" that is available in daily life.

Here, our body-mind conditioning presents an important point of resistance. We have a habitual sense of physical constriction which, as we have found, is intensified in experiences of illness and disability. We feel ourselves to be small, confined within the limits of our skin, separated from others, vulnerable, and ever progressing toward debility and death. This sense of physical limitation must be reconditioned for any sense of the Unlimited to saturate our daily life. We must transform the habitual body, rendering it more free and expansive so that unity with Self and world is not just intellectually investigated but *felt.* I will refer to this as the development of a "transparent body."

What would this mean? In the next section, I will give a suggestive personal example that leans toward an embrace of body and world, not simply their negation. Though there are many other practices we might use, this one progresses through aesthetic dematerialization and appreciation—it might be called "the artist's way." Having begun this book with Perlman's reflections on the "artist's task" to deal with embodied limits, it is appropriate to return to this theme, albeit altered in this final coda.

The Transparent Body

I am walking on a wooded path near my house, accompanied by my dogs. Having studied the teachings previously described, ones that challenge the customary belief in an independent material world, I wish to be more open-minded and open-bodied. I experiment with abandoning what in phenomenology is called the sedimented "natural attitude" in order to see the world afresh. I find it helpful here to regard my visual field as might an artist readying to paint it, or a museumgoer witnessing the result. This introduces the "witness" position favored in Advaitic teaching (Wilber 1999, 86–88) wherein one notices the field of experience, yet from a detached position. I see, as a painter might, that the path stretching ahead rises in my visual field toward a perspectival vanishing point. I witness the tree-lined trail as a play of light and shadow. After all, acquaintance with Impressionist art has taught me that shadows themselves are substantive and beautiful elements, and no less visually important than the "material objects" that cast them. Continuing my walk, I begin to have a deepening sense of the landscape's beauty. As Van Gogh wrote in a letter, "I have a terrible clarity of mind at times, when nature is so lovely these days, and then I'm no longer aware of myself, and the painting comes to me as if in a dream" (Van Gogh 2009, 284). Of course, the artist's gaze can light up plain terrains as well, like the green and red poolroom of Van Gogh's *Night Café.*

As I look around I am struck by an uncanny sense that the entirety of the world has been "painted in" without omission. I playfully search for spots of blank canvas but am unable to find them; the rich blue sky, the grass and trees dappled in multifarious shades of green—every last inch has been filled in by content. I can, however, also imagine a blank canvas lying underneath this world-painting. In a Buddhist context, this might be called *śūnyatā*, or "emptiness"; the term has many meanings, including the kind of formlessness from which all form springs (Davis 2013). In Advaita, that empty canvas stands for the open, empty Awareness which allows for the infinite play of experience. In daily life I can focus on all the *con*tent (accent on the first syllable) coming at me from the busy world, or I can become con*tent* (accent on the second) by making greater space for stillness and emptiness. This lovely, painterly world seems to unite the two, with outward beauty fostering inward quiet.

But of course, this world I stroll through is not truly static as in a painting. With every step my vantage point shifts and the world flows and changes. It is as if a new painting comes into view and disappears each moment. Thereby it is like a movie, my earlier metaphor. As I travel it's as if there is a camera continually tracking my POV shots as I glance right and left. I maintain my position as witness, but also appear as an actor in this film. This too is an Advaitaic trope and one emphasized in the *Bhagavad Gita*: that we should go through the world like an actor playing a part, never fully associating with life's melodramas (Smith 1991, 30–31).

Of course, there are more than just movie visuals and sounds; my experience is also informed by the feel of the wind in my face, the hard stones beneath my feet, the kinesthetic sense of my body in action. Shifting technological metaphors, I can imagine this as a "virtual reality" in which I wear a "haptic body suit" allowing even for tactile sensation. I feel the (simulated) wind, the virtual pebbles beneath my feet. It might be thought that such a high-tech image would diminish the beauty of the woods, but my experience is the opposite. Regarding every single pine needle and stone as remarkably designed or simulated, I am overcome by a sense of awe at this technologically marvelous accomplishment.

This progression leads me to an even-further mode of virtual experience: *What if this were all a dream*? Yes, why not? Again, I find this Cartesian/Vedantic experiment not so much disturbing or diminishing, but as rendering the world more magical. Earlier the world had seemed so—well—mundane. I had walked this path literally hundreds of times, the landscape having long ago lost its luster, the hard soil and stones an irritant to my feet. But when experienced as a dream-world it takes on lightness and fascination.

Yet who am I in relation to all this? First, it seems I am the small dream-figure from whose perspective the world is perceived. But I did not create this world or, if the Advaitic perspective is true, even my own consciousness.

The true source of awareness would really be that of the Dreamer, albeit channeled through my lived body. I can play with a gestalt shift between experiencing myself as the individualized dream-figure and as the all-encompassing Dreamer (Atman) within which world and self appear.

Earlier, I suggested that these forms of aesthetic dematerialization were not dependent on special surroundings, such as my lovely forest walk. For example, I can play with "dreaming" the plain office in which I now write. But it is true that certain settings help me open to an expansive embodiment. When I look up at the rich, blue sky and sense its vastness—and perhaps even more so, the nighttime sky wherein stars shine from what, in the spatiotemporal framework, are thousands of light-years away (and a single light-year is 9.7 trillion kilometers!)—and then realize that somehow this is all fitting within my indefinitely expansive consciousness—I get a stronger sense of limitless Awareness than I usually do sitting in an enclosed room.

Of course, a Zen practitioner might achieve satori in a small meditation hall. Yet it is no coincidence that Zen has a particular appreciation for mountains and rivers, paintings of cloud-colored peaks, Japanese gardens, seasonal haiku poems, and asymmetrical ikebana flower arrangements. These help the world to shine forth in immensity or in delicate beauty such that we feel our oneness with this ordinary, extraordinary world (D. Suzuki 1970).

In Zen, this sense of identity with the world is sometimes called the "big mind" experience as opposed to that of the small egoic mind. In the words of Shunryu Suzuki (1970, 35): "Big mind experiences everything within itself. Do you understand the differences between the two minds: the mind which includes everything, and mind which is related to something?" Yet one might also speak of this as the *big body* experience. Something like this may be at play in the words of the Zen master Dōgen:

> The body comes forth from the study of the Way. Everything which comes forth from the study of the Way is the true human body. The entire world in ten directions is nothing but the true human body. (Dōgen 1985, 92, trans. slightly altered)

As I continue my forest walk, I can flip between two different senses of what exactly constitutes "my body," one far more constricted, the other expansive. That is, I can identify with my physical body, 5 feet 11 inches tall, now 68 years old, well-caffeinated but also laden with aches and fatigue. But if I flip awareness, I realize that my *big body* includes everything passing before me, around me, and above me, which also thereby travels *within* me. As Alan Watts (1957, 120) says of the Zen perspective: "When we are no longer identified with the idea of ourselves . . . it becomes vividly clear that in concrete fact I have no other self than the totality of things of which I am aware." At this very moment my multisensory awareness fills with oak and pine trees rising loftily into the sky, melodious bird calls, leaves fluttering in the wind, the hard-packed soil, and so on. This is all my expanded body as it exists right here and now.

Yes, I can differentiate between interoceptions that seem "inside me" and those of the external world "outside." But this distinction is only possible because both sides make their appearance in my one experiential field. A realization of this non-dual perspective is not just conceptual but deeply embodied. Ken Wilber describes the experience thus:

> The clouds are arising within you—so much so, you can taste the clouds, you are one with the clouds, it is as if they are on this side of your skin, they are so close. The sky and your awareness have become one, and all things in the sky are floating effortless through your own awareness. (Wilber 1999, 203)

To continue with the theme of artistic exploration, John Keats may have entered something like this expanded awareness as recorded in "Ode to a Nightingale," one of the great poems of the English language. He was already sick with tuberculosis, having nursed a brother who died from the same disease. He was thus acutely conscious of the limitations of the ill and impaired body, perhaps the possibility of his own death, and in desperate need of a kind of transcendence—yet one that incorporated, rather than rejected, the sensual richness that so characterized his life and poetry. Reputedly, sitting outside on a friend's lawn he heard the song of a nightingale and writes of how his rapt attention and poetic sensibility release him:

> 'Tis not through envy of thy happy lot,
> But being too happy in thine happiness,—
> That thou, light-winged Dryad of the trees,
> In some melodious plot
> Of beechen green, and shadows numberless,
> Singest of summer in full-throated ease.
> . . .
> Away! away! for I will fly to thee,
> Not charioted by Bacchus and his pards,
> But on the viewless wings of Poesy,
> Though the dull brain perplexes and retards:
> Already with thee! tender is the night. . . . (Keats 2009, 458)

Within the poem, the words “Already with thee!” inaugurate a shift in point of view. Thereafter he is as if in the forest and adopting the nightingale’s perspective. “I cannot see what flowers are at my feet, / Nor what soft incense hangs upon the boughs. . . .” Yet this identification does not last. “Forlorn! the very word is like a bell / To toll me back from thee to my sole self!” At the poem’s end, sad and uncertain, he asks of the fleeting experience, “Was it a vision, or a waking dream?” (Keats 2009, 459–60). It was both, Advaita would answer: a glimpse that all of life is a waking dream, with ecstatic body-states providing both a clue to, and a consequence of, non-dual Awareness. In Spira’s words:

> The expansion of our sense of ourself from the temporary, finite, separate mind to universal consciousness is accompanied by an expansion of the way we feel our body. Just as the separate self feels its body to be this limited physical body, so universal consciousness, unlimited, ever-present consciousness wears the universe as its body. . . . Our body loses its feeling of contraction and limitation, it expands to include everything. (Spira 2021, audio)

What to call this experience? To name it “big body” (like the Zen expression “big mind”) might make it sound like one has just put on extra weight, or in other ways is occupying more physical space. So too with speaking of the “expanded body,” though this is a more evocative term. I am tempted to refer to the “exploded body,” since one blasts past one’s usual sense of skin-bound containment in a way that could also be called “mind-blowing”—but this sounds too violent when the experience can be quite serene.

I instead prefer a term implied by Jean Klein, the direct path teacher with both an Advaitic and hatha yoga background—that of the *transparent body*. In dialogue he said, “The nature of the body is transparent. When you come to the purely transparent feeling of your body that is the healing body” (Klein 2020, 24). To speak of the “transparent body” implies a body that has become porous, and open to the non-dual experience that transcends the rigidity of self–other separation.

This is not to deny that the body also has important boundaries. On the material plane we need our skin and its extensions—clothing and shelter—to protect our body heat, and an immune system to fight off certain pathogens. We take in oxygen and expel carbon dioxide. We could not possibly survive physically without the distinction of “inner” and “outer.” It is also psychologically true that in the face of this troublesome world it can be healing to nurture one’s boundaries. In the words of the Zen master Thich Nhat Hanh:

> Our senses are our windows in the world, and sometimes the wind blows through them and disturbs everything within us. Some of us leave our windows open all the time, allowing the sights and sounds of the world to invade us, penetrate us, and expose our sad, troubled lives. . . . Why do you torture yourself in this way? Don't you want to close your windows? (Hanh 1991, 13)

I have found, for example, that when I take in too much disturbing news (and what else is the majority of what is published as "news"?) it can stimulate gastric distress, depression, headaches, and other stress-related symptoms. When I'm unable to engage in disinterested witnessing, or compassionate well-wishing, I find it most healing to simply drastically lower my news consumption. This is not a denial of the transparent body but rather an acknowledgment of it. The body as ecstatic, both inside-out and outside-in, will be affected by our environment, and wise selectivity is appropriate in relation to such exposures.

The boundary between "self" and "other" also makes available to us rich encounters with different people, perspectives, and cultures. We would not wish to give this up even if we could. Our individual differences open up opportunities for exchange and communion. We earlier explored the empathy we feel for the experience of the ailing other. In another vein, when we appreciate the works of a great painter, we feel privileged to see what the world looks like through their eyes and heart. This can open up for us entirely new modes of perception. And when we read a compelling novel we are sharing in the world as experienced and created by another. How magical this can be!

Yet, all too often our sense of a thoroughly "separate self" is the source of anguish, giving rise to profound feelings of vulnerability and limitation. Or it can surface as selfish drives, with anger and fear directed toward the others. This sense of separation feeds racism, sexism, economic inequality, and xenophobia, and thus is a source of the embodied injustice described earlier. And as Siddhartha saw, and we have explored in depth, the separate body renders us vulnerable to aging, disease, and death. If we are fully identified with the body our long-term prospects seem bleak.

The experience of a transparent body which channels a transpersonal awareness can relieve this woundedness. In a sense we are *healing from the body* as ordinarily conceived. Yet, at the same time, this non-dual experience can also help with the *healing of the body itself.* It is on this last point that I will close the book.

Non-Dual Bodily Healing

Again drawing on a personal example, I will refer to a simple form of qigong I have used, one termed *la qi*, and first developed by a Chinese master, Dr. Pang Ming, specifically for healing purposes (Gu 2011). It involves opening up to all the rich sources of qi that surround one in the universe (qi, sometimes spelled ch'i, is a vital energy recognized in Chinese philosophy and medicine, bridging the Western mind–matter duality). An earlier book of mine closed with the notion that we "form one body with the universe" insofar as we all participate in the same circuit of qi, a central neo-Confucian notion (Leder 1990, 149–73). As Wang Yang-ming (1963, 222) writes: "Wind, rain, dew, thunder, sun and moon, stars, animals and plants, mountains and rivers, earth and stones are essentially of one body with man. . . . Since they share the same material force [ch'i] they enter into one another." Qigong was one practice that helped me *experience more deeply what I had previously written about theoretically*. In this practice you use the breath to open to the qi around you, revitalizing energy centers (*dantian*), while sending qi to any parts of the body in special need of healing. (Of course, breathing as a hinge between dis-ease and healing was the theme of this book's previous chapter.)

As I continue the forest walk I spoke of earlier, on the physical in-breath I experience myself going outward, expanding to embrace all the qi that surrounds me. Then, on what in Western physiology would be considered the out-breath, I send that vital qi inward to the damaged nerve I wrote of earlier. As one manifestation of the "inside-out" body thematized in this third part of the book, I think of this as "outside-in breathing." I use it to draw in the energy of growth and vitality embodied in the trees. I do the same with the qi of the open sky; my nerve needs that cool expansiveness to relieve inflammation and constriction. I breathe in the flowing clouds so that my nerve transmissions can become similarly free and fluid. I breathe the qi of the stabilizing earth, and send it to the region which has for me been so destabilizing. I even breathe in the birdsong; like Keats, my fatigued body can absorb the joy, "being too happy in thine happiness." In a transparent state, there is no true barrier between my ailing, aging body and the healing energies of the Dao that surround me.

On occasion, I use a transitional image of my personal body expanding gradually beyond its customary limits. As if blowing up a balloon, each in-breath makes me larger and larger. Concomitantly, the expanding balloon that separates inside from outside becomes thinner, more translucent (as would a real balloon)—until finally it pops! There is no more division between self and the forest-world.

I have found that I don't even need to be in the woods—at home I can use outside-in breathing activated by visualization. Practicing for anywhere from ten to thirty minutes, I could visualize such a forest scene, or more often would place myself on an imaginary beach, breathing in the fresh breeze, the flowing ocean, the warm sun and sand. In this form of qigong, which can be done standing, sitting, or lying down (I prefer the latter, the lazy man's exercise), one doesn't even need to move the body at all. Qi is circulated by our mental/bodily intentionality. As such, it is an example of a healing method even for those whose impairment makes any movement challenging, one that utilizes the healing strategy of *imagining*. Bodily limitation and disability need not block access to what I am calling the "transparent body."

Last winter I severely aggravated my peripheral neuropathy by walking on slippery ice and twisting my ankle enough to set off a resurgence of nerve pain. Despite the earlier effective surgery discussed in chapter 4, wherein I used the healing strategy of *being-objectified*, the stabbing pain and limitation returned for several months without relief. With gritted teeth I prepared myself to again go under the knife. The procedure this time would involve cutting the nerve entirely, causing numbness in a large part of my leg and the possibility of future complications as the severed nerve-endings might grow back. Needless to say I wasn't looking forward to this—especially since my excellent surgeon no longer accepted my current insurance.

However, within two weeks of using this form of qigong the nerve pain vastly decreased. From having trouble walking to the bathroom I soon progressed to walking a good four or five miles a day. My dogs were delighted! Of course, they, not as constricted by neurotic mentation, already had more expansive bodies than I, and so I was also communing with their joyous energy. My experience of the "transparent body," activated by qigong, helped heal my pain and give me back my world.

I recount all this not to pat myself on the back, recommend a particular form of treatment, or assert that miracles always await those who suffer from chronic problems. I am still on medication, and I do have some minor intermittent pain in my ankle, though I know better how to treat it when it arises. In my case the "placebo effect" may also have played a role in healing. What we believe in tends to have more efficacy, and the "direct path" teachings helped me to believe in my intimate connection with the universe; why wouldn't all that fine qi heal my body? (Though I was honestly quite shocked by how well and quickly it worked.) Perhaps my belief that help was at hand also lowered my anxiety level around the nerve pain, which itself lessens the pain signal. As mentioned in chapter 2, the circuit of chronic pain is perpetuated when we anxiously attend to the source of our distress, "tuning up" its cortical signals. Conversely, relaxation and expansion can bring relief, setting off a "virtuous circle" of healing.

When I went to China twice to receive our two adopted daughters I remember seeing many, particularly older, people gathered in the park early in the morning for communal qigong. (This too is a wise mode of "eldering," the topic of chapter 7.) I enjoyed watching their flowing movements, which united them with the natural world but also with each other, illustrating the power of embodied *communion*. Qigong is used in China not only for healing purposes but to elongate the life span, an instance of the Daoist fascination with life-extension even unto legends of immortality.

But that said, our physical body sooner or later does wear out. What Siddhartha saw—the sick man, the old man, and the corpse—awaits us all. In this book we have examined the experience of illness and other afflictions, but also the many healing strategies that individuals use to survive, and even thrive, in the face of embodied challenges. This included a focus on populations facing special struggles, such as those caught in systems of embodied injustice, including incarcerated persons and the aged in a youth-oriented culture. We have phenomenologically probed certain regions of the body—our visceral awareness, our breathing—for their significance in illness and healing. Yet at the end of the day—and we all come to the end of our day—the body must inevitably wear out and break down.

Perhaps the "ultimate medicine" is then to move beyond identification with this limited form to a trust in our inherence in Awareness, Atman, God, the Dao, Buddha Nature, Being, the universe, call it what you will. Yet this need not be conceptualized and practiced only as an *escape* from the body. Rather, it also suggests practices for *embracing* the body, rendering it fluid and responsive as long as it remains alive. In closing, I return to Jean Klein's words (2020, 24), as well as to the very title of this book: "When you come to the purely transparent feeling of your body that is the healing body."

Works Cited

AARP. 2017. "About the AARP Purpose Prize Award." http://www.aarp.org/about-aarp/purpose-prize/.

Abram, David. 2011. *Becoming Animal: An Earthly Cosmology*. New York: Vintage.

Ahmed, Sarah. 2007. "A Phenomenology of Whiteness." *Feminist Theory* 8, no. 2: 149–68.

Aho, James, and Kevin Aho. 2009. *Body Matters: A Phenomenology of Sickness, Disease, and Illness*. Lanham, MD: Lexington Books.

Aho, Kevin. 2018. *Existential Medicine: Essays on Health and Illness*. Lanham, MD: Rowman and Littlefield.

———. 2019. "Notes from a Heart Attack." In *Phenomenology of the Broken Body*, edited by Espen Dahl, Cassandra Falke, and Thor Eirik Eriksen. New York: Routledge.

———. 2020. *Existentialism: An Introduction*. 2nd edition. Cambridge: Polity.

———. 2022. *One Beat More: Existentialism and the Gift of Mortality*. Cambridge: Polity.

Alcoff, Linda Martin. 2006. *Visible Identities: Race, Gender, and the Self*. Oxford: Oxford University Press.

Alexander, Michelle. 2012. *The New Jim Crow*. New York: New Press.

Ardiel, E. L., and C. H. Rankin. 2010. "The Importance of Touch in Development." *Paediatrics & Child Health* 15, no. 3: 153–56. U.S. National Library of Medicine. https://pubmed.ncbi.nlm.nih.gov/21358895/.

Aristotle. 2011. *Nicomachean Ethics*. Translated by Robert Bartlett and Susan Collins. Chicago: University of Chicago Press.

Ashar, Y. K., A. Gordon, H. Schubiner, et al. 2022. "Effect of Pain Reprocessing Therapy vs Placebo and Usual Care for Patients with Chronic Back Pain: A Randomized Clinical Trial." *JAMA Psychiatry* 79, no. 1: 13–23. doi:10.1001/jamapsychiatry.2021.2669.

Atmananda, Sri Krishna Menon. 1978. *Atma-Darshan—At the Ultimate*. Austin, TX: Advaita Publishers.

Baltes, Margret M. 1995. "Dependency in Old Age: Gains and Losses." *Current Directions in Psychological Sciences* 4, no. 1: 14–19.

Bankei, Zen Master. 2000. *The Unborn: The Life and Teachings of Zen Master Bankei, 1622–1693.* Translated by Norman Waddell. New York: North Point.

Baraz, James, and Shoshana Alexander. 2012. *Awakening Joy: 10 Steps to Happiness.* Berkeley, CA: Parallax.

Baron, Richard. 1985. "An Introduction to Medical Phenomenology: 'I Can't Hear You while I'm Listening.'" *Annals of Internal Medicine* 103: 606–11.

Beauvoir, Simone de. 1996. *The Coming of Age.* Translated by Patrick O'Brian. New York: W. W. Norton.

———. 2011. *The Second Sex.* Translated by Constance Borde and Sheila Malovany-Chevallier. New York: Vintage.

Behrendt, Kathy. 2017. "Narrative Aversion: Challenges for the Illness Narrative Advocate." *Journal of Medicine and Philosophy* 42, no. 1: 50–69. https://doi-org.proxy-ln.researchport.umd.edu/10.1093/jmp/jhw031.

Benner, Patricia. 1994. *Interpretive Phenomenology: Embodiment, Caring, and Ethics in Health and Illness.* Thousand Oaks, CA: Sage.

Benson, Herbert, and William Proctor. 2010. *Relaxation Revolution: Enhancing Your Personal Health through the Science and Genetics of Mind Body Healing.* New York: Scribner.

Blanchard, J., and N. Lurie. 2004. "R-E-S-P-E-C-T: Patient Reports of Disrespect in the Health Care Setting and Its Impact on Care." *Journal of Family Practice* 53, no. 9: 721–30.

Bollnow, O. F. 1961. "Lived-Space." *Philosophy Today* 5, no. 1: 31–39.

Bourdieu, Pierre. 1989. *Outline of a Theory of Practice.* Cambridge: Cambridge University Press.

Brown, Richard P., and Patricia L. Gerbarg. 2009. "Yoga Breathing, Meditation, and Longevity." *Longevity, Regeneration, and Optimal Health: Annals of the New York Academy of Sciences* 1172 (August): 54–62.

Broyard, Anatole. 1992. *Intoxicated by My Illness and Other Writings on Life and Death.* New York: Fawcett Columbine.

Burtt, Edwin A. 1952. *The Metaphysical Foundations of Modern Science.* Atlantic Highlands, NJ: Humanities.

Bury, Michael. 1982. "Chronic Illness as Biographical Disruption." *Sociology of Health and Illness* 4, no. 2: 167–82.

Büssing, Arndt, Thomas Ostermann, Edmund Neugebauer, and Peter Heusser. 2010. "Adaptive Coping Strategies in Patients with Chronic Pain Conditions and Their Interpretation of Disease." *BMC Public Health.* https://doi.org/10.1186/1471-2458-10-507.

Butler, Judith. 2006. *Gender Trouble: Feminism and the Subversion of Identity.* London: Routledge.

Butler, Robert N. 1974. "Successful Aging and the Role of the Life Review." *Journal of the American Geriatrics Society* 22, no. 12: 29–535. https://doi-org.proxy-ln.researchport.umd.edu/10.1111/j.1532–5415.1974.tb04823.x.

———. 2002. "The Life Review." *Journal of Geriatric Psychiatry* 35, no. 1: 7–10. https://psycnet.apa.org/record/2004-12615-001.

Buytendijk, F. J. J. 1961. *Pain.* Westport, CT: Greenwood.

Carel, Havi. 2014. *Illness: The Cry of the Flesh.* New York: Routledge.

Carel, Havi, and Rachel Cooper, eds. 2013. *Health, Illness and Disease: Philosophical Essays*. Durham, UK: Acumen.

Carman, Taylor. 2008. *Merleau-Ponty*. London: Routledge.

Carus, Paul. 1916. *The Gospel of Buddha*. Chicago: Open Court.

Casey, Edward S. 1997. *The Fate of Place: A Philosophical History*. Berkeley: University of California Press.

———. 2000. *Remembering: A Phenomenological Study*. 2nd edition. Bloomington: Indiana University Press.

Cassell, Eric J. 1985. *The Healer's Art: A New Approach to the Doctor-Patient Relationship*. Cambridge, MA: MIT Press.

———. 2001. "Temporality and Illness: A Phenomenological Perspective." In *Handbook of Phenomenology and Medicine*, edited by S. Kay Toombs. Dordrecht: Kluwer Academic.

Ceunen, Erik, J. W. S. Vlaeyen, and Ilse Van Diest. 2016. "On the Origin of Interoception." *Frontiers in Psychology* 7 (May): 743.

Charon, Rita. 2008. *Narrative Medicine: Honoring the Stories of Illness*. New York: Oxford University Press.

Chernikoff, David. 2021. *Life, Part Two: Seven Keys to Awakening with Purpose and Joy as You Age*. Boulder, CO: Shambhala.

Chödrön, Pema. 1994. *Start Where You Are: A Guide to Compassionate Living*. Boston: Shambhala.

Chuang Tzu. 1964. *Basic Writings*. Translated by Burton Watson. New York: Columbia University Press.

Clare, Eli. 2017. *Brilliant Imperfections: Grappling with Cure*. Durham, NC: Duke University Press.

Cook, Francis H. 2001. *Hua-Yen Buddhism: The Jewel Net of Indra*. University Park: Penn State University Press.

Couser, Thomas. 1997. *Recovering Bodies: Illness, Disability, and Life Writing*. Madison: University of Wisconsin Press.

Crenshaw, Kimberlé. 2023. *On Intersectionality: Essential Writings*. New York: New Press.

"Criminal Justice Facts." The Sentencing Project. June 3. https://www.sentencingproject.org/criminal-justice-facts/.

Crowther, Martha R., Michael W. Parker, W. A. Achenbaum, Walter L. Larimore, and Harold G. Koenig. 2002. "Rowe and Kahn's Model of Successful Aging Revisited: Positive Spirituality—The Forgotten Factor." *Gerontologist* 42: 613–20.

Dahl, Espen, Cassandra Falke, and Thor Eirik Eriksen, eds. 2019. *Phenomenology of the Broken Body*. New York: Routledge.

Davis, Bret W. 2013. "Forms of Emptiness in Zen." In *A Companion to Buddhist Philosophy*, edited by Steven Emmanuel, 190–213. West Sussex, UK: Wiley-Blackwell.

Davis, Leonard J. 2016. *The Disability Studies Reader*. 5th edition. New York: Routledge.

de La Mettrie, Julien Offray. 1996. *Machine Man and Other Writings*. Edited by Ann Thomson. Cambridge: Cambridge University Press.

De Preester, Helena. 2011. "Technology and the Body: The (Im)possibilities of Re-embodiment." *Foundations of Science* 16: 119–37.

Descartes, René. 1911. *The Philosophical Works of Descartes*, vol. 1. Edited by Elizabeth Haldane and George R. T. Ross. Cambridge: Cambridge University Press.

Diprose, Rosalyn. 2002. *Corporeal Generosity: On Giving with Nietzsche, Merleau-Ponty, and Levinas.* New York: State University of New York Press.

Dōgen. 1985. *Moon in a Dewdrop: Writings of Zen Master Dōgen.* Edited by Kazuaki Tanahashi. San Francisco: North Point.

Doniger, Wendy, and Brian K. Smith. 1991. *The Laws of Manu, with an Introduction and Notes.* London: Penguin.

Drucker, Ernest. 2011. *A Plague of Prisons: The Epidemiology of Mass Incarceration in America.* New York: New Press.

DuLong, Jessica. 2022. "Startling New Science Reveals the Truth about Chronic Pain." CNN Health, June 27. https://www.cnn.com/2022/06/27/health/haider-warraich-chronic-pain-qa-wellness/index.html.

Dusenbery, Maya. 2018. *The Truth about How Bad Medicine and Lazy Science Leave Women Dismissed, Misdiagnosed and Sick.* New York: HarperOne.

Easwaran, Eknath, trans. 1987. *The Upanishads.* Tomales, CA: Nilgiri.

———, trans. 2007. *The Bhagavad Gita.* Tomales, CA: Nilgiri.

Eberwein, Robert T. 2014. *Film and Dream Screen: A Sleep and Forgetting.* Princeton, NJ: Princeton University Press.

Egnew, Thomas R. A. 2018. "Narrative Approach to Healing Chronic Illness." *Annals of Family Medicine* 16, no. 2: 160–65. https://doi-org.proxy-n.researchport.umd.edu/10.1370/afm.2182.

Ehrenreich, Barbara. 2009. *Bright-Sided: How the Relentless Promotion of Positive Thinking Has Undermined America.* New York: Metropolitan Books.

Eisen, Lauren-Brooke, and Inimai Chettiar. 2016. "39% of Prisoners Should Not Be in Prison." *Time*, December 9. http://time.com/4596081/incarceration-report/.

Elmer, Bruce N. 2008. *Hypnotize Yourself Out of Pain Now.* 2nd edition. Bethel, CT: Crown House.

El-Mohtar, Amal. 2020. "Dealmakers and Wanderers: New Science Fiction and Fantasy." *New York Times Sunday Book Review*, November 1. https://www.nytimes.com/2020/10/14/books/review/susanna-clarke-piranesi.html.

Fanon, Frantz. 2008. *Black Skin, White Masks.* New York: Grove.

Farhi, Donna. 1996. *The Breathing Book: Good Health and Vitality through Essential Breath Work.* New York: Henry Holt.

Feuerstein, Georg. 1997. *The Shambhala Encyclopedia of Yoga.* Boston: Shambhala.

Foucault, Michel. 1975. *Birth of the Clinic: An Archaeology of Medical Perception.* New York: Vintage Books.

———. 1979. *Discipline and Punish: The Birth of the Prison.* Translated by Alan Sheridan. New York: Vintage Books.

Frank, Arthur, W. 1991. *At the Will of the Body: Reflections on Illness.* Boston: Houghton Mifflin.

———. 2013. *The Wounded Storyteller: Body, Illness, and Ethics.* 2nd edition. Chicago: University of Chicago Press.

Frye, Marilyn. 1983. *Politics of Reality: Essays in Feminist Theory*. New York: Crossing Press Feminist.
Fuchs, Thomas. 2001. "Melancholia as a Desynchronisation: Toward a Psychopathology of Interpersonal Time." *Psychopathology* 34: 179–86.
———. 2005. "Implicit and Explicit Temporality." *Philosophy, Psychiatry, & Psychology* 12, no. 3: 195–98.
Gadamer, Hans-Georg. 1984. *Truth and Method*. New York: Crossroad.
Gallagher, Shaun. 1986. "Body Image and Body Schema: A Conceptual Clarification." *Journal of Mind and Behavior* 7, no. 4: 541–54.
Goffman, Erving. 1969. *Stigma: Notes on the Management of Spoiled Identity*. New York: Simon and Schuster.
Gogel, Edward, and J. S. Terry. 1987. "Medicine as Interpretation: The Uses of Literary Metaphors and Methods." *Journal of Medicine and Philosophy* 12: 205.
Gordon, Lewis. 1997. *Existence in Black: An Anthology of Black Existential Philosophy*. London: Routledge.
Gramlich, John. 2020. "Black Imprisonment Rate in the U.S. Has Fallen by a Third since 2006." Pew Research Center. https://www.pewresearch.org/fact-tank/2020/05/06/share-of-black-white-hispanic-americans-in-prison-2018-vs-2006/.
Groopman, Jerome. 2007. *How Doctors Think*. New York: Houghton Mifflin.
Gu, Mingtong. 2011. *Wisdom Healing (Zhineng) Qigong: Cultivating Wisdom and Energy for Health, Healing and Happiness*. Santa Fe, NM: Mingtong Gu.
Guenther, Lisa. 2013. *Solitary Confinement: Social Death and Its Afterlives*. Minneapolis: University of Minnesota Press.
Gunnarson, Martin. 2016. *Please Be Patient: A Cultural Phenomenological Study of Haemodialysis and Kidney Transplantation Care*. Lund, Sweden: Lund University Press.
Gupta, Bina. 1998. *The Disinterested Witness: A Fragment of Advaita Vedanta Phenomenology*. Evanston, IL: Northwestern University Press.
Hamington, Maurice. 2004. *Embodied Care: Jane Addams, Maurice Merleau-Ponty, and Feminist Ethics*. Urbana: University of Illinois Press.
Hanh, Thich Nhat 1991. *Peace Is Every Step: The Path of Mindfulness in Everyday Life*. New York: Bantam Books.
Haraway, Donna J. 2007. *When Species Meet*. Minneapolis: University of Minnesota Press.
Hawkins, Anne Hunsaker. 1999. *Reconstructing Illness: Studies in Pathography*. West Lafayette, IN: Purdue University Press.
Heidegger, Martin. *Being and Time*. 1962. Translated by John Macquarrie and Edward Robinson. New York: Harper and Row.
Herbert, B. M., and Olga Pollatos. 2012. "The Body in the Mind: On the Relationship between Interoception and Embodiment." *Topics in Cognitive Science* 4, no. 4: 692.
Hillman, James. 1999. *The Force of Character: And the Lasting Life*. New York: Random House.
Hoffman, Kelly M., Sophie Trawalter, Jordan R. Axt, and M. Norman Oliver. 2016. "Racial Bias in Pain Assessment and Treatment Recommendations, and False Beliefs about Biological Differences between Blacks and Whites."

Psychological and Cognitive Sciences 113, no. 16: 4296–4301. https://doi.org/10.1073/pnas.1516047113.

Holt-Lunstad, Julianne, Timothy B. Smith, Mark Baker, Tyler Harris, and David Stephenson. 2015. "Loneliness and Social Isolation as Risk Factors for Mortality: A Meta-Analytic Review." *Perspectives on Psychological Science: A Journal of the Association for Psychological Science* 10, no. 2. U.S. National Library of Medicine. https://pubmed.ncbi.nlm.nih.gov/25910392/.

Holt-Lunstad, Julianne, Timothy B. Smith, and J. Bradley Layton. 2010. "Social Relationships and Mortality Risk: A Meta-Analytic Review." *PLOS Medicine*. Public Library of Science. https://journals.plos.org/plosmedicine/article?id=10.1371%2Fjournal.pmed.1000316.

Hornbacher, M. 1999. *Wasted*. London: Flamingo.

Husserl, Edmund. 1989. *Ideas Pertaining to a Pure Phenomenology and to a Phenomenological Philosophy, Second Book: Studies in the Phenomenology of Constitution*. Translated by Richard Rojcewicz and André Schuwer. Dordrecht: Kluwer Academic.

Ihde, Don. 1979. *Technics and Praxis*. Dordrecht: D. Reidel.

Inagaki, Tristen K., Kate E. Byrne Haltom, Shosuke Suzuki, Ivana Jevtic, Erica Hornstein, Julienne E. Bower, and Naomi I. Eisenberger. 2016. "The Neurobiology of Giving versus Receiving Support: The Role of Stress-Related and Social Reward-Related Neural Activity." *Psychosomatic Medicine* 78, no. 4. U.S. National Library of Medicine. https://www.ncbi.nlm.nih.gov/pmc/articles/PMC4851591/.

Jahnke, Roger. 2002. *The Healing Promise of Qi: Creating Extraordinary Wellness through Qigong and Tai Chi*. New York: McGraw-Hill.

Johnson, Rae. 2017. *Embodied Social Justice*. London: Routledge.

Johnson, Sandy. 1994. *The Book of Elders: The Life Stories of Great American Indians*. San Francisco: Harper San Francisco.

Jonas, Hans. 1966. *The Phenomenon of Life: Toward a Philosophical Biology*. Chicago: University of Chicago Press.

Jones III, Arlando "Tray." 2010. *Eager Street: A Life on the Corner and Behind Bars*. Baltimore, MD: Apprentice House.

———. 2019. *Old Too Fast, Smart Too Late: A Prisoner's Foolish Journey to Wisdom*. Baltimore, MD: Apprentice House.

Jowsey, Tanisha. 2016. "Time and Chronic Illness: A Narrative Review." *Quality of Life Research* 25, no. 5: 1093–1102.

Jung, C. G. 1933. *Modern Man in Search of a Soul*. New York: Harcourt, Brace.

Kabat-Zinn, Jon. 2013. *Full Catastrophe Living: Using the Wisdom of Your Body and Mind to Face Stress, Pain, and Illness*. New York: Bantam.

Kafer, Alison. 2013. *Feminist, Queer, Crip*. Bloomington: Indiana University Press.

Kalanithi, Paul. 2016. *When Breath Becomes Air*. New York: Random House.

Kant, Immanuel. 1929. *Critique of Pure Reason*. Translated by Norman Kemp Smith. New York: St. Martin's Press.

Keats, John. 2009. *Keats's Poetry and Prose*. Edited by Jeffrey N. Cox. New York: W. W. Norton.

Keet, Corinne A., Meredith C. McCormack, Craig E. Pollack, Roger D. Peng,

Emily McGowan, and Elizabeth C. Matsui. 2015. "Neighborhood Poverty, Urban Residence, Race/Ethnicity, and Asthma: Rethinking the Inner-City Asthma Epidemic." *Asthma and Lower Airway Disease* 135, no. 3: 655–62. https://doi.org/10.1016/j.jaci.2014.11.022.

Kittay, Eva Feder. 2006. "The Concept of Care Ethics in Biomedicine: The Case of Disability." DigitalGeorgetown Home. https://repository.library.georgetown.edu/handle/10822/976687.

———. 2019. *Learning from My Daughter: The Value and Care of Disabled Minds.* Oxford: Oxford University Press.

Klein, Jean. 2020. *Open to the Unknown: Dialogues in New Delhi.* San Francisco: New Sarum.

———. 2006. *I Am.* Salisbury, UK: Non-Duality Press.

Kleinman, Arthur. 1988. *The Illness Narratives: Suffering, Healing, and the Human Condition.* New York: Basic Books.

Kornfield, Jack. 1993. *A Path with Heart: A Guide through the Perils and Promises of Spiritual Life.* New York: Bantam Books.

Krucoff, Carol. 2000. "Breathe." *Washington Post,* May 2, 2000. https://www.washingtonpost.com/archive/lifestyle/wellness/2000/05/02/breathe/16c8ec0b-71e7–47ec-8c88–4f6df47b896f/.

———. 2013. *Yoga Sparks: 108 Practices for Stress Relief in a Minute or Less.* Oakland, CA: New Harbinger.

Lacan, Jacques. 1989. *Écrits.* Translated by Alan Sheridan. London: Routledge.

Leder, Drew. 1990. *The Absent Body.* Chicago: University of Chicago Press.

———. 1997. *Spiritual Passages: Embracing Life's Sacred Journey.* New York: Penguin/Tarcher.

———. 1998. "The Trouble with Successful Aging." *Park Ridge Center Bulletin,* October/November, 10–11.

———. 2000. *The Soul Knows No Bars: Inmates Reflect on Life, Death, and Hope.* Lanham, MD: Rowman and Littlefield.

———. 2016a. *The Distressed Body: Rethinking Illness, Imprisonment, and Healing.* Chicago: University of Chicago Press.

———. 2016b. "The Experiential Paradoxes of Pain." *Journal of Medicine and Philosophy* 41, no. 5: 444.

———. 2018. "Inside Insights: A Phenomenology of Interoception." In *The Interoceptive Mind: From Homeostasis to Awareness,* edited by Manos Tsakiris and Helena De Preester, 307–22. Oxford: Oxford University Press.

———. 2019. "Re-Possibilizing the World: Recovery from Serious Illness, Injury or Impairment." In *Phenomenology of the Broken Body,* edited by Espen Dahl, Cassandra Falke, and Thor Eirik Eriksen, 173–187. New York: Routledge.

Leder, Drew, and Vincent Greco. 2014. "Prisoners: 'They're Animals' and Their Animals." In *Philosophy Imprisoned: The Love of Wisdom in the Age of Mass Incarceration,* edited by Sarah Tyson and Joshua Hall. Lanham, MD: Lexington Books.

Leder, Drew, and Kirsten Jacobson. 2014. "The Experience of Health and Illness." In *The Encyclopedia of Bioethics,* edited by Bruce Jennings, 3:1434–43. 4th edition. Farmington Hills, MI: Macmillan Reference USA.

Leder, Drew, and the Jessup Correctional Institution Scholars. 2014. "The Enlightened Prison." In *Studies in Law, Politics, and Society* 64, 19–32. Special Issue: *The Beautiful Prison*, edited by Austin Sarat. Bingley, UK: Emerald Publishing.

Lee, Emily S. 2014. *Living Alterities: Phenomenology, Embodiment, and Race*. Albany: State University of New York Press.

Levinas, Emmanuel. 1969. *Totality and Infinity: An Essay on Exteriority*. Translated by Alphonso Lingis. Ann Arbor, MI: XanEdu.

Levine, Stephen. 1982. *Who Dies? An Investigation of Conscious Living and Conscious Dying*. New York: Anchor Books.

Lewis, Dennis. 1997. *The Tao of Natural Breathing: For Health, Well-Being and Inner Growth*. San Francisco: Mountain Wind.

Love, Heather. 2015. "Stigma." In *Keywords for Disability Studies*, edited by Rachel Adams, Benjamin Reiss, and David Serlin. New York: NYU Press.

Loy, David. 1988. *Nonduality: A Study in Comparative Philosophy*. Atlantic Highlands, NJ: Humanities.

Loy, Tetsu'un. 2017. "*Shushōgi* Paragraph 1." In *Engaging Dogen's Zen: The Philosophy of Practice as Awakening*, edited by Tetsu'un Jason M. Wirth, Kanpu Bret W. Davis, and Shudo Brian Schroeder. New York: Simon and Schuster.

Lucille, Francis. 2006. *Perfume of Silence*. Temecula, CA: Truespeech Productions.

Lyons, Oren. 1980. "An Iroquois Perspective." In *American Indian Environments: Ecological Issues in Native American History*, edited by Christopher Vecsey and Robert W. Venables, 202–5. Syracuse, NY: Syracuse University Press.

———. 2011. *The Ultimate Medicine*. San Diego, CA: Blue Dove.

Malcolm X. 1971. *The End of White World Supremacy: Four Speeches*. New York: Arcade.

Mann, Thomas. 2005. *The Magic Mountain*. Translated by John E. Woods. New York: Everyman's Library.

Mehling, Wolf E., Cynthia Price, Jennifer J. Daubenmier, Mike Acree, Elizabeth Bartmess, and Anita Stewart. 2012. "The Multidimensional Assessment of Interoceptive Awareness (MAIA)." *PloS One* 7, no. 11.

Mehling, Wolf E., Judith Wrubel, Jennifer J. Daubenmier, Cynthia J. Price, Catherine E. Kerr, Theresa Silow, Viranjini Gopisetty, and Anita L. Stewart. 2011. "Body Awareness: A Phenomenological Inquiry into the Common Ground of Mind-Body Therapies." *Philosophy, Ethics, and Humanities in Medicine* 6, no. 6.

Meltzoff, Andrew N., and M. Keith Moore. 1983. "Newborn Infants Imitate Adult Facial Gestures." *Child Development*. U.S. National Library of Medicine. https://pubmed.ncbi.nlm.nih.gov/6851717/.

Melzack, Ronald, and Joel Katz. 2004. "The Gate Control Theory: Reaching for the Brain." In *Pain: Psychological Perspectives*, edited by Thomas Hadjistavropoulos and Kenneth D. Craig, 13–34. Mahwah, NJ: Lawrence Erlbaum Associates.

Melzack, Ronald, and Patrick D. Wall. 1996. *The Challenge of Pain*. London: Penguin.

Merchant, Carolyn. 1980. *The Death of Nature*. San Francisco: Harper and Row.

Merleau-Ponty, Maurice. 1968. *The Visible and the Invisible*. Edited by Claude Lefort, translated by Alphonso Lingis. Evanston, IL: Northwestern University Press.

———. 2012. *Phenomenology of Perception.* Translated by Donald A. Landes. London: Routledge.

Metzl, Jonathan M. 2020. *Dying of Whiteness: How the Politics of Racial Resentment Is Killing America's Heartland.* New York: Basic Books.

Mikkelson, David. 2007. "Itzhak Perlman Three Strings." Snopes.com. May 16. https://www.snopes.com/fact-check/three-strings-and-youre-outre/.

Minkowski, Eugene. 1970. *Lived Time: Phenomenological and Psychopathological Studies.* Translated by Nancy Metzel. Evanston, IL: Northwestern University Press.

Moerman, David. 2002. *Meaning, Medicine and the "Placebo Effect."* Cambridge: Cambridge University Press.

Moody Jr., Raymond. 1975. *Life After Life.* New York: Bantam Books.

Mount, Matthew P., Arman Lira, David Grimes, Patrice D. Smith, Sylvie Faucher, Ruth Slack, Hymie Anisman, Shawn Hayley, and David S. Park. 2007. "Involvement of Interferon-Gamma in Microglial-Mediated Loss of Dopaminergic Neurons." *Journal of Neuroscience* 27, no. 12.

Muktananda, Swami. 1992. *I Am That: The Science of Hamsa from the Vijnana Bhairava.* South Fallsburg, NY: Siddha Yoga.

Murthy, Vivek H. 2020. *Together: The Human Power of Connection in a Sometimes Lonely World.* New York: Harper Wave.

Nagel, Thomas. 1989. *The View from Nowhere.* Oxford: Oxford University Press.

Nancy, Jean-Luc. 2002. "L'Intrus." Translated by S. Hanson. *New Centennial Review* 2, no. 3: 1–14.

Nettleton, Sarah, Ian Watt, Lisa O'Malley, and Phillip Duffey. 2005. "Understanding the Narratives of People Who Live with Medically Unexplained Illness." *Patient Education and Counseling* 56, no. 2. U.S. National Library of Medicine. https://pubmed.ncbi.nlm.nih.gov/15653250/.

Ngo, Helen. 2017. *The Habits of Racism: A Phenomenology of Racism and Racialized Embodiment.* Lanham, MD: Lexington Books.

Nietzsche, Friedrich. 1954. *Thus Spoke Zarathustra.* In *The Portable Nietzsche,* translated and edited by Walter Kaufman, 103–439. New York: Viking.

Nisargadatta, Maharaj 1973. *I Am That.* Edited by Sudhaakar S. Kishit and Maurice Frydman. Durham, NC: Acorn.

———. 2006. *The Ultimate Medicine as Prescribed by Sri Nisargadatta Maharaj: Dialogue with a Realized Master,* edited by Robert Powell. Berkeley: North Atlantic Books.

Nowen, Henri J. M. 2014. *Out of Solitude: Three Meditations on the Christian Life.* Notre Dame, IN: Ave Maria.

Ortega, Mariana. 2014. "Hometactics: Self-Mapping, Belonging, and the Home Question." In *Living Alterities: Phenomenology, Embodiment, and Race,* edited by Emily S. Lee. Albany: State University of New York Press.

Osler, Lucy. 2021. "Controlling the Noise: A Phenomenological Account of Anorexia Nervosa and the Threatening Body." *Philosophy, Psychiatry, & Psychology* 28, no. 1: 41–58.

Ouchida, Karin M., and Mark S. Lachs. 2015. "Not for Doctors Only: Ageism in Health Care." *Generations* 39, no. 3: 46–57.

Palmer, Richard. 1969. *Hermeneutics: Interpretation Theory in Schleiermacher, Dilthey, Heidegger, and Gadamer.* Evanston, IL: Northwestern University Press.

Parsons, Talcott. 1951. *The Social System.* London: Free Press of Glencoe.

Plato. 1993. *The Last Days of Socrates.* London: Penguin.

Plaut, W. Gunther. 1981. *The Torah: A Modern Commentary.* New York: Union of American Hebrew Congregations.

Plessner, Helmuth. 1970. *Laughing and Crying: A Study of the Limits of Human Behavior.* Translated by James Spencer Churchill and Marjorie Grene. Evanston, IL: Northwestern University Press.

Polanyi, Michael. 1969. *Knowing and Being.* Chicago: University of Chicago Press.

Price, Catherine. 2018. *How to Break Up with Your Phone.* New York: Ten Speed.

———. 2019. "Put Down Your Phone. Live Longer." *New York Times,* April 30, section D, p. 6. https://www.nytimes.com/2019/04/24/well/mind/putting-down-your-phone-may-help-you-live-longer.html.

Prosser, Jay. 1998. *Second Skins: The Body Narratives of Transsexuality.* New York: Columbia University Press.

Proust, Marcel. 2002. *The Guermantes Way.* New York: Penguin.

Quartana, Phillip, Claudia Campbell, and Robert Edwards. 2009. "Pain Catastrophizing: A Critical Review." *Expert Review of Neurotherapeutics* 9, no. 5: 745–58.

Ramana Maharshi. 1988. *Be as You Are: The Teachings of Sri Ramana Maharshi.* London: Penguin UK.

Ram Dass. 2001. *Still Here: Embracing Aging, Changing, and Dying.* New York: Riverhead Books.

Ram Dass and Paul Gorman. 2003. *How Can I Help: Stories and Reflections on Service.* New York: Alfred A. Knopf.

Rees, Lesley, and Andrew Weil. 2001. "Integrated Medicine." *The BMJ.* January 20. https://www.bmj.com/content/322/7279/119.

Remen, Rachel Naomi. 1991. Essay. In *Stories of the Spirit, Stories of the Heart: Parables of the Spiritual Path from the World,* edited by Christina Feldman and Jack Kornfield, 28–31. San Francisco: Harper.

Reynolds, Joel Michael. 2022. *The Life Worth Living: Disability, Pain and Morality.* Minneapolis: University of Minnesota Press.

Ricoeur, Paul. 1966. *Freedom and Nature: The Voluntary and the Involuntary.* Evanston, IL: Northwestern University Press.

Riemer, Jack. 2001. "Perlman Makes His Music the Hard Way." *Houston Chronicle,* August 15. https://www.chron.com/life/houston-belief/article/Perlman-makes-his-music-the-hard-way-2009719.php.

Rogo, D. Scott. 1983. *Leaving the Body; A Complete Guide to Astral Projection.* New York: Prentice Hall.

Rosen, Richard. 2002. *The Yoga of Breath: A Step-by-Step Guide to Pranayama.* Boston: Shambhala.

Roszak, Theodore. 2009. *The Making of an Elder Culture: Reflections on the*

Future of America's Most Audacious Generation. Gabriola Island, BC: New Society.

Rowe, John W., and Robert L. Kahn. 1998. *Successful Aging*. New York: Pantheon/Random House.

Russon, John, and Kirsten Jacobson. 2018. "Existential Medicine and the Intersubjective Body." In *Existential Medicine: Essays on Health and Illness*, edited by Kevin Aho. Lanham, MD: Rowman and Littlefield.

Sacks, Oliver. 1994. *A Leg to Stand On*. New York: Touchstone.

———. 2013. "The Joy of Old Age. (No Kidding)." *New York Times*, July 6. https://www.nytimes.com/2013/07/07/opinion/sunday/the-joy-of-old-age-no-kidding.html.

Sartre, Jean-Paul. 1956. *Being and Nothingness: A Phenomenological Essay on Ontology*. New York: Pocket Books.

Scarry, Elaine. 1985. *The Body in Pain: The Making and Unmaking of the World*. Oxford: Oxford University Press.

Schachter-Shalomi, Zalman, and Ronald S. Miller. 1995. *From Age-ing to Sage-ing: A Revolutionary Approach to Growing Older*. New York: Grand Central.

Sekimoto, Sachi, and Christopher Brown. 2020. *Race and the Senses: The Felt Politics of Racial Embodiment*. New York: Routledge and The Sentencing Project.

Sherman, Nancy. 2011. *The Untold War: Inside the Hearts, Minds, and Souls of Our Soldiers*. New York: W. W. Norton.

Sheikh, Knvul. 2019. "Enjoy 2 Hours a Week in Nature, Doctors Say." *New York Times*, June 25, D4.

Sherrington, C. S. 1906. *The Integrative Action of the Nervous System*. New Haven, CT: Yale University Press.

Sirois, Fuchsia M., Danielle S. Molnar, and Jameson K. Hirsch. 2015. "Self-Compassion, Stress, and Coping in the Context of Chronic Illness." *Self & Identity* 14, no. 3: 334–47.

Sivan, Manoj, Margaret Phillips, Ian Baguley, and Melissa Nott. 2019. *Oxford Handbook of Rehabilitation Medicine*. Oxford: Oxford University Press.

Slatman, Jenny. 2014. *My Strange Body: Philosophical Reflections on Identity and Medical Interventions*. Amsterdam: Amsterdam University Press.

Smith, Huston. 1991. *The World's Religions*. New York: Harper One.

Spira, Rupert. 2007. *The Nature of Consciousness: Essays on the Unity of Mind and Matter*. Oxford: Sahara.

———. 2008. *The Transparency of Things: Contemplating the Nature of Experience*. Salisbury, UK: Non-Duality Press.

———. 2018. "An Impulse of Love." Audio. https://non-duality.rupertspira.com/home.

———. 2021. "Experiencing the Unbound Presence of Awareness." Audio. https://non-duality.rupertspira.com/home.

Stambaugh, Joan. 1990. *Impermanence Is Buddha-Nature*. Hawaii: University of Hawaii Press.

Stanton, Annette, Tracey Revenson, and Howard Tennen. 2007. "Health Psychology: Psychological Adjustment to Chronic Disease." *Annual Review of Psychology* 58: 565–92.

Stepanikova, I., and G. R. Oates. 2017. "Perceived Discrimination and Privilege in Health Care: The Role of Socioeconomic Status and Race." *American Journal of Preventive Medicine* 52, no. 1S1: S86–94.

Straus, Erwin. 1952a. "The Upright Posture." *Psychiatric Quarterly* 26.

———. 1952b. "The Sigh: An Introduction to a Theory of Expression." *Tijdschrift voor Philosophie* 14, no. 4: 674–95.

———. 1963. *The Primary World of Senses: A Vindication of Sensory Experience.* Translated by Jacob Needleman. New York: Free Press of Glencoe.

Straus, Joseph N. 2011. *Extraordinary Measures: Disability in Music.* Oxford: Oxford University Press.

Stryk, Lucien. 1968. *World of the Buddha.* New York: Grove.

Sun, Michael, Tomasz Oliwa, Monica E. Peek, and Elizabeth L. Tung. 2022. "Negative Patient Descriptors: Documenting Racial Bias in the Electronic Health Record." *Health Affairs* 41, no. 2. https://doi.org/10.1377/hlthaff.2021.01423.

Suzuki, Daisetz T. 1970. *Zen and Japanese Culture.* Princeton, NJ: Princeton University Press.

Suzuki, Shunryu. 1970. *Zen Mind, Beginner's Mind.* New York: Weatherhill.

Svenaeus, Fredrik. 2001. *The Hermeneutics of Medicine and the Phenomenology of Health: Steps towards a Philosophy of Medical Practice.* 2nd revised edition. Dordrecht: Kluwer Academic.

———. 2011. "Illness as Unhomelike Being-in-the-World: Heidegger and the Phenomenology of Medicine." *Medicine, Health Care and Philosophy* 14, no. 3: 333–43.

———. 2015. "The Phenomenology of Chronic Pain: Embodiment and Alienation." *Continental Philosophy Review* 48: 107–22.

———. 2017. *Phenomenological Bioethics: Medical Technologies, Human Suffering, and the Meaning of Being Alive.* London: Routledge.

Tavernise, Sabrina, and Robert Gebeloff. 2014. "In a New Divide, Smoking Is Becoming a Habit of the Poor." *New York Times,* March 25, A17.

Taylor, Jill Bolte. 2009. *My Stroke of Insight: A Brain Scientist's Personal Journey.* New York: Penguin Books.

Thoreau, Henry David. 1983. *Walden and Civil Disobedience.* New York: Penguin Books.

Tolstoy, Leo. 1960. *The Death of Ivan Ilych.* New York: New American Library.

Toombs, S. Kay. 1992. *The Meaning of Illness: A Phenomenological Account of the Different Perspectives of Physician and Patient.* Dordrecht: Kluwer Academic.

———. 1995. "Healing and Incurable Illness." *Humane Medicine* 11, no. 3: 98–103.

———. 2001. *Handbook of Phenomenology and Medicine.* Boston: Kluwer Academic.

Turkle, Sherry. 2011. *Alone Together: Why We Expect More from Technology and Less from Each Other.* New York: Basic Books.

van den Berg, J. H. 1966. *The Psychology of the Sickbed.* Pittsburgh, PA: Duquesne University Press.

Van Gogh, Vincent. 2009. *The Letters: The Complete Illustrated and Annotated Edition.* Edited by Leo Jansen, Hans Luijeten, and Nienke Bakker. London: Thames and Hudson.

Warren, Karen J. 2000. *Ecofeminist Philosophy: A Western Perspective on What It Is and Why It Matters.* Lanham, MD: Rowman and Littlefield.
Watts, Alan. 1957. *The Way of Zen.* New York: Pantheon Books.
Wehrle, Maren. 2019. "Being a Body and Having a Body: The Twofold Temporality of Embodied Intentionality." *Phenomenology and the Cognitive Sciences* 19. https://doi-org.proxy-ln.researchport.umd.edu/10.1007/s11097-019-09610-z.
Weil, Simone. 1951. *Waiting for God.* New York: Harper and Row.
Weiss, Gail. 1998. *Body Images: Embodiment as Intercorporeality.* London: Routledge.
———. 2014. "Pride and Prejudice: Ambiguous Racial, Religious, and Ethnic Identities of Jewish Bodies." In *Living Alterities: Phenomenology, Embodiment, and Race,* edited by Emily S. Lee. Albany: State University of New York Press.
Weiss, Gail, Gayle Salamon, and Ann V. Murphy. 2020. *50 Concepts for a Critical Phenomenology.* Evanston, IL: Northwestern University Press.
Wendell, Susan. 1996. *The Rejected Body: Feminist Reflections on Disability.* New York: Routledge.
White, Katherine, M. S. M. Issac, C. Kamoun, J. Leygues, and S. Cohn. 2018. "The THRIVE Model: A Framework and Review of Internal and External Predictors of Coping with Chronic Illness." *Health Psychology Open* 5, no. 2. https://doi.org/10.1177/2055102918793552.
Wijesinghe, Sunny, and Mark B. Parshall. 2016. "Impermanence and Sense of Coherence: Lessons Learned from the Adaptive Behaviors of Sri Lankan Buddhist Nuns with a Chronic Illness." *Journal of Transcultural Nursing* 27, no. 2: 157–65.
Wilber, Ken. 1999. *One Taste: The Journals of Ken Wilber.* Boston: Shambhala.
Wilkerson, Isabel. 2020. *Caste: The Origins of Our Discontents.* New York: Random House.
Woods, Angela. 2011. "The Limits of Narrative: Provocations for the Medical Humanities." *Medical Humanities* 37: 73–78.
Wyllie, Martin. 2005. "Lived Time and Psychopathology." *Philosophy, Psychiatry & Psychology* 12: 173–85.
Yancy, George. 2017. *Black Bodies, White Gazes: The Continuing Significance of Race in America.* Lanham, MD: Rowman and Littlefield.
Yang-ming, Wang. 1963. "Inquiry on the Great Learning." In *A Sourcebook in Chinese Philosophy,* edited by Sang-Tsit Chan. Princeton, NJ: Princeton University Press.
Yeats, William Butler. 2000. *Yeats's Poetry, Drama, and Prose.* Edited by James Pethica. New York: W. W. Norton.
Yogananda, Paramahansa. 1986. *The Divine Romance: Collected Talks and Essays on Realizing God in Daily Life, Volume II.* Los Angeles: Self-Realization Fellowship.
Young, Iris Marion. 2005. *On Female Body Experience: "Throwing Like a Girl" and Other Essays.* Oxford: Oxford University Press.
Zaner, Richard. 1981. *The Context of Self: A Phenomenological Inquiry Using Medicine as a Clue.* Athens: Ohio University Press.
Zeidan, Fadel, Joshua Grant, Christopher Brown, John G. McHaffie, and Robert

Coghill. 2012. "Mindfulness Meditation-Related Pain Relief: Evidence for Unique Brain Mechanisms in the Regulation of Pain." *Neuroscience Letters* 520, no. 2 (June 29): 65–173. https://doi.org/10.1016/j.neulet.2012.03.082.

Zeiler, Kristin. 2018. "On the *Autós* of Autonomous Decision Making: Intercorporeality, Temporality, and Enacted Normativities in Transplantation Medicine." In *Existential Medicine: Essays on Health and Illness,* edited by Kevin Aho, 81–100. Lanham, MD: Rowman and Littlefield.

Zeiler, Kristin, and Lisa Folkmarson Käll. 2014. *Feminist Phenomenology and Medicine.* New York: State University of New York Press.

Zhou, Yanqiu Rachel. 2010. "The Phenomenology of Time: Lived Experiences of People with HIV/AIDS in China." *Health* 14, no. 3: 310–26. https://doi.org/10.1177/136345930935.

Index